Diane
Enjoy the dream...
Enjoy the journey of life
Enjoy the journey of life
C'est la Vie

A
BEACH
LESS
TRAVELED

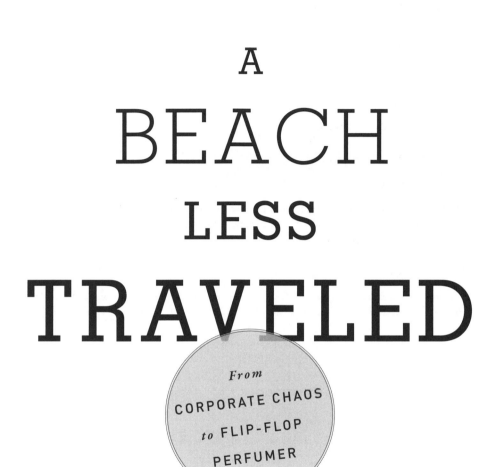

From
CORPORATE CHAOS
to FLIP-FLOP
PERFUMER

JOHN BERGLUND

EMERALD
BOOK CO.

Published by Emerald Book Company
Austin, TX
www.emeraldbookcompany.com

Distributed by Emerald Book Company

For ordering information or special discounts for bulk purchases, please contact Emerald Book Company at PO Box 91869, Austin, TX 78709, 512.891.6100.

Design and composition by Greenleaf Book Group LLC and Alex Head
Cover design by Greenleaf Book Group LLC

Publisher's Cataloging-In-Publication Data
(Prepared by The Donohue Group, Inc.)
Berglund, John (John Frank), 1954-
  A beach less traveled : from corporate chaos to flip flop perfumer / John Berglund.—1st ed.
  p. ; cm.
  ISBN: 978-1-937110-31-4
  1. Berglund, John (John Frank), 1954—Career in business. 2. Businessmen—Saint Martin (West Indies)—Biography. 3. Perfumes industry—Saint Martin (West Indies) 4. Small business—Saint Martin (West Indies) 5. Saint Martin (West Indies)—Economic conditions. I. Title.
HC158.5.Z7 S2624 2012
330.9/72984/051   2012934353

Part of the Tree Neutral® program, which offsets the number of trees consumed in the production and printing of this book by taking proactive steps, such as planting trees in direct proportion to the number of trees used: www.treeneutral.com

Printed in the United States of America on acid-free paper

12 13 14 15 16   10 9 8 7 6 5 4 3 2 1

First Edition

DEDICATION

*This book is dedicated to my traveling business partner, loving
wife of thirty-plus years, and soul mate, Cyndi.
She has supported my dreams and plays a starring role in this story.
It is also dedicated to all who are dreaming of a
holiday or a move to a tropical island.*

CONTENTS

AUTHOR'S NOTE

"St. Martin" is used regularly throughout the book in reference to the entire island, which is the smallest land mass divided by two countries. "Saint-Martin" is technically the name for the French side of the island, while the Dutch side goes by "Sint Maarten."

St. Martin offers a time for reflection. This tropical Caribbean island means many things to many people: holiday, romance, adventure, home. To Cyndi and me, St. Martin conjures vivid images of the unparalleled natural beauty of the land, the sea, and the people who call this place home. This memoir is my attempt to capture that beauty from a perfumer's perspective: a blending of history, insight, and personal recollections. Enjoy the memories and reflections.

ACKNOWLEDGMENTS

I wish to acknowledge and thank our children, Rachelle and Tyler, who assisted in our business conception and design. My gratitude also extends to the people of St. Martin, who have welcomed us with open arms, and to all who have gone before me, and go after, to explore the world as we find it.

PART I
DREAMS

PERFUME FACT

Not only do perfumes
smell nice, they can change
moods, help us remember
things, or help us dream
and create.

CHAPTER 1

THE BIG PICTURE

I was completely entranced in the ecstasy of my surroundings. I was lying on one of the most beautiful French Caribbean beaches imaginable, next to my amazingly gorgeous wife. She was tan and topless, her black top dangling over the edges of her lounger. The swaying palm trees that surrounded us provided a gentle shade that worked in perfect harmony with the ocean breeze that gently stirred the tropical air.

My eyes were closed, and I listened intently to all the sounds or lack thereof. The repetitious crashing of the surf provided a soothing rhythmic background for the quiet serenity that can only be found in a place like this. I lazily raised my tropical beverage and savored the realization that life was good; life was meant to be enjoyed.

Tomorrow, work would be calling my name, but that was okay. Today, I had this, and it was something to be thankful for. We had no problems managing the staff at the small boutique we owned; we were the only employees. At work, I would reach out to the tourists and offer them our unique wares. It was always interesting to tell the visitors about our shop and witness their looks of enthusiasm and intrigue. Most of these tourists had slightly sunburnt faces and tan lines that easily identified them as not being island locals. There's definitely something desirable about island life, and I remember well the first feelings I had about it. I carry them with me like the breeze carries the scent of blue oceans.

The evening promised to be divine. I was eager to savor a delicious and leisurely meal filled with some of my favorite French cuisine. My wife and I had our favorite island place. Just a few blocks from our home, it always promised a tantalizing meal that we were guaranteed to enjoy.

The next day came quickly, and it was 8:00 a.m. before I knew it. One of my favorite things about living on the island was that I didn't have to wake to an alarm clock. Waking up a bit drowsy to the sounds of roosters crowing and goats crying was pleasantly different than being abruptly awoken by a ringing, electronic noise.

My breakfast routine is one that I cherish. I sip on a steaming cup of French roasted coffee every morning while I read the local paper. The front-page politics and international updates are omnipresent but of no direct interest to my business or lifestyle. There is nothing more liberating than taking away the power of the dips and doodles of the stock market.

It is invigorating to know that I don't have to sit in any chaotic rush-hour traffic, because I only have to walk next door to open the boutique. There are no long, taxing hours during my day. My shop is open from 10 a.m. to 1:00 p.m., Monday through Friday. At 1:00 p.m. comes the perfection of an outing to the beach. Then the boutique reopens at 6:00 p.m. for a couple hours so we can capture business from the dinner crowd. I'm still somewhat fascinated by how such minimal hours can bring such amazing personal rewards.

Life is simple and suits me well. My toolshed consists of a variety of shovels for moving sandy soil and whatnot. I just purchased a car, and it doesn't need a heater because I'm living in a paradise that never gets cold. One of the most gratifying days I've had since being on the island was the day when I got rid of all my dress shoes. Today, I'm a flip-flop wearer. In fact, all I own are flip-flops, and I wouldn't change it for anything. Of course, I had to also make sure there were no more stuffy suits or ties within a ten-mile radius after I got on the island. They have no place in this casual Heaven on Earth.

Every day my wife and I go out and pick the amazing fresh fruit that grows right in our backyard. Coconuts, bananas, limes, papayas, pomegranates, and star fruit have become a part of our daily diets. Watching the fruits go from blossoms to being ready to pick is a delight in itself.

There is way more fruit than my wife and I can eat alone, so we always share with our island friends and neighbors when we visit.

* * * * *

Aah! I've had another short and fabulous work week, and it's Friday afternoon—beach time. I signal the waiter to bring me a tropical beverage. "*Monsieur, un ti punch s'il vous plaît.*"

"Honey, you're talking again," my wife says. Cyndi shakes my arm.

"What, hon?" I'm so drowsy.

"You're talking in your sleep again. Might as well get up. It's almost six anyway, and it snowed a lot last night. You go shovel, and I'll make the coffee. Did you want your usual Pop-Tart?"

Reality has abruptly awoken me from the perfected bliss of dreamland. Today it's twenty degrees below zero in Hudson, Wisconsin, and I have to travel through a slow-paced, black-ice-coated commute from the scenic but frozen river town to St. Paul, Minnesota's capital city, to prepare for a 7:30 a.m. meeting. I turn and look at Cyndi. "Oh, you won't believe the dream I had."

CHAPTER 2

THE DREAM BEGINS

Is this scenario insanity or inspiration? After all, my family and I were born in the United States, an incredible country, the home of freedom and opportunity. Multitudes of people from other countries are trying to sneak into the place where we were fortunate enough to be born.

When it comes to our standard of living, we've never experienced anything short of outstanding. We enjoy working utilities and modern amenities that make life easy. However, despite having lived the good life, I realized I had a dream and a deeper purpose to fulfill.

I dreamed of moving to a foreign island and submersing myself in the lifestyle of island natives who spoke a language I didn't understand. For income, I planned on opening a business that I'd never competed in, in a country with laws I was unfamiliar with. Most people would have called my dream a midlife crisis, a foolish risk, a fanciful folly, or some other term to symbolize its craziness. Is there a doctor in the house?

THE BERGLUND CARIBBEAN VACATION, PART I, CIRCA 1996

Our family of four—Cyndi, Rachelle, T. J., and I—engaged in an exciting and memorable island-hopping adventure. We explored the lands of four saints, one of them home to two queens, starting in St. Thomas and weaving our way to St. Martin, Saba, St. Barts, and St. John. To make our adventure more affordable, we traveled during an extended Thanksgiving vacation to take advantage of off-season rates.

As we left the Minneapolis airport, we smiled. It was five dreary degrees below zero, which was colder than usual, but not unheard of for the end of November. When we landed in St. Thomas, the thermometer read 27 degrees Celsius. We didn't need to know what that converted to in Fahrenheit to know it was wonderful and welcome.

It was great to shed the winter coats and boots that we had donned back home so early in the season. The upper Midwest's dreary brown earthtones splotched with dirty snow couldn't compare to the green tropical beauty and swaying palm trees of our Caribbean destination. Equally enticing, clear, turquoise-blue waters glimmered like sapphire in the sunlight.

We left the land of "you betcha" and were greeted by the thick accents of "yah, mon." That amazing welcome from the St. Thomas natives hit me like a big snowball in the face. I was eager to discover how refreshing it must be to be an islander. Island life, mon . . . I be jammin'!

Outside the airport, Cyndi and I grabbed two rosy-red rum punches and the kids each got a soda. We toasted to the start of the Berglund Caribbean vacation. Little did my wife know that my enthusiasm for the kick-off of our island life was quickly turning into a plan to make the island life our only life.

The rum punch cooled our mouths, drizzled down our throats, and tingled our tummies. I thought of family and friends back home and recollected a favorite saying from the *Farmer's Almanac*: "A real friend is someone who takes a winter vacation on a sun-drenched beach and doesn't send a card."

We've all seen those beautiful postcards with the perfect sunset or some other backdrop to paradise. But there's absolutely nothing that can compare to seeing the real thing. There are more shades of color in a Caribbean sunset than we would have ever known to be possible.

Taxis were lined up, and the drivers each tried to capture our attention and earn a fare. We flagged one to deliver us a mere nine blocks up the big hill to a small, inexpensive, one-room basement unit at

Bluebeard's Castle Hotel. Our first stop would be for two nights on the cheap side.

I was on holiday from my work gig in St. Paul, Minnesota: an attorney/lobbyist/trade-association manager on a rare hiatus. Cyndi operated our family's bed and breakfast inn, which was thirty miles away in Hudson, Wisconsin. The B and B was a historic, 1884 Queen Anne Victorian mansion that we'd converted. We lived in the basement, which gave us some valuable perspective on our present circumstances. Our family was pretty darn good at living in basements!

A few days and a few islands into the trip I found myself relaxing on the patio of our room before dinner at a place called the Captain's Quarter Resort. We were in Saba, and it was November 29, my forty-second birthday. Amazingly, there were no locks on the hotel doors—and no need for any. I had indulged in a few tantalizing tropical beverages and had decided to verbalize what had been brewing in my head since arriving here. I abruptly declared that the Swede Family Berglund should move to Paradise.

My lovely, cynical Cyndi inquired, "And do what for a living?"

I, the closet chemist, raised my hands toward the tropical rainforest overhead. I pointed to its abundance of plants and nutrients and blurted out, "Cosmetics."

I'd be remiss if I didn't mention that Cyndi had heard a few of my desires before. The passion in my voice had her attention, though, and I continued with my narrative. I think she ordered another of those tantalizing drinks, for medicinal purposes.

I used all my corporate skills to diagram the simplicity and necessity of my idea. I explained how the beautiful and popular Cyndi would greet in-store customers; the intense and intelligent Rachelle would be vice president of worldwide marketing; and T. J., the very definition of style and cool, would be the inspiration and designer. In essence, I had just given the most brilliant opening statement of my career.

Cyndi had always found it difficult to cross-examine her attorney husband, but she did give it a try. She peppered me with concerns and lectured me about hurricanes with a fiery rhetoric all her own.

But I had my game on, and I pointed to our historic host hotel, which had several times housed Queens Juliana and Beatrix of the

Netherlands (the "queens" of our tropical adventure). I shared that fact with great animation, mentioning how this, the oldest building on the island, had stood untouched by a hurricane for over one hundred years. Point to me.

I managed to keep that point for three years. But in 1998, Hurricane Georges demolished the entire resort, and it hasn't been rebuilt as of this writing.

Point to Cyndi.

Have no fear; the battle wasn't lost.

* * * * *

What was my motivator for proposing such an insistent, tropical dream? Forever etched in my mind is a visit to my father when he was in hospice. I looked at this once incredibly strong man and saw him attached to numerous tubes. That was back in 1989, and I was starting to get on in years myself. I didn't want that man in the hospice to become me.

I was only thirty-five at the time and was well on my corporate ascent as a lobbyist for the liquor industry. My dad had worked until the day he went into hospice, because he loved to keep busy. He was only seventy-two when he spent his final week here on Earth.

By Tom Brokaw's definition, my father was a member of the Greatest Generation. He had survived the Depression, despite his father's death in a car accident in 1930, and had served his country in World War II as a lieutenant in the infantry. Returning from the war, Dad became a corporate staffer of a regional hardware chain. He left corporate life to open a small hardware store at age forty-seven, and he never looked back.

His entrepreneurial spirit led him to open other retail outlets. He worried only about *his* agenda, *his* successes and failures—not about those of some distant corporate exec. His future was on his own shoulders, and he loved it.

My dad was a man of action and knew that deeds were more powerful than words. In light of that, it's sort of ironic that I spent so many years educating myself for a profession that relied on my words to get the actions I wanted. His only professional advice to me while I was growing up was to get as much education as possible and to work for myself. He had witnessed too many friends in their forties and fifties being laid off and having difficulty securing new, meaningful employment.

Thinking of our own mortality is a peculiar thing. It makes our minds reel with all the what-if's, would-have's, could-have's, and should-have's that such an abrupt awareness brings to one's life. That morbid thought followed me throughout my corporate work years. What if I ended up lying in a hospice bed, knowing I'd never leave? Would I question whether I had lived life to the fullest? Could I have done things differently and changed my habits for a more fulfilled life? Should I have worked more for fun and less for a paycheck?

I had an indescribable desire to do something different than what I'd been doing. My ideas of change were a bit more extreme than Cyndi perhaps realized. However, our desired end result was the same: we wanted to live out our days together and know, without question, that we had enjoyed as much of our lives as possible.

I preferred a warm breeze to a cold freeze. These thoughts were wildly invigorating and reminded me of something that Zig Ziglar once said: "Will you look back on life and say, 'I wish I had,' or 'I'm glad I did'?"

In 1989, a few months after my father's death but before my tropical illusions, Cyndi followed my then-current dream. I'll admit it was enhanced by the popular Bob Newhart TV show about Vermont innkeepers who wanted the lifestyle of bed-and-breakfast owners.

We purchased the Queen Anne Victorian in Hudson, thirty miles across the border from Minneapolis-St. Paul. We rezoned, remodeled, and opened our beautiful B and B for business in October 1990. It had six rooms, and each had its own private whirlpool and fireplace. It was a beautiful and wildly romantic place for a couple's retreat or for St. Croix River lovers to stay the night.

Oddly enough, the first night we'd ever stayed at a bed and breakfast was the night we opened our own. It may be evidence that my experiences come from some abnormal, deep-down calling. Back in college I took my first ever airplane ride just to jump out of it and join a skydiving club.

Cyndi became queen bee of our beautiful inn while I continued working in my corporate capacity in St. Paul. On weekends and evenings I transformed into the inn's dumbwaiter. For nine years we labored at a life of love in the cold tundra and met countless wonderful guests who arrived from all areas of the United States. We even had a few international guests.

During those years I had an opportunity to invest in a new venture with two other B and B owners. We purchased an old, three-story brick building on the St. Croix River in Stillwater, Minnesota, only ten miles away from Hudson. I was an equal but silent partner in the venture as we took out a $3 million loan for renovations and updates. That was a ridiculously high amount for three families who had little money. This brick building was converted into a forty-room historic inn and conference center named the Lumber Baron's Hotel.

The "newly antiquated" hotel opened to revenues in excess of projections. Unfortunately, the expenses were also well over projection. We changed managers, but the struggles continued. We were close to losing the business and our B and B's, which were also our homes.

One month later, and a mere twenty-four hours before we were to hire a bankruptcy attorney, our primary lender approved a new loan. It saved the day. We hired a new manager who would be more effective, and a few years later we sold the business at a slight profit.

Martha Hubbs, wife of one of the partners, was asked a defining question about the Lumber Baron's Hotel by the local Stillwater press prior to its opening. The reporter asked what would happen if we didn't succeed. Her response was something to this effect: "We'll just pick up the pieces and find something else to do." The statement was brilliant, and it clearly stated that competent people could find a way to make a living.

Her observation has given me great comfort in my endeavors over the years, and I remembered her words when Cyndi and I invested our life savings in a new business venture on a foreign island. In fact, as I sat on the patio during our first tropical adventure in 1996 and began spinning my dream vision for my somewhat skeptical family, Martha's words were probably bouncing around inside me.

One of our society's most overrated beliefs is that a job involves no more than chasing a certain quality of life through toys, trinkets, and retirement savings. On the other hand, the most underrated truth is that we can find something we love to do and gain the important things in life without even realizing that we're working. The rat race is a sure path to stress and potential misery, but it doesn't have to be that way.

I spent far too many years of my life working for money, then continuing to work for more. Career building was my focus, starting with being a prosecuting attorney, then moving on to being an attorney-lobbyist, and then finally a trade association executive. I was so focused on the corporate ladder that I often missed incredible opportunities awaiting me.

Thankfully, some of my peers rendered me sane advice, not that they realized it. One lobbyist, after losing a Senate vote on his issue, rationalized, "Life is a bitch, and then you die." This particular person was a few years younger than I and wore his stress outwardly. He was becoming a heavy drinker and noticeably gaining weight. Another lobbyist, a former legislator, counseled me after a senator ignored my attempt at a hallway discussion. He told me, "They don't understand that when they're out of office, people no longer care about who they are or what they think."

Careers in the United States involve forty- to eighty-hour work-weeks, annoying alarm clocks, and the weeklong hope for the relative freedom of a peaceful weekend. For thirty years Cyndi and I accepted this premise as we climbed that ladder in Minnesota, Georgia, and Texas. After sixteen years as a lobbyist for the liquor industry, I experienced my first personal political hit. In 1998, a state senator filed an ethical complaint against me after his bill lost on the Senate floor by one vote for the second time. I was the face of his opposition, or in this case, the poster child.

The complaint was over a flyer that listed my name as the author. Others in our coalition had drafted this particular piece, and I had agreed to put my name on it for a variety of reasons involving expediency for my clients, some of whom wished to keep a low profile. The senator characterized some of the contents as misleading.

This was the first time in roughly forty years that an ethical complaint had been filed by a legislator against a lobbyist. In fact, the higher-ups were clueless about the process that should follow. Meanwhile, I was emotionally crushed; taking one for the liquor-industry lobbyist team wasn't something I cherished. I called my wife and mother to alert them before they heard it on the news.

Soon after, the senator and I met for a private discussion. He told me he would withdraw his complaint if I would publically proclaim I was wrong on the issue. In other words, I could sell out my client and get off the hook. I ignored his offer.

The chair of the ethics committee happened to be a cosponsor of the senator's bill—you know, the bill that had just been defeated. Not only that, but she was also the author of another liquor bill that I had beaten weeks earlier after she and I had vigorously debated its merits on a CBS national morning news show.

The entire hullabaloo was, of course, quite newsworthy, and reporters embraced every opportunity to call and question me about it. I felt sick to my stomach for days.

The day of the hearing came. The newspaper reported that over a hundred lobbyists packed the hearing room, protesting the procedures being utilized. Many of those lobbyists had done battle with me or against me, but all could testify to my integrity.

The complaint was dismissed in the follow-up hearing. I trudged home, feeling no sense of victory, and mixed two tropical libations to share with my ever-faithful Cyndi. I knew I hadn't done anything wrong, but one day a few weeks later I received a bit of salve for my wounded soul. A lobbyist friend shared his experience of having been in the middle of a well-documented scandal. He said, "John, believe it or not, I was actually able to raise my hourly fee; I was better known and in-demand. You know the old saying, 'All publicity is good, just spell my name right.'" Incidentally, in the next Minnesota legislative session the rules were changed for future ethical complaints, requiring a due process hearing before the complaint could go public.

If I had any doubts about getting the hell out of Dodge and ultimately landing in the Caribbean, those doubts were long gone. The dream intensified. But until I could act on it, I knew I had had enough of Minnesota's "clean" politics, and a few months later I took a position in Atlanta, representing a physician's association.

The doctors were wonderful people to work for, and there was no doubt that everything they fought for was to make things better for their patients. Still, it was the same daily corporate rat race: fighting the insurance lobby, trial attorneys, pharmaceutical companies, and others that impacted the doctors' roles.

Many nights I lay awake, longing for a simpler life. My mind would always return to the soothing sounds of the ocean, the soft lapping of the waves on the beach. I was able to transport myself there mentally, and it was a welcome vacation from the reality of my current career.

The tropical setting increased my dream's therapeutic value and continued to come in handy a few years later, after I accepted a national position in Texas, running the bowling-center trade association. At least I kept physically moving farther south.

There were days when the corporate climb, with its associated politics, agendas, and long hours, was comparable to scaling Mount Everest in a bitter, blinding snowstorm without an oxygen tank. I sometimes had to postpone family outings or miss them altogether.

For thirty years I climbed and climbed without getting any stronger. I concluded I was working for money and that it was time to work for myself, to set my own workday agenda.

I knew the why, but how, when, and where? Those were all questions I needed to answer.

I found some amazing resolve one day and made a commitment: I was determined to make the present day our family's first day of success by transforming my dream to one of means, not ends. There were four basic tenets that helped convert my idealistic fantasy into a real possibility:

1. Work for myself. Maybe Papa had it correct after all. Why do we always find out those things when it's too late? A 2009 Gallup-Healthways Well-Being Index, from a poll of 100,000 people, found that business owners scored highest as the happiest Americans.

2. I had to live in a tropical area where people pay to vacation. Growing up in Minnesota, the land of 10,000 frozen lakes, made this a tantalizing prospect. I used to proudly announce that, while attending law school at the University of San Diego, I graduated in the top 5 percent of my class . . . in beach activities.

3. My required foot attire had to be nothing more formal than a pair of flip-flops; I wanted the freedom of having my toes exposed. As I was growing up, helping my father in his hardware store, I admired the professionals who dressed to the max. The suit, tie, and fancy, polished shoes represented success, and I wanted to be like them. But I reached that goal and discovered it wasn't so special after all. I no longer wanted to be like them; I wanted to free the toes.

4. I wanted to be in a position to help others. I had been too busy ascending the corporate ladder, and the time had come to start giving something back.

I'm fully aware that many people viewed my dreams of abandoning civilization and moving to a tropical island as childish fancy, unpractical nonsense. But the fact is that many people have similar fantasies in varying intensities. In fact, I believe that a majority of people momentarily experience such dreams but dismiss them as insanity or, the worst of all words, impossible. Still, others dream longingly of such a move, but never act on the impulse. Thankfully, inspiration can be drawn from the select few who take their given dreams and "just do it." Count Cyndi and me in that last category.

My island dream embraced cultural learnings, new opportunities, fashionable lifestyles, exotic lands, working for myself, and helping people. I believed in Walt Disney's observation: "If you can dream it, you can do it."

These visions provided a necessary escape from the tedious routines of my daily corporate life. I came to think of it as pulling the trigger on our aspirations: sometimes the metaphorical bullet might hit the target, sometimes the gun might shoot blanks, and other times it could backfire and explode in our faces. But the dream would not die.

My dreams also served as appealing alternatives to the medications that some depend on to remain stable. When we dream, we're stable and visualizing how great it is to try something different. You take a shot at it and simply follow the trajectory of the bullet. My exploratory trips to the Caribbean were exhilarating and helped me create the direction I wanted to go in my life.

However, I still needed to determine how to break into the cosmetics business. Gift shops, restaurants, and beach bars were all possibilities. On the other hand, though these were fun jobs, they were labor intensive and, unless converted to a multiple-location operation, had limited upside potential.

Thus, the manufacturing part of the business was my preferred choice. Retail by itself was limited to the products and their cost and was controlled by distributors. Conversely, few items for sale to tourists were actually made on the island. I considered that a big advantage for manufacturing.

I had been studying botany and chemistry for years and decided to start focusing on the Caribbean's abundance of natural resources available for fragrance and cosmetic creations. I drafted a business plan, not for a client, a bank, or a corporate boss, but for Cyndi and myself. Energy and enthusiasm flowed . . . as did the homemade tropical libations.

To minimize the prospect of failure, I envisioned sales of perfumes and related unique gift items originating on multiple, concurrent paths:

- Sales to tourists at the manufacturing location

- Sales to distributors or other retail operators

- Sales worldwide via the Internet

A necessary caveat to the dream and the planning was to ensure there was sufficient time to research—at the beach. I know: it's a dirty job, but . . .

So now, the fantasy was in its beginning stages. And the rest of the story was beginning to unfold.

PART II

RESEARCH AND PREPARATION

PERFUME FACT

The combinations of scents that most increase male sexual arousal are lavender and pumpkin pie; the combinations that most increase female sexual arousal are cucumber and Good & Plenty candy (licorice, or anise).

CHAPTER 3

THE SEARCH FOR AN ISLAND

In order to open a business in Paradise we needed a location—duh! After our first family Caribbean vacation in 1996, when I had boldly blurted out that we would live and work in the tropics, I smartly narrowed it to "somewhere down there." But which island?

We had visited five islands under the guise of a family holiday. But my pronouncement required a second visit to acquire a business perspective. Considerations for schooling were irrelevant, so that helped a titch; both of our children would be in, or beyond, American colleges before we could financially act on our dream.

Berglund Vacation Part II transpired in 1998. The fab four traveled from Tortola to St. Kitts to St. Martin, adding two new islands to our repertoire. In two trips we had visited a total of seven islands, and it was no coincidence that St. Martin was the only dot on the map visited twice.

Each island definitely tempted us with its unique beauty and attraction. I discovered with each passing year that it took less time to fly to the Caribbean and more time to drive to work. Those are the thoughts one gets when one is ready to take the next step and is building up justifications for every element of the transition.

St. Thomas was a popular cruise stop, and real estate values were a bargain after recent hurricanes. It offered secluded beaches, national parks, tremendous shopping, world-class diving, tropical forests, superb sailing, island art, and a great nightlife. Plus, all of those benefits were wrapped in the security and efficiency of the American flag. We couldn't ignore the locals, though, when they told us not to walk downtown at night.

St. John's, also an American territory, was two-thirds national park, had lush vegetation, and possessed a small-town atmosphere. We rented a Jeep and explored the hilly terrain. The people were friendly and spoke English. However, from a business perspective, the island was relatively non-commercial and low-key. The tiny island is only accessible by boat or ferry.

Tortola, part of the nearby British Virgin Islands, is the sailing capital of the Caribbean, an island of contrasts. I could look one direction and see the hustle and bustle of Road Town. Turn my head another direction and I'd discover the peace and tranquility of Sage Mountain National Park. That area has secluded beaches and is comparable to St. John's for its tropical beauty—and its limited number of tourists.

St. Kitts is a former British colony, filled with plantation history. It is home to a well-preserved fort and a rainforest adorning the majestic, cloud-fringed peak of Mount Liamuiga, which provided habitat for the elusive green vervet monkey. We enjoyed lunching in the capital city of Basseterre while witnessing a local judge dine nearby, frocked in his black robe and white wig.

Its sister island, Nevis, was a short ferry ride away. All in all, though, the island, while beautiful, appeared to be in transition as a tourist destination. It wasn't the right choice for us.

Saba, with less than 3,000 inhabitants, was truly unique. The entire land mass was a volcanic peak with a tropical rainforest at the cloudy top. I'd expected a beach at the bottom, but that was not to be. There was, however, a national water park that lent its beauty to a drive with breathtaking views.

St. Bart's, the most elegant and expensive Caribbean island, was French in all ways and had beautiful beaches to boot. On this intimate and alluring island of 8,000 residents there were no casinos, no mega resorts, and no cruise ships to clutter the view. English, however, was a limited commodity.

As it turned out, St. Martin was the winner of the Berglund lottery because of its beautiful contrasts, French culture, and the mother country's historical role in the perfume industry. It had history, culture, and tourism. It remains the smallest island shared by two countries, giving residents and visitors unique choices.

St. Martin has a bustling economy based on tourism, but also retains an abundance of undeveloped tropical vegetation shared by cattle, sheep, and goats. Did I happen to mention that a goat's bleating is actually a delightful sound to wake up to in the morning?

Our business plan called for us to produce one of only a few items island-made for the shopping tourists: perfume.

We received an insider's perspective during our 1998 trip. Cyndi and then-seventeen-year-old Rachelle met a young, good-looking, twenty-four year-old sailor, Colin Campbell, on a catamaran tour of the island. Colin, a Canadian with sandy brown hair and a muscular build, could have passed for a California surfer dude. He was well educated and had outstanding manners. He had worked at Club Med as a sailing instructor, bartender, and chief gopher prior to landing in St. Martin. Now he assisted with catamaran tours and did some bartending.

Colin and Rachelle hit it off, and at Colin's invitation we all got together at the Arawak Café in Marigot. His information, perspective, and counsel on island life were invaluable. In our many returns to the island, often without our daughter, we would check on Colin and enjoy watching his career progress from sailing crew to top bartender (once voted best bartender on the island during the annual *Daily Herald* poll) to co-owner of the successful Red Piano bar in Simpson Bay.

According to popular legend, St. Martin/Sint Maarten's boundaries were established in 1648 by a walking contest around the island's perimeter. Setting off in opposite directions, a wine-drinking Frenchman paced off twenty-one square miles, while a less speedy, gin-drinking Dutchman wound up with only sixteen square miles. As scissors beats paper, so does wine beat gin. Good information to know should such an opportunity present itself.

St. Martin was once known for its salt ponds. Other islands were known for sugarcane, tobacco, and cotton plantations during the brutal centuries of Caribbean slavery. Salt is thought to have first been extracted in St. Martin around 1631, and the industry thrived until the

1920s. At that time, salt was used more for preserving food than for flavoring it. There was a modest sugarcane industry on the island from 1770 to 1850, and a few plantations remain today, including a popular and impressive tourist spot known as Lotterie Farms.

Today St. Martin is a popular cruise stop with an enjoyable nearby shopping district in Phillipsburg. The island offers a Las Vegas–type nightclub atmosphere in Maho, Parisian elegance in Marigot, and a sleepy French seaside village in Grand Case. Grand Case is often referred to as the gourmet capital of the Caribbean. We like to eat, so we couldn't help but like the sound of that.

St. Martin was also inviting because of the combination of its Dutch gentility and French sophistication. It's the only truly duty-free port in the Caribbean that's coupled with trade preference within the European Union and the United States. Not even the U.S. Virgin Islands are totally duty-free. If you ship something from the United States to yourself in St. Croix, it goes through customs, and most items incur a duty.

St. Martin became duty-free in 1939 as a practical matter. Prior to that time there were guardhouses on the island's Dutch-French borders that charged import fees for liquor and other products. This resulted in smuggling both at the border crossing and over the mountainous hills. It was a cumbersome burden to manage, and it became so difficult that it was easier to abandon the duty concept. This made St. Martin a shopper's haven and an advantageous place to do business.

The clincher for the family patriarch in choosing St. Martin, after discovering it was duty free, was that its beaches enjoyed the French tradition for topless bathing. Upon the stark discovery of the latter, I did as any reasonable man might do and lost a contact lens in the sand.

Baie Orientale, or Orient Beach, is to St. Martin what a mountain full of fresh snow powder is to Aspen. If one jaunts to St. Martin for the thirty-seven beaches, then one must visit Orient, the most populous and active beach on the island, if not the entire Caribbean. Labeled the French Riviera of the Caribbean, Orient is a beach we love. The smell of the salty water, the wind in our faces, the gentle tumbling of the surf, along with the surrounding activity and French culture, combine to create a sense of tranquility. Orient Beach forms a crescent of two miles of beautiful sand, surf, water activities, a few gift shops, and a multitude of beach bars, many serving fine French foods.

Topless bathing is *au naturel*, and if one wishes a full-body experience, it is available at the far end of the beach, just past some low-lying rocks. Beyond those boulders lies the world-renowned naturist resort, Club Orient. Their turf is clothing-optional. One of the delightful older "Club O" guests told me she used to be a 34-B, but now is a 34-long.

We were hesitant to check out Orient on our first St. Martin visit, since we had young children in tow. We were enjoying a breakfast in Marigot and asked the restaurant owner, a handsome young French Canadian, for his suggestion.

"Monsieur, what beach do you recommend we first try?"

"Orient Beach, but of course."

"Is it okay to go there with our young kids?"

"Yes, yes, 'tis beautiful, with many things to do. Many families there. Your children love it, trust me."

Trusting that his word was as good as his food, we nervously drove through Grand Case to Orient. We took a left and went in through the first entry to the lengthy beach, putting us at Boo Boo Jam, an active beach bar at the far northern end, next to the Mount Vernon resort. We couldn't afford beach chairs on that vacation, so we instead placed our towels near the water's edge and enjoyed the surrounding beauty. We weren't completely relaxed, but we were completely curious.

We swam, bodysurfed, walked the length of the beach, and ate and drank fantastic fare. It was fascinating to be surrounded by such beautiful people in such varying states of dress. The restaurant owner was dead on: T. J. and Rachelle loved it, and we returned the next day. We did get bitten by a few sand flies (a.k.a. "no-see-ums"). But even those pesky bites were a source of inspiration, as years later I concocted an all-natural insect repellent with lemon eucalyptus.

Not surprisingly, we periodically get asked the same question from first-time visitors: would they enjoy Orient Beach? Our answer is always an emphatic yes. Topless bathing is not a big deal; it's a personal preference, and, in fact, most Americans simply choose to keep their tops on.

A primary reason we chose to live in St. Martin is the abundance of

French culture, something visiting Americans easily recognize whether they appreciate it nor not. The French are known for their *savoir vivre*, the ability to live life well, with intelligent enjoyment: meeting every situation with poise, good manners, and elegance. We're unabashed Francophiles. The French-side restaurants, cafés, and designer boutiques all possess a quaint charm that is distinctly *je ne sais quoi*.

The Dutch side was formerly part of the Netherlands Antilles, along with the islands of Curaçao, Saba, St. Eustasius, and Bonaire. This collection was considered an autonomous country of the Kingdom of the Netherlands until Sint Maarten voted to be an autonomous country within the Netherlands Empire, which it attained in October 2010. The Dutch side posts prices in a local currency and dollars. The American tourists perceive this as more Caribbean in flavor than Dutch. That's definitely not so for the French side.

St. Martin is a *collectivité territoriale* of France. This means that it's part of France itself and is governed by the mother country through its appointed *préfet*. A few years prior the island was designated as merely a *commune* with its regional headquarters located on the island of Guadeloupe. The laws and the euro currency of France apply to St. Martin.

Working in France or its territories means a thirty-five-hour workweek, four weeks of vacation, many holidays, free health care, and a good night's sleep. A 2009 survey by the International Organization for Economic Cooperation and Development found that the French spend more time sleeping, on average, than those in any other developed country: eight hours and fifty minutes per night. It's amazing how productive one can be while living a carefree lifestyle when you get great night's sleep!

Another study claimed that only 57 percent of Americans used their entire allotted vacation days, while 89 percent of the French do. Who is the better hire? The Americans. Who enjoys life more? The French. And does it matter how many extra days you worked when you're lying in hospice?

Since 1871, France, including St. Martin, hasn't categorized people according to their alleged ethnic origins. The usage of ethnic and racial categorization is avoided to prevent discrimination. This explains why there's considerably less racial tension on the island than in America.

Interracial blending is a vibrant and boasted feature of French culture. Bob Marley, the first pop superstar from Jamaica, offered his perspective on race many years ago. "I don't have prejudice against meself. My father was a white and my mother was black. Them call me half-caste or whatever. Me don't dip on nobody's side. Me don't dip on the black man's side nor the white man's side. Me dip on God's side, the one who create me and cause me to come from black and white."

The French are perceived as taking great pride in their national identity. Americans assert the French are arrogant, while the French make a comparable claim of Americans. Perhaps we're much alike.

The most memorable event of our first visit to St. Martin in 1996 occurred one evening as Cyndi and I journeyed to dinner. We made our way from our mostly French-speaking Nettle Bay Beach Club in Sandy Ground to the famed dining village of Grand Case, about thirty minutes away. We left Rachelle and T. J., fifteen and twelve at the time, respectively, back at the hotel with an unusual but delicious non-American pizza.

We enjoyed an exquisite dinner at L'Bistrot Caraibes, owned by two young brothers, Thibault and Amaury Meziére. We would get to know Thibault and Amaury years later as wonderful business neighbors. Cyndi ordered a crisp mixed salad and roast duck breast with a sweet and sour honey sauce. I tried the braised red snapper in a creamy mussel sauce with saffron. A delicious French chardonnay accompanied our meal. Prior to ordering, our transplanted Parisian waiter, likely Thibault or Amaury, politely asked in broken English if we'd be so kind to move to another table. They wished to combine our table with another for a larger group. We were happy to comply with their request.

After dinner, our server gave us a gift of gratitude to thank us for relocating: an after-dinner drink of our choice. Cyndi chose the Scottish Drambouie and I, being in a French restaurant, chose Grand Marnier. Shockingly, our waiter brought out the bottles and two empty glasses, setting each before us in a pour-your-own manner. We poured our own, and poured our own again. This wasn't like the States, where liquor law liability would make such generosity unthinkable to a restaurateur.

After the delicious dinner, we carefully retreated to Nettle Bay on the winding and unfamiliar narrow roads. We parked and casually meandered to our darkened villa on the beach. After locating the key and unlocking the door, our children rushed from the darkness into our arms. They anxiously explained they had been without electricity in their hot, stuffy room for hours. They had dutifully called the hotel desk, only to be blockaded by the language barrier.

I followed the unlit sidewalk to the hotel lobby and articulated the issue with the help of hand signs. We were quickly and graciously moved to a nearby unit with electricity in good working order. A memorable evening for all, although definitely more pleasurable for Cyndi and me than the kids.

Our tropical dream now had a destination: St. Martin. It was more difficult than ever to return to the snowy Dairy State, Wisconsin. I actively started to research and study skin care and the creation of fragrances while visualizing the concept for our business.

At this time, I was in the process of accepting the position in Atlanta to work for the physicians' group. That opportunity opened new doors to medical research. I also spent every minute I could lusting for the quieter tropical lands of St. Martin. This evolving dream would require having a home lab to test concoctions, and it would also necessitate numerous future visits to St. Martin in search of a great piece of property.

CHAPTER 4

DR. FRANKENSTEIN
CREATES PERFUMES

Creating perfume requires a dream, a vision, knowledge, patience and—if you're doing it for commercial purposes—money. My dream was a lifestyle change to a Caribbean island; my vision was a new career aligning my life with my passion. I had acquired the knowledge through years of chemistry and fragrance study that continues every day. The patience . . . well, maybe I didn't need all of the attributes. I may always have a challenge with patience no matter how laid back my environment. We were saving the money for our goal, though we tried not to dwell on the fact that this was putting our children's inheritance on the line.

I vividly recall Christmas 1965. I was twelve and received a chemistry lab set complete with chemicals, microscope, test tubes, and a Bunsen burner. I couldn't have been more excited about any gift. After an early church service amidst the snow and frozen temperatures in Minneapolis, I retreated to our semi-heated basement washroom and its freezing cement floor and unfinished bare walls. It was there that I set up my first lab. It wasn't an inspirational space per se, but the thoughts, innovations, and ideas in my head were delighted nonetheless to have a place to call home. In quiet solitude I could mix, design, invent, concoct, and enjoy chemistry. Eventually I ordered more items for my set, and I spent as much time as possible in my basement castle.

The youthful memories of creations and formulations transferred to college chemistry classes and the associated lab work. After college I had a choice of attending graduate school or law school, and I chose the latter, believing it presented better financial opportunities. I had initially chosen money over passion and hoped someday to have the financial wherewithal to return to my true love, figuring it would someday be more fun to create than to argue.

In the many years leading to the opening of our business, I religiously studied the history of fragrance, famous perfumers, and formulas. I was amazed and fascinated by how one could mix two chemical compounds together and end up with a new third compound that was all its own in scent and properties.

It was astounding to see how oil and water would mix with the use of certain emulsions. Blending single-note oils to create perfumes was an adventurous journey that had potential to create heavenly results.

The move to Atlanta in 1999 resulted in relocating to a country home on five acres of wooded land with thick underbrush. Even Dr. Frankenstein couldn't have asked for better privacy.

I converted the walk-out basement to a working lab with an array of chemicals, equipment, and denatured alcohol, which I had purchased with a permit from the Bureau of Alcohol, Tobacco, and Firearms. If the house were to blow, neighbors would be unaffected. Thankfully no threatening incidents or explosions took place.

My lab included a library full of various journals and papers dating from the most recent and trending back to discoveries in the 1800s. I studied biology and biodynamics. I consulted with a local chemist and conducted extensive interviews with perfumers, dermatologists, and numerous cosmetic suppliers. For me, school was seriously in session and would continue into our next move in 2002, to Arlington, Texas.

Phase one of our product development concluded with the partial opening of our Caribbean parfumerie in December 2007. It was slowly taking place. And when I say slowly, I mean turtle pace. Remember, patience wasn't my particular virtue; I was in torment, wanting things to move faster.

Chemists and perfumers whom I studied for countless hours ranged from W. A. Poucher, who authored the 1923 masterpiece *Perfumes and*

Cosmetics, to Ernest Breaux, who had left Russia when the czar was overthrown to accept a position making perfumes for Coco Chanel.

I was a regular at department store fragrance counters, asking more questions than most women would ever consider. I would smell, sample, and read the labels until I had them memorized. I devoured biographies of noted designers with namesake perfumes, trying to gain an insight into their entrepreneurial success.

I began to notice common traits. I decided that our business would differentiate itself by manufacturing the perfumes itselve rather than subcontracting the development to a highly regarded industrial fragrance house. Admittedly, by going solo we had fewer industrial resources, but we gained greater product control. Perhaps that was my father's influence.

As I'll explain more fully later, we chose the name "Tijon" (pronounced "Tezhon") for our business. Actually, the idea came to me one lonely evening as I waited for my family to join me in Atlanta. It was a blending of our son's nickname—T. J., short for Tyler John—with a French-sounding twist.

Entrepreneurial pioneers I studied and respected included Coco Chanel, my scent hero and a businesswoman of incredible acumen. Although some scholars suggested it started with Frances Coty, I submit that modern day perfumery began with Chanel. Born Gabrielle Bonheur Chanel, Coco grew up poor in France and was orphaned in her early teens. In 1921 Coco introduced Chanel No. 5 to the world, a scent formulated by her hired perfumer, Ernest Breaux. It was the first fragrance to be introduced by a clothing designer; now they all do it. Coco, as she became popularly known, set both industry and society standards. Her darkly tanned appearance steered society away from Victorian pale.

I also gained a deep admiration for Estée Lauder, born Josephine Esther Mentzer in Queens, New York. She was an intense marketing master who began with her own name change, initiating her empire by selling lotions made by her uncle in their basement. She was a cosmetic pioneer in marketing efforts that included calling on stores to not only carry her products, but to allow her trained staff to instruct customers on proper use of the products.

Born Ralph Rueben Lifshitz in the Bronx, Ralph Lauren similarly understood the value of a name change. He was always interested in men's fashion, yet he never attended a fashion school. His career began as a sales associate with Brooks Brothers. Later he would design and sell ties, which, in turn, opened the doors in 1972 to his creation of the famous men's short-sleeve mesh shirt with the polo logo.

Calvin Klein, although four years younger than Ralph Lauren, grew up in the same Bronx neighborhood. Klein began with a coat shop, featuring his own designs in the city's York Hotel. Similar to Coco Chanel, he was later described as "the supreme master of minimalism." As Lauren had done, he worked with an industrial fragrance house to create namesake perfumes.

A few years after our boutique opened, I had a fascinating visit with Terri Lawton, a world-renowned provider of innovative organic and holistic approaches to skin care and age management. There she was, in my boutique, and I was excited to take advantage of her expertise and share mine. Terri formulated two nice fragrances from the oils on our perfume organ, both of which became customer favorites and, as we discovered later, were worn by a Hollywood A-list actress. I do my best to never stop learning all I can, from anyone I can.

Knowledge of fragrance history was also necessary and similarly fascinating, so for me it wasn't a daunting task to absorb a load of information. *Parfum* comes from the Latin phrase *per fumum*, meaning "through smoke." The first fragrances consisted of incense for religious purposes in Arabia, China, and ancient Egypt—interesting, when you consider that most would assume that the French invented perfume. Well, they may not have invented it, but they certainly redefined it.

Historically, perfumes were used to mask odors, too. The fear of bacteria-filled water existed in the Middle Ages due to deadly bouts of bubonic plague and other diseases. Known as the Perfume King, France's Louis XIV reportedly bathed only once or twice in his entire lifetime, opting to dose himself heavily each day with different perfumes. Perfumes were prized possessions, considering the stench of city life during those times.

Grasse, France, became world perfume headquarters in the eighteenth and nineteenth centuries, evolving as the perfume capital subsequent to being a popular leather glove–making region. When scented gloves became the rage across Europe in the 1700s, Grasse adapted and created the fragrances by growing what they could and importing the other flowers and oils needed. It turned out that Grasse had the perfect climate for roses, lavender, and jasmine. At one time over 20,000 people were employed in Grasse's flourishing perfume industry.

My search for knowledge even embraced fiction and movies. *Perfume: The Story of a Murderer* by German writer Patrick Suskind, originally published in 1985 as *Das Parfum,* was adapted into a 2006 movie starring Dustin Hoffman, Alan Rickman, and Ben Whishaw. The story explores the sense of smell and its relationship with the emotional meaning that scents carry. Its plot centers on Jean-Baptiste Grenouille, an unwanted Parisian orphan and misfit who has no personal body scent but who possesses a superior olfactory sense. In the story, he creates the world's finest perfumes.

Grenouille's work, however, takes a dark turn as he embarks on a career as a serial murder of beautiful virgins. His goal is to capture their body scents in an effort to create the perfect fragrance. The ending was twisted and captivating.

After reading that book and later viewing the movie, I couldn't help but wonder: if I succeeded in creating a beautiful scent, in addition to advertising it as "no animal products used" and "not tested on animals," did I also need market it as "no virgins killed in the making of this perfume"? Hmm . . .

I had discovered my own perfect blend of passion and inspiration: studying chemistry and perfumes was definitely my passion, and learning how one could become rich and famous selling fragrances was both educational and inspiring. Putting the two together was the challenge. But I embraced the challenge and prepared to conquer it. I remember taking a bar review course in preparation for the California and Minnesota bars, back at the beginning of my professional career. A professor teaching the course offered valuable insight into the bar exam when he said, "Think of all the lawyers you know. How tough can it really be?" I found this recollection oddly encouraging as I prepared my assault on the fortress of fragrance manufacture and marketing.

* * * * *

To create perfumes is to blend fragrant oils. This requires an acute sense of smell acquired at birth and further developed through training. My sense of smell is crucial in judging single fragrances and blending them. Similar to the taste buds of a wine connoisseur or the endurance of a marathoner, your sense of smell can improve with training, and train I did.

Women generally have a better sense of smell than men. Cyndi has a good nose made better by smelling and critiquing my creations for fifteen years. Years after we opened the business, a customer asked Cyndi, "Who has the better nose, you or John, the perfumer?" Cyndi responded, "I think I do, but John the perfumer-attorney will convince you he does." We enjoy a competitive marriage, and I like to give her the illusion of victory on occasion . . . just kidding, my love!

Most people are unaware of the significant role that our sense of smell plays in our lives. At this given moment you're using your sense of smell and probably don't realize it. I bet you also took a sniff of the air after that last sentence. Of all our senses, smell triggers the strongest memories and emotions and can change our mood. Bruce, a cruise director, once explained that his mother died while he was young, and he remembers her vividly through her perfume, White Diamonds. To this day, when he's lonely, he sometimes places a few drops of that fragrance behind his ears.

Our sense of smell also plays a large role in eating, too, because 90 percent of taste is attributed to smell. If you hold your nose while eating a piece of chocolate, it'll taste like cardboard. Mature at birth, the olfactory sense is one of the first that a newborn baby experiences; it is at work even while we are sleeping. People who suffer from *anosmia* have lost their sense of smell and are often prone to depression.

A multitude of perfume fragrances exist simply because no two people smell odors the same way—even when they're sniffing the same thing! A debate is ongoing in the scientific and medical community in regard to whether people acquire likes or dislikes for certain scents or whether they are present at birth. The consensus appears to support acquisition.

Perfumes are made from over 3,000 possible ingredients in the plant world, derived from flowers, roots, leaves, stems, seeds, resins, herbs, bark, lichens, moss, and fruits. Perfumes wouldn't exist today if we couldn't extract the oils from their raw materials. A variety of techniques have been used over the years, but the most common extraction method remains steam distillation, invented around the year A.D. 1000 by the Persian scholar Ibn Sina (Avicenna). In this method, the flowers, twigs, or roots are submerged in boiling water, and the resulting steam is captured and cooled. The steam then condenses back to water, and the oil separates and goes to rest on the surface to await collection.

At Tijon we utilize steam distillation to create oils from locally grown products such as jasmine, gardenia, rosemary, and sometimes frangipani. Other oils are imported from many sources throughout the world, and we pay close attention, because the quality varies greatly. For example, the original sandalwood groves have been overharvested, and there are now about nineteen varieties. We need also be careful, as many supposedly "pure" oils are diluted with alcohol or other chemicals. Testing is always paramount with the ingredients we wish to use to make a fragrance.

Possessing oils means little, of course, without knowledge of how they blend. One perfume will often include from thirty to three hundred different scents. All oils are categorized into three "notes," although some are flexible, fitting into more than one category. The notes are based on evaporation rate. The unique balancing act in this mixture is what gives a fragrance its distinct personality.

Top notes, often citrus scents and the lightest of the bunch, disappear within five to ten minutes. A nice perfume could be made with lime oil only, but the fragrance wouldn't last long. Middle notes provide three primary purposes. They help define a perfume's character, help classify its fragrance family, and can modify its base notes. It takes approximately ten minutes for middle notes to develop on the skin, and, with the assistance of other top and base notes, they can last for hours. Middle notes tend to be rich in floral scents. We could make a nice perfume of rose oils only, but without the top and base notes, its scent would shortly disappear on the skin.

Base notes tend to be the heaviest scented and longest lasting ingredients. They're the last thing we'll smell from our fragrance. Many of the scents in this category smell hideous to the untrained nose. Base notes are frequently referred to as fixatives because they prolong the evaporation rate or dry down. They give perfume its depth. Ambergris, civet, castoreum, and musk are all base oils that were extracted from animals and used as common fixatives in earlier perfumes. Today, they've been replaced by synthetics.

Ambergris is a solid, waxy substance of a dull grey or blackish color occurring naturally as a biliary secretion from the intestines of the sperm whale; it can be found floating upon the sea or in the sand near the coast. When heated, it melts to a resinous liquid. Cyndi and I thought we had found a large clump on Galleon Beach in St. Martin and sent off a piece to France for testing, but the negative results left us disappointed.

Civet, highly valued as a fragrance and stabilizing agent for perfume, is derived from the perineal glands of the cat-like civet. It's harvested by killing the animal and removing the glands or by scraping the secretions from the glands of a live animal. The popular Chanel No. 5 replaced its civet component with a synthetic in the 1980s.

Castoreum is a strongly odiferous oil from the abdominal glands of the North American beaver. It was an object of trade for the frontier trappers and produced a sharp, tar-like odor. When diluted with alcohol, the odor transforms to a pleasantly musky scent.

Musk is the name originally given to a substance obtained from the anal gland of the male musk deer, now one of the most expensive animal products in the world. Makes me wonder: who discovered this, and why?

An *accord* is the mixture of fragrant oils chosen for the perfume. Perfumers call it the *juice*. Today, store-bought perfumes, whether branded by Estée Lauder, Ralph Lauren, or Calvin Klein, are typically made by one of seven mega-industrial fragrance houses located worldwide. These houses—factory-style behemoths such as International Flavors & Fragrances (IFF), Givaudan, Firmenich, Quest, and Drom—create and manufacture perfumes in guarded secrecy. Nowadays, the primary ingredients in these popular brands are synthetics, as opposed to natural essential oils. Synthetics offer greater variety, are more stable, and are less expensive.

Typical synthetic replacements today include chemical blends such as Phenylethylalcohol 2 for rose, Methyl Diantilis 0.5 for carnation, or Vanillin 0.05 for vanilla. But of course, commercial perfumes purchased are never described as a combination of Phenylethylalcohol 2 and Methyl Diantilis 0.5. Instead, they focus on what the synthetics are intended to represent: in this case, rose and carnation.

My desire and determination to revert to the French traditions of perfumery directed the utilization of more essential oils in Tijon's juice. Cyndi and I estimate that we've formulated over 1,000 different scents to arrive at our initial ten offerings.

All perfumers undertake the same process: we mix ingredients, whether natural or synthetic, until we find a unique and attractive scent; we then recreate that scent numerous times, each time adding a droplet of another fragrance to determine if it improves the outcome. This process is repeated hundreds of times. That may seem tedious to some, but to me it's exciting to see how the subtlest difference can completely change a scent. Friends tell me there are medications for people like me. Fortunately, in the corporate world I managed a number of wonderful people. I've become known as the guy who greets employees and friends with an arm extended and the words, "Smell me."

Once the accord is finalized, we add a touch of deionized water to cool down all but the strongest of concentrations, and benzophonene-4, a powdery substance that assists the duration of the fragrance. Benzophonene-4 brought us a discovery; when we added this powder to the mixture it was exceedingly difficult to dissolve it, despite numerous stirrings and shakings. We ended up having to toss many of our first mixtures. We finally learned that it was better to first melt the powder with the water before the oils and alcohol were added. Adding too much altered the fragrance over time, which resulted in still more finished bottles being tossed and the formula altered. As you can see, creating perfume is an extraordinary learning process, and perfecting a blend creates a sense of exultation that's hard to describe.

The remainder of the perfume is denatured alcohol. Alcohol is a carrier that sustains the fragrance on the skin and helps it diffuse in the surrounding air. Without it, not many would smell the perfume, even if just a few feet away. Denatured alcohol is ethyl alcohol to which a toxic substance, such as acetone or methanol, has been added to make it unfit for consumption. It's denatured, not to make one ill, but for taxation purposes; if it's not drinkable, it's industrial and therefore not taxed.

The alcohol becomes apparent when a person actually spritzes the perfume on, thus the need to wait a few seconds to allow its dissipation before we evaluate the scent. The *dry-down period* occurs when the final phase of a fragrance develops on the skin, usually fifteen to thirty minutes after application.

As a perfumer I closely monitor the tenacity of the fragrance during the dry-down stage. That's also why other perfumers and I recommend smelling a scent for a period of time to see how it changes and to observe the feelings it creates.

The tradition of perfumery has an even older and richer vocabulary than the arcane but more familiar descriptions of fine wine. The scent's bouquet can be subtle, full, or pungent. A subtle bouquet blends demurely with the body's own chemistry, while a full bouquet is distinctive and assertive. A pungent bouquet tickles the nose, filling our environment with essence.

* * * * *

In our basement labs in suburban Atlanta and Texas, we prepared, tested, reformulated, re-tested, and tossed numerous concoctions. The process was admittedly frustrating on occasion, but with each try we learned something valuable that has helped us today. Plus, we had the best smelling trash in our neighborhoods.

We took copious notes on all formulations and modifications. Hundreds, if not thousands, of formulas reflected the thousands of dollars spent on ingredients. If the IRS had audited, I would have failed the initial business-expense test that dictates a profit for two out of five years to avoid the activity being categorized as a hobby. I was fortunate to have a hobby that was serious business with an end-game plan— even if the end was clouded in a chemical haze.

Cyndi and I also prepared multiple formulations for skin care and sun care. We located the hard-to-find and expensive natural ingredients, though frequently we had to purchase in bulk quantities that were never fully used prior to their expiration date. We wrote that off as part of our needing to work extra hard to find the right concoctions that would work for us. We also purchased Caribbean plants and herbs to cultivate.

Sometimes we'd chuckle about not having neighbors that lived a bit closer. They would have definitely voted our dwelling as the area's best-smelling residence, if there were such an award. In keeping with the industry's evolving standard, our motto was "Tijon: not tested on animals; tested on family and friends instead." Prominently displayed in my home lab, and now at Tijon, I have a poster containing some nuggets of popular chemistry humor:

RULES OF THE LAB

When you don't know what you're doing, do it neatly.

Experiments must be reproducible. They should fail the same way each time.

First draw your curves; then plot your data.

Experience is directly proportional to equipment ruined.

A record of data is essential. It shows you were working.

To study a subject best, understand it thoroughly before you start.

To do a lab well, have your report done well in advance.

If you can't get the answer in the usual manner, start at the answer and derive the question.

If that doesn't work, start at both ends and try to find a common middle.

In case of doubt, make it sound convincing.

Don't believe in miracles; rely on them.

Teamwork is essential. It allows you to blame someone else.

All unmarked beakers contain fast-acting, extremely toxic poisons.

Any delicate and expensive piece of glassware will break before any use can be made of it.

CHAPTER 5

THE HUNT FOR FRENCH-CARIBBEAN PROPERTY

Our corporate jobs were good in the sense that they afforded Cyndi and me vacation time for the required trips to "The Friendly Island." We were on high alert for that precious parcel of land that nestled near the tropical beauty of the beaches, had a glorious view of the sensational sunsets, and kept us just steps away from some tasty tropical beverages and gourmet dinners. Planning for a life in paradise was inspirational.

Our property requirements were relatively simple—or so we thought. We needed to purchase an affordable commercial building on the French side that was easily assessable and visible to tourists. But as we walked the streets, there were no for-sale signs to be found.

We turned to local newspapers for leads. We understood the papers produced on the Dutch side, because they were in English. Unfortunately, they advertised properties only on that side of the island.

The newspapers for the French side were, well, all in French. That might have been fine if we were looking at a dinner menu, but since we were looking for real estate, we had no idea of their contents. To keep the process moving without having to take a crash course in French, we enlisted the help of some island real estate agents. The Dutch-side agents were polite. They also never found any French listings. Still, they left us with the assurance that they would contact us if they did come across one. We never heard back.

The French-side agents were similarly of little help finding any suitable buildings, but they, too, assured us they would contact us if any became available. They must have been busy talking to the Dutch-side agents, because we never heard from them, either. What did two Americans with a dream need do to find some property in St. Martin?

Every vacant building we came across got a serious evaluation for our new venture. We were consistently told they weren't for sale because of title issues. French law, to the delight of our children, doesn't allow parents to disinherit children; a portion of the real estate holdings is required to pass on to the little cherubs.

This French law created title issues when the deceased had multiple children—especially when not all the children shared the same two parents. When I asked one island friend how many siblings she had, she replied, "One on my mother's side and twelve on my father's side. My father was like his father, who stopped having children because he died."

Some of these children leave the island after they reach adulthood. Inevitably, some cannot be located to approach about a sale or, even worse, they fight with their siblings over what that sale price should be. We suspected there were French legal procedures to circumvent these title issues, but apparently it was costly and took considerable time. Did I mention that we're talking about French legal procedures?

Islanders are proud of their lineage and wear it like a badge of honor. One local, a lady named Patricia, shared her ancestry with us. She told us how her grandfather on her mother's side proudly fathered thirty-four children, obviously not with the same woman, making title transfer of his property understandably difficult.

Island families also consider land sacred. One islander explained why he would never sell his beachfront shack: "The land was my parents', and it shall pass to my children." The result: there was little property ever for sale in French St. Martin. Leases were available, but of no interest to me.

Thoughts of dejection and defeat entered my mind, but I stopped them from completely deterring me and continued to religiously surf the web for property listings for this specific little domain.

In the summer of 2004 I found a large house on the ocean in Grand

Case. I suspected it could qualify for a commercial conversion, and I was eager to act quickly, despite the fact that it was at the upper end of affordability. I e-mailed the Dutch-side listing agent for a showing and made air reservations for Cyndi and myself for two weeks out.

Grand Case (pronounced "Grahn Kahss") is one of the oldest sites of human settlement on the island. Its first settlers are believed to have arrived from Venezuela by boat around 1800 BC. Their successors, the Arawak Indians, settled here around 550 BC. The area offered an abundance of fishing and hunting.

Old maps from the early 1700s mention La Grande-Case (the Great Cabin) as one of the four districts on the French side of the island. Some believe that this "large cabin" was the master house of a large sugar mill.

In the early 1800s there were seven or eight houses in the community. Its principal industry centered on exploiting salt from nearby ponds, bringing wealth to this hamlet until the early 1900s. At that time, Grand Case became St. Martin's center of communication. This lasted until 1970, when much of the island's sea traffic docked here, offloading vegetables on the wharf and picking up the cattle that hillside farmers raised. In 1971 the L'Esperance airport was built in this village and, as the only airport on the French side, is used for smaller regional and private planes.

When we went to visit the property that was for sale, Cyndi and I were anxious. We stepped off the plane in St. Martin, breathed in the warm sea air, and drove our rental car to the tiny, three-story L'Atlantide Hotel, located on the beach in Grand Case. Our appointment with the real estate agents wasn't until the next day.

The next morning, Cyndi and I met the agents at our hotel, and they drove us the short distance to the listed property. They were a mother-son team who had transplanted to the Dutch side of St. Martin from South Africa. The mom, Betty, did the office work, and John, the son, assisted with the property showings. Betty and John were the only Dutch-side English-speaking agents we had found who were open to showing properties on the French side. We were thankful.

We pulled up to a large, two-story, square, cement structure abutting the beach. An expansive yard stretched between the road and the house. A tenant, who apparently served as property manager, walked us through the house while our hearts skipped a beat—unfortunately, mostly from the shock of the pungent, stale odor that filled the air. Keep in mind, we had our scent sniffers well trained by this point.

The place smelled like a chemistry experiment gone wrong. The dirt was as plentiful inside as the cement, and the walls showed many large cracks. The windows were tiny, and the house had a layout similar to a 1930s hotel. It was easy to see that property repairs and remodeling would cost as much as the purchase itself.

Cyndi had a "deer-in-a-headlights" look, but came back to Earth when I assured her in a whisper that we couldn't afford this property. The building later sold, but couldn't close for lack of a clear title from the seller. Seems there may have been some missing or disagreeable heirs.

After the showing, I visited with our agents about other possible properties. Cyndi badly needed a break and an opportunity to forget about what she'd seen. She walked across the street where a sign read TI POTTERY. She entered through a small door on the side of a two-story house. Inside was a shop complete with a pottery wheel and a pretty, petite potter with trimmed brown hair, who greeted Cyndi in perfect English: "Hi there."

"Hi, I'm Cyndi. What a beautiful shop."

"Thank you. I'm Cecile."

"Did you make all this pottery?"

"Yes, feel free to browse. Are you visiting?"

"Believe it or not, we're looking at property to purchase in the neighborhood. What can you tell us about the area?"

Cecile Petrelluzzi generously gave Cyndi an audio tour and explained her origins. She was an avid surfer who later accepted our invitation to dinner as we peppered her with questions on property ownership and other doings in St. Martin.

Although the initial showing was nixed, John and Betty eagerly volunteered to show us other possibilities. They tried to veer us to the Dutch side. We were kind and looked at a few tempting properties. Although disappointment accompanied most showings, the exploratory trips were never for naught. We took refuge in fending off disappointment at the beach, the bars, and the gourmet restaurants. We wanted St. Martin to work, particularly the French side, and would keep pursuing that route.

On this particular trip, two days before we would return stateside, we explored an Italian menu while sitting on the porch of Spiga, a small but elegant eatery on a side street in Grand Case. The sun had set as I ordered the osso buco; Cyndi was tempted by the pumpkin ravioli.

Between sips of wine, mouthfuls of savory food, and more sips, our eyes were drawn to a spot directly across the dimly lit street, a two-story villa that was showcasing a FOR SALE sign. Our eyes kept wandering to the left to the house next to it, a one-story home on the corner that definitely had commercial potential. There was also a similar FOR SALE sign posted by it. This particular house faced the street on a fairly popular intersection. It was also across the street from the ocean.

"Madame, another bottle of Brunello, *s'il vous plaît*?"

"*Oui, monsieur.*"

We talked excitedly about the possibilities as questions swirled through our minds. Could these two properties be combined for a commercial and residential venture? Would they be affordable? We did what all reasonable wanna-be property owners would do when on St. Martin: we split a delectable homemade tiramisu with limoncello.

Before our walk back to the L'Atlantide we ventured across the street and jotted down the listing info on the signs.

The next morning I contacted our South African friends, who arranged a showing with the French agent that afternoon. We were immediately impressed by the swaying palm trees and the other full-growth vegetation consisting of lime, banana, gardenia, jasmine, rosemary, aloe, and starfruit plants.

The properties were within our budget and consisted of two villas, each having a smaller carriage house. The two-story villa was a duplex with an upstairs and downstairs unit. The French agent only had keys for the corner one-story villa and the downstairs unit of the two-story villa. The upstairs villa and the two carriage houses were viewed only from the exterior. What we inspected looked acceptable.

If we wanted this property, it would have to be sight unseen for the upstairs and the carriage houses. We believed in signs and received one while touring the outside of the property: a tour bus filled with cruise-ship passengers drove by. *Voila*! Maybe our property search was over.

Cyndi and I were definitely overcome, but in different ways.

"I think we should make an offer on both properties," I proclaimed.

Cyndi's eyes filled with tears; they weren't joyful. They indicated panic, and she started to throw out questions: "Do we have the money? Are we really ready?" In other words: what the hell were we thinking?

"But, honey, we've been talking about this for years, and here we are, in our final planning stages, and you're objecting now, after all the work?"

"I had fun with the dream, the travels, and plans, but I didn't think you'd really do it."

"You know me better than that, honey. I've never taken that approach to life. Look around this place. It's beautiful. We're in paradise, a paradise where we can work and play. It's understandable that you have some nerves and fear. I do, too. Remember though, you also have me, and as a team, we can do amazing things."

I went on to give a most eloquent summation, tapping into my courtroom skill set. I assured her she was reacting naturally and understandably. It was a classic case of buyer's remorse; it had just happened before the actual buy. In reality, it demonstrated our differences, but those differences are what make us an amazing team.

Cyndi has a popular, winning personality and disposition; everyone likes her. She enjoys games without a burning desire to win. She's less ambitious and enjoys her family and friends while taking time to smell the flowers and appreciate life. She routinely scheduled days off at our bed and breakfast, even if we had customers calling. She had once worked for my father's retail business for years and was such a tremendous, hardworking employee who had no burning desire to take on managerial duties. She is content in the role she has chosen for herself, though she keeps me in check by introducing me as her "first husband."

Now, I'm the complete opposite. I'm a type-A personality and an alpha male. Enough said. Cyndi and I do find common ground with one trait: we both have a strong Midwest work ethic. Maybe we inherited it or perhaps it was environmental (in Minnesota, we needed to keep moving to stay warm).

Despite the obvious differences between Cyndi and me, we share threads of a similar destiny. Cyndi enjoys antiques and taught me to restore furniture. Entering our tenth year of marriage, we first became business partners with the purchase of our bed and breakfast. Cyndi was the decorator, the cook, the cleaner, and the greeter. She was the face of the business that made guests into friends, creating a significant return clientele. But she had no desire to market or work the business side. I did the latter, and we made a terrific team.

Now, my finger was set to pull the trigger that would shoot us into paradise on a permanent basis. I had told our real estate agent we'd likely put an offer in to purchase the two side-by-side properties. Cyndi cried. This wasn't a thirty-mile drive from St. Paul across the Minnesota border to Wisconsin to open an inn. This was a 3,000-mile trek to a foreign country with different laws and a language we didn't speak.

Business was a difficult proposition anywhere, but in a foreign land?

Anyone observing us likely saw Cyndi's tears, making them recall a dramatic movie and probably wondering what the heck was going on.

I ordered a second round of rosy-red rum punches and verbally rewound the dream while offering Cyndi a tissue. Leaving the bar, I escorted Cyndi to a beachside table overlooking the ocean cliffs below and ordered a bottle of a crisp, bone-dry, but highly aromatic Sancerre, a wine with intense flavors.

Cyndi cheered slightly and ordered sautéed *filet de boeuf* tenderloin with goat cheese and truffle on potato rings roasted with thyme. I followed with a locally caught red snapper with sauce vierge. We splurged by ordering separate desserts: Cyndi enjoyed the *palette de sorbets et glaces maison*, an assortment of homemade sorbets and ice cream, while I stuck with my favorite, *profiteroles*—a delectable French cream puff.

Cyndi was a trouper that night. After the typical complimentary after-dinner flavored rum came, she put on her happy face. Before our walk back to our hotel, with red eyes and a reluctant smile, she calmly said, "Let's go for it."

CHAPTER 6

WOULD THE OFFER CLOSE?

Cyndi and I retreated to our Texas home to reexamine our savings account and make sure we were organized. A few weeks later, in August 2004, we submitted a formal offer via fax on both properties in Grand Case. "Formal," by island standards, was a one-page piece of paper, hand-typed by our Dutch-side realtor, indicating the property address and the money we offered, 10 percent down and the balance due at closing. Each offer was contingent on the success of the other and further contingent on the corner building being approved for commercial use. We were moving along.

The separate owners of the property were both in the United States. Luckily for us, they quickly agreed, and the real estate agents delivered the file to Nadia Jacques, a sharp young French notary who, consistent with French procedures, would act as attorney, title examiner, and closing agent for both parties. Although she was from St. Martin, she had completed her advanced schooling in France. A notary under French law, unlike in the United States, is one step above an attorney, or *avocat*.

For our purchase, Nadia had the added challenge of securing the corner property for commercial usage. She provided us the list of required documents for closing: it included our marriage license and the birth certificates of our children.

Foreign real estate purchases are understandably filled with unfamiliar nuances, not the least of which is the inability to finance. It's cash on the barrelhead—cash we didn't have. Our options were two: attempt to acquire a loan against our U.S. holdings or sell a small strip center we owned in Atlanta, the proceeds of which would almost pay for the two island buildings.

It was an easy decision; the strip center was becoming difficult to manage. The stars seemed to be even more aligned when an offer came forward on that property. After a bit of negotiation, during which we managed to keep the buyer unaware of our dire financial need, we agreed to the sale and prayed it would close quickly.

However, closings on commercial properties typically require a lot of due diligence, inspections, financing, and renegotiation. Our Atlanta property was no exception. It took eight months to close, despite a hasty effort and some quick give-ins on our part.

This delayed closing could have presented problems if not for even greater delays in St. Martin. The commercial usage was the obstacle. The owners periodically threatened to pull the plug unless we waived this requirement. Not wishing to have all of our cash and then some tied up in two residential foreign properties, we declined.

The cat was chasing the mouse, but which one were we? The anxiety of wanting our dream to come true didn't deter us from holding strong. After all, the dream would be no closer to coming true if we couldn't get commercial approval on the corner property.

Fortunately, the wife of one of the owners of the two-story villa that was to be our residence was a St. Martiner. Although we were all in the United States, she had her relatives contact the notary to accelerate the process. Nine months after our offer was accepted, the notary produced a signed letter from the *Marie*, the local government office, approving commercial usage, provided that the regional office in Guadeloupe signed off on the final architectural plans.

We instantly had a huge list of "did nots" to consider: we did not have any plans drawn, did not know what plans were needed, did not have any guarantees that Guadeloupe would sign off, and did not wish to close the sale with such ambiguity. We weren't even sure where the island of Guadeloupe was! We were at a loss for what to do.

Once again, the owner's wife came to the rescue by offering to procure a meeting with the local elected official, comparable to a city council member in the United States. We made our flight reservations for a Saturday, and the villa owner had his island buddy, Julian Brooks, accompany us to the Tuesday-morning meeting. Julian's presence was reassuring, if only for his assistance in finding the office and serving as a translator. We were to meet Julian at the buildings we were attempting to purchase.

We drove the ten minutes to the meeting spot with Brooks and arrived early; this was not a day to be late. We found a large blue commercial truck parked there. The driver saw us approach and jumped out. He was a tall, good-looking guy with broad shoulders, large hands, and dark skin. His hair had a touch of grey, and he wore it closely cropped.

"You Julian Brooks?" I asked.

"Yea, me Brooks. You Berglund?"

"Yes, nice to meet you. And thanks for doing this." Brooks, like many islanders, went by his last name only.

"I do anyting for Bill Davis. He a good friend," Brooks said. Davis was one of the owners of the two-story villa; his wife was the islander who had arranged the meeting.

We followed Brooks for twenty minutes in traffic to the Sous Prefecture in Marigot, the capital of French St. Martin. Our appointment was with Daniel Gibbs, who not only spoke excellent English, but also was most professional and accommodating. While he would offer no guarantees, he reassured us that, with architectural plans for commercial usage along with the Marie's letter, Guadeloupe would approve.

Our properties appeared preordained for business, with an Italian eatery and a local Creole restaurant across the street. A little *parfumerie* and gift shop sandwiched in could add nicely to the mixed-use neighborhood.

I was impressed with Mr. Gibbs. I had met many statesmen over the years and predicted to Cyndi that someday Mr. Gibbs would lead the *Collectivité*, the democratically elected French island government. Sure enough, at the time of this writing he is serving as St. Martin's vice president and planning a run for the presidency.

To proceed, we needed plans drawn by a local architect. Brooks was the go-to man. He knew virtually every person who was anybody of affluence on the island. After introducing us to an insurance agent, he arranged a meeting with a man we believed to be an architect. Apparently, years ago this man had been on the school bus route driven by Brooks.

Brooks introduced us to someone whose name sounded like Carti. Carti had a young friend standing nearby whom he introduced as Jym. Short and thin, with light brown skin and closely cropped, curly black hair, Jym barely looked old enough to drink. But then, we weren't sure there was a drinking age in St. Martin. We restated our problem to Carti.

"That's no problem, mon. The plans get drafted, Jym sends them to Guadeloupe and secures approval. He take care of it all for you."

Now, no offense against Carti or Jym, but we had clearly experienced that nothing was quick or simple in St. Martin. No procedures for anything were streamlined. I asked, "But what if Guadeloupe says no?"

"They won't say no, trust me. You get approval, then Jym works on specific drawings."

"Do you have a business card?"

"No, but Jym here will be your contact, and he'll tell you how to reach him."

"And what will this cost us? Can we afford it?" I asked.

"No worries. It's a small percent of the building cost, and Jym does all. He watch over the building, too." They explained three levels of percentages that depended on how much work we wanted them to do, and it was in line with previous experiences in the States.

Jym, who had been born in Guadeloupe, said he would rush the plans, but couldn't rush a response and predicted it would take a few months. The continued delay would again break another negotiated deadline with sellers who were now claiming they would abort the sale if we didn't close immediately. The thing was, short of having a new offer, there would be no motive for them to truly abort the sale, so we tried not to let them sway us toward making any hasty decisions.

It was time for a business break and a reminder of why we were in the Caribbean. The meeting with Gibbs, Brooks, and our prospective architect occurred on a fact-filled Tuesday. That was good, because we had a boating appointment on Wednesday. We could reflect on our situation while enjoying the crystal blue tropical water.

We had ended up booking out this boating adventure quite by coincidence. During a relaxing afternoon at Orient Beach, Cyndi and I had met Joe and Marie, two New Yorkers who had a winter condo on Simpson Bay, on the Dutch Side. They were planning a boat trip to the nearby islet of Tintamarre and asked us if we'd like to join them. The answer was obvious: "Love to."

Tintamarre was fascinating to the chemist in me; the island is famous for its therapeutic mud. "You take a bucket and fill it with sea water," Joe explained when we arrived at the island. "Then you collect the soft, rock-type pellets that are found at the bottom of that ledge over there," he said, pointing to his left. "Mix them with the water and they create mud."

Joe was right; it was absolutely invigorating to apply the mud to our skin and start feeling it work its magic from head to toes. The medicinal mixture exfoliated our skin, and Joe and Marie assured us that it also provided minerals to boost the immune system.

Cyndi and I were refreshed from our boating adventure, and returned to the hotel to concentrate on our dream project. We both felt good about our young new architect, Jym. We decided to throw caution to the winds and boldly informed the notary on the day we flew out that we were ready to close. When we went to her office to sign the papers, we explained we had an architect who was helping us push our plans through Guadeloupe. We asked if she knew him and told her that we thought his name was something like Carti, but he didn't have a card. We also mentioned his assistant, Jym.

"Was Carti a younger, taller, thinner, good-looking man?"

"Yes."

"He's not an architect," she laughed. "He's what you would call a building inspector for the island government. I believe Carti is dating Jym's sister."

Fortunately Jym was an architect, although we would discover later that our project was the first he would be doing as a lead architect rather than as an assistant. Before leaving, we made a final inspection of the properties, and I noticed a teeny black line going up the base of the interior cement wall of what would be our home. There was also a fine trail of cement dust on the floor. I turned to Cyndi. "Look at this. What do you think?"

We didn't need experienced inspectors to recognize the likely markings of termites. That was hard to comprehend, considering this was a cement-block house. Cyndi had a predictably "Cyndi" response: "We can't buy this thing; the house may be infested. We don't know anything about termites."

I tried to calm Cyndi by making one final stop on the way to the airport that day: the local Terminix office. The experts assured us that with proper, periodic spraying, there shouldn't be a lingering problem.

As soon as we landed back in the States we called the villa owner, Bill Davis. He was a genuinely nice man in his seventies who had married an island girl in her twenties. When we mentioned the termites, he promised to have it immediately sprayed and to provide certified documentation that it was termite-free. He did exactly what he said he would do, and the termite situation was resolved in less than a month.

Our day finally came. About ten months after the offer was initially accepted, we wired the funds and closed on both properties *in absentia*. Cyndi and I were the proud, excited, and nervous owners of two termite-free properties with a clear title in French-side St. Martin: one hurdle crossed, but another on the way.

Now we had to exercise patience as we anxiously waited to hear from Jym.

PART III

CHALLENGES IN OPENING THE BUSINESS

PERFUME FACT

The alcohol in perfume allows the fragrance to emanate from your skin. Without alcohol, you would most likely be the only person aware that you're wearing perfume.

CHAPTER 7

THE REMODEL

Jym the architect was a man of his word; he delivered the approval from Guadeloupe. We eventually learned his real name was Jhigai Yves-Marie; "JYM" was actually his three initials. We were pleased to call him Jym. He needed to meet with us regarding specific architectural renderings. We loved and embraced Caribbean culture, beaches, sunshine, foods, vegetation, and architecture, so we wanted everything represented in some capacious way.

A wide range of environmental factors has influenced Caribbean architecture. The geographical surroundings—mountains, volcanoes, flatlands, forests, and deserts—each affected building material availability and presented unique demands for comfort.

St. Martin's building styles are also influenced by the island's respective cultures. Since we had located on the northern side of the island, we focused on trying to create something French and fabulous. French-Caribbean architecture is a living thing in its modern expressions and its relation to the French Creole style, which remains prominent in New Orleans.

The early Creole homes in St. Martin were built with crisscrossing wooden slats of cherrywood and logwood. The homes were built to face the rising sun, to maximize access to the light and the cooling trade winds. Roofs were made of sugarcane straw, later to be replaced by corrugated steel canopies.

Wooden shutters protected the homes from bad weather and allowed air to circulate when open. In areas subject to flooding, some houses were built on short stilts. Most had two rooms with two interior hallways, one for the bathroom and one that served for sleeping and cooking. Relaxation and family living occurred on the open-air porches.

The island's commercial structures, also infused with French-Creole influence, often feature intricate wrought iron and fretwork. Some offer pillared collonades along the street, with working and living spaces set farther back so they're sheltered from the sun and rain.

Today, cement blocks are the primary building components. Zinc roofs are embedded in the masonry structure to strengthen resistance to tropical winds and hurricanes. Bright colors and influences from prior years continue the unique Caribbean flavor.

We flew to the island and met with Jym to give our input and vision. A few days later he drafted specific plans for the one-story former dwelling that would be our business. We instantly fell in love with the draft.

Jym had found a way to tap into our descriptions and bring them to life on paper. The design included interior archways, the necessary parking, and a new sloped zinc roof on what had previously been flat cement.

Jym created a front patio and incorporated decorative glass block windows that added an airy openness to what had previously been three small, 1950s-style bedrooms. The former kitchen was to the left side upon entering, and would be converted to the commercial lab, with a window separating the lab and boutique so that customers could watch products being made. The carport would be walled in for storage and a packaging room. The outdated exterior tiles would be removed and replaced by a smooth beige plaster.

Jym estimated the entire cost of the project, minus his fees, at €70,000. That seemed reasonable and was also within my conservative U.S.-dollar budget of $100,000. Still, I recalled the entire remodeling experience with our bed-and-breakfast conversion and knew about cost overruns. Jym suggested, and we approved, an engineer to test the structural integrity of the current cement roof, as some interior walls would be demolished and some of the flat roof was to remain. The tests revealed the entire roof needed replacement, which surprised none of us, since chunks of cement had been lying on the kitchen floor.

Bids came in over the next two months, and we were absolutely shocked at even the least expensive of them: €170,000. The exchange rate at that time was about $1.20 to €1.00, meaning the remodel would cost in excess of $200,000. Our choices were to sell short or scale back the work, both difficult to do after being blown away by the plans. We closed our eyes, held our noses, and nervously accepted. And, unbelievably, Jym generously kept his fee percentage based on his original €70,000 estimate. We were grateful for his kindness.

The winning bid became a twenty-page contract that required signatures. I had drafted many such agreements in my life, but had never seen anything similar to this one. It was in French, and I had been too busy to open my *French for Dummies*. Who was feeling like a bit of a dummy now?

"Jym, what the heck does this thing say?"

Jym interpreted the key portions and had our complete trust when he said, in his calmly soft, high-pitched voice, "It's okay, it's a standard-type contract."

I asked the contractor, who spoke virtually no English, "Can Cyndi and I sign our names in English?"

Either he didn't catch my veiled humor or simply had no clue what I was saying. He responded, "*Oui, oui.*" In my nervousness, I'd attempted a joke, and it earned me one of Cyndi's award-winning smiles.

A deposit was required to make the contract official, and it depleted the last of our available cash. All the funds from the sale of our small shopping center in Atlanta had gone toward the purchase.

Nevertheless, we were feeling great. Per island tradition, our motto was, "No worries, mon." We figured that since it had taken ten months to close the deal, the remodel would most likely take longer. One island neighbor advised us that when workers tell you they will be finished by, say, October 1, you need to ask them, "In what year?"

We stopped by one morning at 10:30 to check on the progress of the demolition. One worker was sitting on the cement floor drinking a Heineken, and another was taking a nap. Thankfully we weren't paying by the hour. They weren't doing anything unusual by Caribbean standards, but U.S. expectations would certainly process the scene differently.

Word travels quickly on a small island, and it didn't take long for the locals to hear the details of our venture. They all knew that the small corner house was being remodeled for a lab and a parfumerie. Although nobody had ever said so to our faces, we did suspect they thought we were two crazy Americans who didn't mind throwing their money away.

Similarly, fifteen years earlier, when we remodeled the old Queen Anne Victorian in Wisconsin into a bed and breakfast, the local architect who drafted the plans, an older man, told us how important it was to allow enough flexibility for the inn to be converted back to a single residence if needed. We could sense he didn't believe in the viability of our commercial concept.

But island surprises never end. The construction crew stayed with the project, and further payments became necessary more quickly than anticipated. Whoever said "timing is everything" definitely wasn't referencing the exchange rate for the euro. It had climbed to a then-all-time high of $1.30. Construction was completed in four months, requiring us to proverbially rob Peter to pay Paul. After Peter was depleted, we secured financing from the mother of all banks: my mother.

Our beautiful building was complete. However, we were in the middle of a catch-22: I needed to keep my day job to repay Mom. Our consolation came in receiving weekly progress photos, e-mailed by Jym. Peter may have been broke, but he had an awfully nice looking building.

So, by the end of 2005 our property remodel was complete, and we would spend the next few years saving money, preparing for our physical move, and completing product formulations. Our goal was to open in December 2007.

At this point, contrary to conventional wisdom, all our eggs were in one basket, so you can bet we kept a close eye on that basket! During the next few years, we made many trips down to St. Martin to check on our property and to complete various aspects of the preparation necessary for opening and running our business. Naturally, we had many truly memorable experiences during this transition period. One of my favorites among these memories was when we participated in a quintessential island experience: a concert by the one and only Jimmy Buffett.

We had been on the island for two weeks during a visit in March 2007 when we read in the local paper that Buffett would grace the neighboring island of Anguilla with a concert.

Each year, some members of our Lutheran church in Texas hosted a Jimmy Buffett Parrot Head poolside party on Labor Day weekend. One of my favorite Buffett sayings is, "Let me remind you: we are party people, and things will get better."

Even more than most Parrot Heads, we felt a special connection to Jimmy Buffett. I'm positive he'd have felt it, too, if he'd known us. In the early 1980s, while we were investing in our bed and breakfast, he had invested as a co-owner in the Autor de Rocher, a hotel and restaurant/bar on the nearby French island of St. Bart's where he reportedly maintains a home. It's widely known that his hit song "Cheeseburger in Paradise" focuses on the burgers at Le Select bar in downtown Gustavia. Except for the Green Bay Packers poster on the wall at Le Select (hey, we're Vikings fans all the way), we had enjoyed our visit there on our first family trip to the Caribbean.

Jimmy Buffett would be performing at the Bankie Banx beach hotspot known as the Dune Preserves in Anguilla. It was just a twenty-minute ferry ride from Marigot, and the concert proceeds went to local charities. Banx was an international reggae icon and Anguilla's favorite son. This most likely explains how he acquired either ownership or license to the strategically located Dune Preserve, an outdoor, standing-room-only amphitheater on the beach facing St. Martin. Nestled into the white, sandy beach was a tall, ramshackle wooden fence that surrounded the amphitheater and stage.

For us, this concert was a "don't miss" event. Because of unlimited standing room in this seatless arena, we easily purchased tickets in Phillipsburg. To get to and from Anguilla was another matter; the newspapers announced there would be extra ferries running, which suggested long lines and a risk of being left behind.

As we contemplated our options, by chance we bumped into some acquaintances who later became good friends, Mark and Robin. When we ran into them at Orient Beach a few days prior to the concert, they told us that they had tickets to both the concert and a private catamaran, the *Golden Eagle*. They informed us how to purchase tickets on the same boat. Problem solved.

On a sunny Sunday morning, with forty other souls, we boarded the seventy-foot catamaran in the Phillipsburg marina for an hour's sail to Anguilla. An onboard trashcan quickly filled with empty rum punch containers, and the vivacious Robin discarded her top, liberating her girls. A delightful sail ensued. Soon we neared an anchoring spot about thirty yards from the Dune Preserves.

When we anchored, we had the option of boarding a dinghy or swimming to shore. We chose the latter. We packed up our tickets, money, and sunscreen into a watertight baggie and dove in.

Meanwhile, helicopters swarmed overhead, presumably to take photos of the rich and famous, including Mr. Buffett. I often suspected celebrities dreamed of a normal lifestyle, while we normal people dream of celebrity status: *Yes, I'm John Berglund, operator of the island's most widely known parfumerie . . .*

We jumped into a lengthy line on the beach and waited an hour or so to clear local security. Standing in line behind us was a woman who introduced herself as Elisa Cohen. She was the well-known American owner of the Bikini Beach Bar on Orient. Learning of our future business move, she offered counsel and recounted her early days in business.

We stared hard at another lady nearby who returned a quizzical look. It turned out she was the agent who had sold our bed and breakfast in Wisconsin nine years earlier. She'd been on holiday in St. Martin when she learned of the concert. Have we said that island life resembles that of a small town?

Entering the Dune Preserve reminded me of sardines being packed into a tin. The heat was sweltering as the pulsating sunlight bounced off thousands of bodies. The tall wood fence surrounding the venue kept out non-ticket holders . . . along with any hint of a breeze.

We pushed and zigzagged through the crowd to the back, only to stand in a line to purchase some ice-cold beer and water. Jimmy Buffett took the stage to a roaring ovation, and life was good. The crowd cheered wildly to "Margaritaville," "Cheeseburger in Paradise," "Fins," "Changes in Latitudes, Changes in Attitudes," and other hit songs.

I was wearing a baseball cap with a big O; it was from Osakis High School, nestled in rural Minnesota, where Cyndi's sister and brother-in-law were teachers. Two young, attractive girls, both of whom fit nicely into their tiny bikinis and had obviously swilled a few cold ones, saw the cap and shouted, "Go Ohio State!" Not desiring to disappoint, I may have hinted I was from Columbus.

There were no rules for an adventure like this. Thankfully Bankie Banx himself saved me from having to come up with more Ohio adventures. He joined the maestro on stage to add a splash of local flair.

Alas, all good things must come to an end, even the good-time music of Jimmy Buffett. We swam back to the catamaran for a pleasant and fairly quiet sail back to Phillipsburg. Our energy was left behind at the Dune Preserve. Although thousands had attended the concert, we were perhaps the only two souls in the world lucky enough to witness Jimmy Buffett performing on a beach in the Caribbean while concocting our own move to paradise. If other fans were Parrot Heads, we were the entire parrot.

During that same trip to St. Martin we celebrated St. Patrick's Day 2007 by attending a green celebration at the Baywatch bar on Orient Beach. Today, it's simply called Andy and Cheryl's. We stopped in near sunset for hamburgers and rum punch. We were surrounded by couples wearing only body paint and little green hats, singing in unison to the recorded music. The party had apparently been underway a few hours. It was packed, boisterous, and fun, although we felt a bit overdressed . . . and under-painted. We left after a few drinks and some fun conversation.

The uniquely Caribbean experiences we were living were fascinating. We flew home to Texas that March and rested from our trip as we continued to work, save money, and strategize in preparation for our unofficial, soft opening the following December. Life was an adventure. We were working hard, but now with a new purpose.

CHAPTER 8

A CAST OF CHARACTERS: MEETING NEIGHBORS AND MAKING FRIENDS

During our visits to oversee the remodel and the preparations for opening the business, we proudly stayed at our newly purchased, termite-free villa, conveniently located next door. We were looking forward to a meet-and-greet with our neighbors in this tranquil, small-town atmosphere. They were likely quite curious to meet their new American neighbors, too.

Leaving friends behind for a new adventure can be a glass-half-full or a glass-half-empty experience. Many times it comes down to whether one is moved by choice or demand. As a child, Cyndi relocated often within Minnesota as her father climbed his professional ladder. Each move became less painful because of the realization that the loss of old friends coincided with the creation of new ones.

We had spent most of our lives in Minnesota, "Land of 10,000 Lakes," and now we were making our home on St. Martin, "The Friendly Island." It was indeed friendly to tourists. Would it be equally friendly to two soon-to-be American expatriates? The time to find out had arrived.

Americans can endear themselves to most people in foreign lands if they will simply take an interest in local culture and shed any perceived arrogance. At first, locals may eye an American with suspicion because of a negative personal experience, rumor, or innuendo. Cyndi's childhood equipped her with the perfect antidote to local distrust: smile, be friendly, and the same will be returned.

The French categorized island residents in three tiers. At the top were themselves, "Metropolitans": French citizens born in the mother country. Next were the St. Martin "*Ois*," pronounced "wahs," comprising those born and bred on the island. The third category was the "others," meaning expatriates, with Americans at the top of that otherwise bottommost list. We "others," by the way, regarded the usually friendly islanders in two classes: friends and potential friends.

There is no official definition of who's a St. Martiner as the debate plays out in public. Is it someone born on the island, even though his or her parents may have immigrated there only a year ago? Or must they trace their roots on the friendly island back for thirty or more years?

Those born in St. Martin are relatively few in comparison to those who have immigrated. The island has a mostly friendly heritage and a complex history. Early inhabitants were the Arawak, who claimed the territory from 550 BC to shortly before the arrival of Columbus, when this friendly tribe was run off by the warlike, cannibalistic Carib. The island was known as Sualouiga, an Arawak word meaning "land of salt."

With the discovery and naming of the island by Columbus on November 11, 1493, colonization proceeded, on and off, by the Dutch, French, and Spanish. Europeans introduced slavery for salt harvesting and cultivation of cash crops on the plantations. Ships laden with salt, cocoa, sugar, cotton, and coffee departed from the bays and headed overseas for trade.

Slavery was abolished in 1848 on the French side and 1863 on the Dutch side. This virtually crushed the plantation system. The population continued to shrink for a hundred years, until the growing popularity of air travel and a new economy based on tourism sprang up. A 1957 *Saturday Evening Post* article highlighted the island and referenced its population at 6,500, with approximately 4,000 on the French side and 2,500 on the Dutch side. This compares today to an estimated 45,000 on the Dutch side and 35,000 on the French side.

Those born on the island are primarily of African descent and typically multilingual, with the Dutch side natives speaking English and

Dutch and those on the French side speaking English and French. Some Creole may also apply. Surprisingly, the Dutch rarely speak French, and the French wouldn't think of speaking Dutch. That makes it sound like the island could be a racially or ethnically tense area, but that tension is minimal.

On our visits, Cyndi and I began to introduce ourselves and mingle with neighbors. We were blessed to be between two popular restaurants whose food was only outdone by the personalities of the owners. Carl Phillips of Ti Coin Creole restaurant lived and worked in the building he grew up in. He was a tall, broad-shouldered, well-built man of African heritage in his late thirties or early forties. We went to introduce ourselves to Carl.

"Hi, we're John and Cyndi, your new neighbors across the street." He saw us, smiled, and nodded. "Okay, I'm Carl. So ya bought da property next door?" We nodded, and he stuck his large hand through the open window to firmly grip our hands. "Well, den, I have someting for ya. Wait da minute, sit oder dere."

A few minutes later Carl walked out of his kitchen with two beautiful red rum punches in tall glasses, reminiscent of the Hurricane at Pat O'Brien's in New Orleans. "Here's a welcome-to-da-island drink."

Carl told us how he had served as a limo driver years earlier, but his true passion was cooking. He prepared the best goat and Creole mahi mahi on the island. Across the street from his front door, behind our shop, was a large hill where goats regularly roamed. Cyndi teased him, suggesting that this animal population thinned coinciding with his customer count.

Carl, who also cooked off-menu vegetarian fare that our daughter would be eternally grateful for, offered to cook our family an exclusive, free turkey dinner for our first American Thanksgiving as property owners. Carl was married to his long-time Asian girlfriend, Bella, and they had a beautiful son named C. J., short for Carl Jr. We've enjoyed watching this little guy grow.

Before our December 2008 grand opening, a year after our "soft" opening, we were under a major time constraint to fill small sample lotion bottles but lacked the proper equipment to make it easier. This meant we had to suck up the lotion with large plastic veterinary vaccine holders and squirt the mixture into tiny bottles. It doesn't sound that difficult, but it is, evidenced by the lotion squirted all across the lab and us.

Carl good naturedly, and perhaps foolishly, volunteered his services and enlisted his younger brother Kenneth to help us. Kenneth was shorter and of slighter build than Carl, with long, dreadlocked hair. He was an immensely talented woodworker. The two brothers loved to banter and give each other a hard time. When they worked in our building, the scene was akin to a school cafeteria food fight: lotion flew every which way. We never did ask Kenneth how he washed the lotion out of his dreadlocks.

When we later decided we needed a second car, we ended up purchasing a used one, a little blue Daihatsu Sirion, from a younger Jamaican. He added a bonus to the deal by giving me two jackfish he'd caught earlier that morning in his little wooden boat. When I arrived home after making the purchase, I called out, "Hi, honey, I'm home with the car. Guess what else I got?" With a big smile I showed Cyndi the two wrapped jacks.

"What are we going to do with those?" Cyndi asked with a twisted look. Neither of us knew a thing about how to clean a fish. "Well, let's give them to Carl. He'll cook 'em up for us." Carl did just that, and later that evening we enjoyed the bonus to our car purchase. He made some delicious sides and a rum punch for each of us. When we asked for the check, Carl refused and told us that it was our fish, and cooking it was his gift to us.

The other neighboring eatery, Spiga, was owned and operated by a St. Martiner with Italian heritage, Lara, and her northern-Italian chef husband, Ciro. Spiga offers gourmet northern Italian foods and has consistently ranked in the top-ten island restaurants. Their food lineage is remarkable. Lara's father, Livio, for many years owned and operated a well-known Italian restaurant on the Dutch side. Lara and Ciro met in London while working at the Ritz Carlton, where Ciro was a chef and Lara was in sales.

As with C. J., we have enjoyed watching Lara and Ciro's two children, Nicholas and Sebastian, grow from birth. Like Carl, they kept an eye on our property when we were off-island.

Other neighbors included the eighty-plus-year-old, frail but popular Bessie—known to all as Thwanty, a nickname that had some connection with Auntie—and her friend a few blocks toward the village, Jeannie Larmony. Jeannie was in her early nineties when we first introduced ourselves to her as she sat on her porch one evening.

A few years later, in a book entitled *35 Miles From Shore*, we read a captivating account of ALM (Antilliaanse Luchtvaart Maatschappij, a Dutch Antilles airline) Flight 980, which crashed in 1970 on its way to St. Martin from New York City. The plane ran out of fuel after bad weather prevented landing in St. Martin and ditched in the ocean, thirty-five miles from St. Croix. The impact of the crash killed about half of the passengers. Jeannie crawled out with a broken back and was believed to be the last person out of that doomed plane. She's still living in her house at this time of writing, with some accounts listing her age at ninety-six and others at ninety-eight.

Another fascinating encounter occurred with neighbor Vic Laurence. I was repairing our front gate when I noticed this elderly gentleman, with a great tan, a white beard, and neatly trimmed, thinning white hair, coming down the road toward us. He was outfitted in a cream-colored, loose-fitting cotton shirt.

"Are you da owner of dis property?" His island accent matched his appearance.

"Yes. Hi there. My name is John. My wife Cyndi and I bought the property."

"I'm Vic Laurence, an' I live behind you over dere, and I own dat vacant land next to you. I was wondering if you know who is dumping grass and leaves behind your wall over dere?"

"Oh, I'm so sorry. I suppose it's the guy who's been cutting our grass."

"It's no good. It attracts da mice and other rodents."

"No worries, I understand. I'll get it cleaned up and tell our guy to stop doing that." I didn't bother to tell him that "our guy" was actually Cyndi.

"You need to meet Cyndi. Won't you please come in?" I found Cyndi inside and brought her out to meet our new neighbor. I had recognized the Laurence name as the family who had owned much of the land in our area, including ours, at one time.

A lasting friendship followed with Vic and his lovely American wife, Jeanine. As we urged him on, Vic provided a glimpse of his fascinating family history that included many brothers and sisters. He was born on the then-tranquil island in a home without electricity, the son of a cattle-raising father. His father had acquired considerable land for grazing over the years.

Vic reminisced about riding his bike on the main street of Grand Case when the road was dirt and the present-day restaurants were dwellings. As an adult, Vic moved to New London, Connecticut, for work and, as a dual citizen, retains homes in both countries.

Cyndi and I learned about the connection between New London and Grand Case. Some years ago a cargo ship from New London foundered outside of Grand Case. This situation forced the sailors to spend a few months visiting in the village, waiting for the repairs to their ship to be completed. Naturally, friendships developed between the islanders and the Americans and, in turn, the crew invited their new Grand Case buddies to visit them in New London. When jobs on the island became scarce, some accepted that invitation and immigrated to the States, specifically, to New London.

A few days later Vic stopped by to introduce us to some of his friends. He walked us a few blocks to an upstairs apartment belonging to Mike and Marilyn, retired expats from the States who had previously owned a beachside restaurant across the street.

Mike, an Italian-American chef, looked like a retired Dean Martin, while Marilyn looked every inch the corporate executive she had been during their life in Boston. We visited with Marilyn, and she threw out the offer to help at the shop if we ever needed it. We would later take her up on her offer and appreciated her assistance.

Prior to this time, on one of our property-hunting trips Cyndi got to the island ahead of me, where she met up with our daughter, Rachelle. They took a break from the property search and went to Orient Beach, where they then meandered into a new beach bar called L'String.

There they met a most engaging guy by the name of Jean Henri, running the beach chair concession. "Jean" in French is pronounced similar to Sean, with an "S-J" sound. Most Americans simply call him "John." Jean, about 5'8", had a smile and a dark-skinned, muscular, stocky body that reminded me of the late baseball Hall of Famer, Kirby

Puckett. His personality and customer service skills were as good as they got. We became friends and visited him most every trip.

One evening we offered to treat Jean and his wife Mary to a dinner of their choice. Like Vic and Ed before them, they chose Carl's neighboring Ti Coin Creole. Jean and Mary were originally from Haiti, but Jean had spent a number of years in Guadeloupe. These transplanted locals fit a profile of other Caribbean natives who had moved to the friendly island to pick up some friendly cash. Tourism on the island was good, construction was booming, and jobs were available. And for the native French, the adventurous move to an island paradise was an attraction by itself.

In November 2005 Cyndi and I were on the island inspecting our new property when Jean insisted that he and Mary were going to take us to dinner for my birthday. They were to pick us up around 6:30 p.m. It was our last evening on-island, and Cyndi had promised me a celebratory dinner, but we gladly accepted Jean's sincere invite.

At 8:00 p.m. there was still no sign of Jean Henri, and Cyndi was initiating alternate plans. A few minutes later, Jean and Mary pulled up in their rickety car and completely astonished us; they carried in pots of delicious home-cooked shrimp, chicken, rice and beans, salads, and other foods, plus champagne, a French rosé wine, and a birthday cake. I was speechless. I would be hard-pressed to recall a more kind and heartwarming birthday celebration.

One day in July 2010, we stopped by to say hello to Jean at his beachside business. We hadn't been there for about four weeks because of a busy run at work. Our buddy Jean was rather somber in his greeting and said he wanted to talk with us after we chose our beach chair. Later he came over and began the conversation.

"Last Friday my father dead," Jean blurted out.

Stunned, I replied, "Jean, your father is dead?"

"Yea, him dead."

"What happened?"

"He was in Guadeloupe. He back hurt, he went Haiti. Was see a doctor on Monday, but Friday him dead."

"Was it cancer?"

"No, the muscle," Jean said, pointing to his heart.

"Jean, we're so sorry," both Cyndi and I said. "Is there anything we can do?"

"No, he was eighty-four."

"Well, then, he lived a good life."

"Yes, he lived good life."

"How's your mother doing?" I inquired. She was in Guadeloupe and had been diagnosed with a severe stage of breast cancer two years earlier.

"She okay, best she can, I tink," Jean replied.

We continued the conversation with our dear friend and together mourned the loss of his father. Jean had spent much of the little money he had to give him a proper funeral.

Our conversation with Jean represents just how important and deeply connected the friendships are that we've developed in St. Martin.

In the period leading up to our taking up full-time residency on St. Martin, we needed a reliable caretaker to watch the property while we were off-island. We inherited our caretaker from the prior villa owners, and thankfully, she was magnificent. Jackie was her name, and her physical beauty was surpassed only by her trustworthiness. She was a divorced mom originally from St. Kitts. Jackie and her then-boyfriend became our closest island allies.

Jackie's boyfriend, Derryck Jack, was a well-built, handsome, and industrious man with a shaved head; he hailed from Trinidad. His job was managing the three island Kentucky Fried Chicken outlets, and he did an exceptional job. He had an impressive résumé, having worked for a few resorts and also spending time with Häagen Dazs. While with that company he had completed training at their corporate headquarters, located in our hometown, Minneapolis. Derryck would have been a top-ranking corporate executive if he had resided in the States. His skills and work ethic were impressive.

Since most island men go by their last names, Jackie and others called him "Jack." That meant the couple were known as Jack and Jackie, complicated by their subsequent marriage when they became Jack and Jackie Jack. Sounded like a local band.

If we had a property crisis when we were back in the States, we would call Derryck, who had the pull to get a local person out to our place pronto to put out the proverbial fire. Herman Wouk's character in *Don't Stop the Carnival* might still be living island life if he'd had someone like Derryck.

When Derryck and Jackie had their first child together, we were honored when they chose us to be the godparents. His name was Jaiyel, and we're enjoying watching him grow as much as if he were our own. Two years after his birth, he would be the ring bearer at our daughter's on-island wedding. At the crowded church baptismal service for Jaiyel, we later recounted that we were the only white people, with the exception of one young boy. At the time, we had given no thought to it because of the comfort of the surroundings. We truly felt local, and it was fantastic.

CHAPTER 9

OBTAINING A BUSINESS LICENSE, ESTABLISHING RESIDENCY

Having a business license is a requirement for opening a business in any civilized country. St. Martin, being a part of France, was no exception. The only problem, and it was fairly huge, was that I was the partner designated to handle that task, and I had dropped the ball. I failed to check on the licensing requirements prior to purchasing the property. Uh-oh. When we discovered the difficult process that awaited us, my lovely Cyndi became the disgruntled-at-John-but-still-lovely Cyndi.

"This is getting past the point of ridiculous. We should just sell the property and move on with our lives."

"We can't sell now," I pleaded. "We've got too much money invested, and there's no way we'll get most of it back in a rushed sales process."

"But who knows what issues will be next?"

"I understand, but trust me. We'll get it figured out. Remember, life is a journey, not an end. Besides, this could just very well be our last obstacle."

"Yes, but our journey right now is a roller-coaster ride that's giving me a headache." Cyndi was still distraught about the requirements for residency, which we were simultaneously researching.

The addition of the business license problem was just too much for her to take. I tried to take care of as many of the details alone as I could.

I couldn't help but think that the "technical side" of island life was anything but easygoing. It wouldn't be terrible if they could infuse some of their laid-back flavor into the corporate and governmental environment.

I drove alone to an office that would best be described as the French Chamber of Commerce. Unlike Chambers in the States, however, this Chamber was the part of the government that issued licenses. After waiting in line, I got my turn at the desk, and a nice lady told me what we needed: in addition to the list of required documents, I had to take a class at the Chamber office on tax and business procedures. Naturally the class would be in French, and my *French for Dummies* was still collecting dust. The most important thing was to file our articles of incorporation, and we needed a managing director who was a resident. We also needed a French bank account.

My attorney/lobbyist mode kicked in as I tried to find effective ways to document the criteria. I asked the nice lady at the Chamber, in my sweetest voice possible, "Could you help me?" She said no but gave me a list of names of people who might.

Every person I approached for help turned me down. Our venture was either too small, not of interest to them, or just merited a flat-out "*non.*" I was down to one name left on the list: Gladys, whom I found in a cramped upstairs office in Marigot. Gladys was a young assistant in an accounting-type firm who said she would be glad to help. God bless Gladys.

Gladys took our information and said she would have the corporate papers drafted. She inquired about our resident director, and we asked our caretaker, Jackie, if she'd be interested in the job. Jackie would need to collect and deliver her personal documents, including birth certificate, proof of residency, and the like. We didn't have any other choice and were thankful she graciously agreed to help.

Jackie, despite having four children at home and feeling nauseous, since she was two months pregnant, looked at her to-do list.

Having concluded our agenda for this short, hectic island trip, we headed back to the States. My first mission upon arrival was to determine the process for the long-stay visa needed for our residency. The Internet explained the procedures, but it was somewhat confusing as to where St. Martin fit within the French empire. Different rules applied to regions and territories, and St. Martin wasn't specifically listed. We gathered that our chosen island fell within the requirements of Guadeloupe, which was then the territorial headquarters.

Next, I searched the Internet for a French attorney who could assist. I discovered an attorney in Paris who specialized in immigration. For an exorbitant fee in euros that had to be wired to his account, he was put on the clock to collect our documents and bundle our visa package. As an added bonus, he informed us that a French law had passed a few years earlier that allowed nonresident American owners of a business in France to serve as managing director. He e-mailed the text of the new law to Gladys, who changed the managing director designation from Jackie to Cyndi and me.

Our Parisian attorney forwarded us our visa package, and we received our corporate papers from Gladys. It was time to make an appointment with the French Consulate in Houston for the visa, and we authorized Gladys to file the articles of incorporation. Gladys claimed we didn't have to take the Chamber class. Now our list of requirements to obtain our license was down to just getting a French bank account. Easy, right? Wrong!

Cyndi returned to the island in December 2007 to open the business for the island high season, which is December through April. She believed she could secure a bank account in a few days to finalize our license, and Tijon—the name we had chosen for our business—would be official.

Cyndi closed the shop one day and stopped at a bank in Marigot. She was none too thrilled to learn that the process involved first making an appointment; unlike at an American bank, she couldn't just drop in.

At the scheduled time, Cyndi returned and received a list of approximately twenty documents to collect and bring back. We were just plain lucky that Cyndi had copies of them all back at the villa. A few of the items included were our marriage certificate and our children's birth certificates. We would have never suspected those things would be needed for a corporate bank account. I guess we should have, though, since the French laws did say that the account would be the children's upon our demise.

Cyndi collected the necessary papers and returned for the third time to the bank. The bank's personnel told her the documents would be sent to the bank's regional headquarters in Guadeloupe; they'd be in touch in two weeks. Cyndi was such a trouper through this process.

Three weeks later, without having received a call, Cyndi stopped in and, upon investigating, learned that the bank had lost the paperwork, and we needed to resubmit. Could we trust a bank with our money if they lost our papers?

Cyndi promptly made a call to Gladys and she, in turn, recommended a different bank, Banque Française Commerciale (BFC). She also helped Cyndi schedule the appointment. The same process occurred again, including the long delay, but at least the banker, Mrs. Mussington, was most helpful. After a few months we'd been approved for a bank account.

From the time Cyndi had stopped by the first bank to receiving final account approval, four months had passed. Gladys then filed everything with the Chamber and, *voilà*, the business license was issued in March 2008. The relief of receiving that license breathed renewed energy into us and our vision.

Tijon, which had been open and operating during this time, was now official. We could apply for residency as the owners of a business. This was particularly important, because I wasn't in a position to live on the island for more than six months; I still needed to work at my primary job in Texas in order to pay back the Bank of Mom.

* * * * *

Business license accomplished. Obtaining residency status was next on the list.

As visitors, Cyndi and I could stay in St. Martin's for a mere three months at a time, and then we had to leave. Obviously, we couldn't operate Tijon in that manner, so we had to do some fast work and hope that we got some prompt responses—at least prompt by island standards. Sure, we could have chosen Hawaii or the U.S. Virgin Islands as our place of business, but we sought a beach less traveled.

Our research suggested we would be best served with French

residency for three reasons: to be legal as workers in St. Martin; for tax purposes in the United States; and to proudly walk through the shorter, "residents only" line at airport customs in St. Martin (travelers know the appeal of that reason).

Under U.S. tax law anything we earned in a foreign country would be taxed both by the foreign country and good old Uncle Sam. As much as I love Uncle Sam, I wasn't eager about the thought of double taxation. That rule wouldn't apply, however, if Cyndi and I obtained residency status in that foreign country. In that case, the U.S. tax code would exclude up to $80,000 of foreign income earned per person, or $160,000 per couple.

I asked our French notary at the time of our real estate closing in 2004 what was needed for residency, and she advised, "You need go to the Prefecture, up by the Fort, and bring your passport, your driver's license, your birth and marriage certificate, your children's birth certificates, a letter from your American bank, a note verifying medical insurance, and the deeds to your St. Martin properties." As you may recall, the Prefecture is the French governmental entity overseeing the territory. I scribbled notes down as we returned to the States.

After a few months we collected the necessary documents and booked another flight to St. Martin. Even though we wouldn't be permanently moving to the island for another few years, we proudly marched up to the Prefecture, a group of small offices at the base of Fort St. Louis, overlooking the harbor and the capital city, Marigot. Applicants nervously crowded outside under a porch roof in the sweltering heat. Only two people were allowed in at any given time. "In" was a space equal to a walk-in closet. This particular closet had two glass windows that the government workers sat behind in their air-conditioned offices.

When we initiated this process, St. Martin was a commune, similar to a city within the Guadeloupe Department of France. Today, because it's a direct territory, when we're in French St. Martin, we're legally in the Republic of France.

We first arrived at the Prefecture on a weekday morning around 10:00. We had no idea where we should go or whom to ask. The little signage that existed was in French, and we hadn't begun to master that, yet. After a few minutes of wandering about we recognized a friendly face. There, before our very eyes, was Jean Henri.

"Monsieur Jean! What are you doing here?"

"I apply for travel documents," he told us.

"We were told to come here for our residency. Where do we go?"

"Oooh, that a problem. You need get a number over dere, but dey stop giving numbers at nine o'clock. Dey open eight but you need get here before den to get in line."

"What do we do with a number?"

"Number gets you appointment. You come back for appointment."

Dejection set in, discovering this so late into the day. We returned the next day with the sun rising in the background, around 6:00. We counted fourteen in line ahead of us, others sitting in chairs. We guessed at the line's end and took our place.

The line was mostly *non anglais*. People from Haiti, the Dominican Republic, and other non-English-speaking lands anxiously stood in the cramped, body-to-body line, their expressions downcast and grim. The air was permeated with sweat and despair. Women, tiring of holding their babies, waved magazines to combat the sweltering heat under the porch, where any hint of a breeze was blocked. One woman sat off to the side to breastfeed her newborn.

As per another custom at the Prefecture, everything turned into complete chaos at 8:00 a.m., when the door opened. The crowd, which had grown to thirty-five, crashed forward—everyone but us, that is. The others flew by; we froze in shock.

The Prefecture turned instantly mob-like. People were pushing, shoving, and shouting, demanding their rightful spot in line . . . or at least we assumed they were; the words were all in French, Spanish, or Creole.

Later on we learned this was the norm every morning at 8:00. Realizing the other applicants desperately needed papers in order to work to feed their families, we tried to be both patient and understanding.

We weren't alone in our quest. The local newspaper reported in July 2005 that there were 13,896 foreigners of 117 nationalities registered on the French side, with 8,374 in the process of applying for residency. Excluding Europeans, who could come and go at will under the laws of the new European union, Haiti accounted for the largest concentration of foreigners, with the Dominican Republic second and Dominica third.

Another common event occurred at about 8:05 a.m., when the tiny window from the office to the outside opened, and a government worker shouted, "*Arrêtez de pousser, ou nous nous arrêterons pour le jour!*"

What did they say? Finally, another person in line explained that if the pushing, shouting, and shoving didn't cease immediately, the Prefecture would lock their door for the day. Apparently this wasn't an idle threat; order was quickly restored.

At 8:10 a.m. I counted twenty-five people in front of us. Sixty minutes later, with twenty people having entered and departed the cubicle, Cyndi and I were number fifteen in line; people seated in chairs kept jumping into what they perceived as their rightful place in the queue.

Our turn to enter the walk-in closet finally arrived, and we proudly presented our paperwork, gleefully requesting residency. The young man behind the glass was polite and spoke English.

"Who gave you a list?"

"The notary who closed on our property."

"Notaries don't know what you need. Only our office tells you what you need. You first need a long-stay visa."

"The notary told us we didn't need a long-stay visa," I argued, to no avail.

"And I tell you, you *do* need a visa. Whom do you believe?"

"Is there a list of documents we need?"

"You come back with your visa, get a number for an appointment, then we give you a list of documents needed."

Shock set in as Cyndi and I slowly left the walk-in closet with our heads lowered. We felt like two school kids who had just been reprimanded by the principal. I meekly said, "*Merci,*" on our way out.

So, back to the States we traveled, with no date set for becoming residents of St. Martin. We had to figure out how to get a long-stay visa, or *carte de jour.* To obtain the visa we had to compile numerous documents and make an appointment with one of the French embassies in the States. However, to avoid a repeat catastrophe like that experienced at the Prefecture, I hired the *avocat*/attorney in Paris via the web.

Our appointment at the French embassy in Houston came on a

rainy Monday morning. It was only a four-hour drive from our home in Arlington, near Dallas. Our documents, thanks to our Parisian attorney, and our application fee in euros were in hand.

Unlike the island, we had an appointment at a specific time in a nicely furnished, quiet, air-conditioned office. There was no standing in line, pushing, nor shoving. The consulate who met with us, from France, was professional and polite. She looked through our documents and told us that everything appeared in order and that she would send everything to Paris for final approval. Our visas were to be ready in four to six weeks. Her words were like music to our ears.

A few weeks before the official arrival of our visas, Cyndi, back in St. Martin to open the shop, went to the Prefecture to set a time for our appointment and receive the list of needed documents we would bring, along with our visas. She endured the cattle chute experience on her own. And you wonder how I know she's so dear?

I joined Cyndi on the day of the appointment with our *cartes de jour* and our ten other needed documents. Island appointments, unlike at the French embassy, meant we were given a number, and we arrived at 9:00 a.m. From that point, we just waited until we were called. Our call came around 10:30 a.m. Again, the Prefecture staff was polite and spoke English. We left smiling, holding our initial residency cards. Time to celebrate and do some hard work!

We also acquired two new friends on this particular trip to the Prefecture. While there, we noticed another white couple, approximately twenty years older than us, sitting in the cattle call. Typically we were the only whites in line; most applicants were Antilleans from nearby islands, immigrating for better work opportunities.

I struck up a conversation with the woman, who introduced herself as Carol and the man as her husband, Paul. They spoke English! Carol was slim, attractive, and athletic, and Paul sported a distinguished, trimmed white beard and thinning hair. The two had retired to St. Martin because of a love for its culture and climate. They were established and had three grown children. Their experiences and love of St. Martin made them close friends and island mentors for Cyndi and me.

Technically anyone who spends over ninety consecutive days on the island need be a resident with the appropriate documentation. Paul and Carol, on the island for six to nine months at a time for many years, understood that enforcement was becoming more stringent after 9/11, and so began their official residency quest.

The old adage that it's not what you know but whom you know was proven true with this lovely couple. Paul was a Rotarian, a member of the French club where the important leaders and business people participated in giving back to the community. We naturally had a number of local business issues, whether it was our license or the need for an accountant, and Paul advised us on whom to see. Dropping his name brought immediate and successful assistance.

Paul generously donated to Cyndi and me a Rosetta Stone French language course that he'd abandoned long ago. He could understand a bit of French, but wasn't to the point of speaking.

Paul and I immediately hit it off on our first couples' dinner at L'California restaurant, overlooking the ocean in Grand Case. His neighbor was serving as chef, and my ordering the local rum-based ti punch sealed the deal with our friendship. It turns out that the tasty little rum drink was Paul's favorite libation.

The rules required us to return every three months to the Prefecture for the first year of our residency application. It was difficult, but not impossible. We were considering our options and thought it would work best if Cyndi ran the shop from December through April. I would continue working in Texas, flying over as needed to make product. The last admonition we'd received at the Prefecture office indicated that we would be receiving further instructions in the mail.

The first mailing surprisingly arrived about a month prior to our scheduled appointment in July. We weren't on the island, but our trusty helper Jackie collected the mail and relayed the information. It instructed us to complete a physical at the island hospital and to obtain approval from the gendarmes. We immediately changed our airline bookings to arrive on the island a day earlier than our appointment.

Our visit at the Prefecture was set for a Friday. Jackie told us that the hospital gave these required physicals only on Wednesdays, and she made our hospital appointments. We scheduled our arrival for Tuesday. Cyndi was coming from Minnesota, where she was visiting family, and I was on my way from Texas. Cyndi's plane was delayed by thunderstorms, and her arrival was changed to Wednesday evening. Uh-oh.

I landed on schedule and proudly beamed my way through the "residents only" line at airport customs. With a big smile, I produced my passport and my French residency card. I was excited about the time savings I'd had by not waiting in the long visitors' line. Unfortunately, it wasn't that easy. The local customs worker began to quiz me.

"Do you live on da island?" she asked. She also looked surprised, as if the notion was crazy.

"Yes, I live in Grand Case."

"But are you from the United States?"

"That's where I am from, yes."

"Why would you want to live here?"

"Well, ah . . . because we like it here?" I replied. It sounded like more of a question because I honestly wasn't sure what she was getting at. She kept looking at me, so I continued. "It's warmer than where I'm from, and you have nice beaches and nice people."

"But we want to live in da United States," she proclaimed with a smile.

"That's nice, too, but we live here and can go back to visit in the States when we want." I experienced the sudden realization that paradise is definitely in the eye of the beholder.

I trekked to the hospital on Wednesday morning with Tijon gift samples in hand to offer the gatekeeper. She was a kind woman and the one who processed the appointments. Luckily, she was sympathetic to Cyndi's plight and graciously agreed to reschedule Cyndi's appointment for the next morning.

My next step was to make an appointment with the gendarmes. I went to their secure complex located in a neighborhood known as Orleans, or the French Quarter. I saw a telephone box outside the gate that said the phone was for emergencies. I didn't believe my request was an emergency, so I didn't pick up the phone. There was no need to risk annoying the very people whose help I needed, I reasoned. I walked around the side through an open gate, entered the compound, and approached the office. The front door was locked. Not to be deterred, I walked around back, where the door was slightly ajar, and let myself in.

What happened next was both surprising and scary. A gendarme was moving his hand toward his gun, because he saw me, a strange man, entering the supposedly secure building. He was angrily shouting at me in French.

In this brief commotion, someone found an officer who spoke a bit of English. Once he understood what I wanted, and after scolding me for barging in, he told me their next appointment would be Friday afternoon. Explaining that was too late, as we were meeting with the government Friday morning, the officer calmed down and graciously scheduled an appointment for Thursday afternoon.

Cyndi arrived late Wednesday on her postponed flight, passed her physical Thursday morning, and joined me in meeting the gendarmes that afternoon. I brought Tijon samples and was warmly greeted by an officer whom, we suspected, spoke no English. He sat us down at his desk and asked questions in French while an officer at a nearby desk graciously translated. After some friendly give and take, they said something to the effect that we were good to go.

On Friday morning we met with the Prefecture and had our residency extended for a full year. We had to return in three months to pick up our cards, but then we were good until the following June. Upon receiving that information I leaned over to Cyndi and said quietly, "There is a God." We walked down the steep hill to an outdoor Creole restaurant in Marigot to celebrate over lunch.

Two months prior to the end of our first one-year residency, in May 2009, we needed to hop back in the cattle call at 8:00 a.m. to make an appointment for our one-year extension. We received an appointment date and a list of documents to bring in order to receive our second one-year residency. We visited with our French friends, who interpreted our list of needed paperwork. They certainly didn't make year two residency requests much easier than year one.

We recognized the woman behind the glass as a supervisor who had always been kind and helpful. She took our papers and started shouting to her colleagues in French. She then explained to us that we had been given the wrong list of documents to bring and provided us the correct one. She told us we needed to come back, and that we would have a thirty-day extension. I kept reminding myself, *That's island life, mon.* It was difficult to understand, but I kept my cool.

This particular wild-goose chase was on a Wednesday morning. I asked her if we could meet again on Friday morning, as I had flown in specifically for this meeting and was leaving on the weekend. The cost for airline tickets was adding up, and their office was only open from 8:00 a.m. to 12:30 p.m., Monday through Friday. She graciously gave us an appointment for Friday, warning us, however, that it would be difficult to obtain the documents in such a short time frame. Thursday was a holiday, and all offices and businesses were closed. It's a good thing we had both passed our physicals the year prior, because the scramble to collect information was on, and not for the faint of heart.

Cyndi and I rushed out of the Prefecture to find someone to translate our new list of needed documents. It included insurance papers that were at our home in Texas, an updated business license, called the *Kabis*, from Guadeloupe, and some type of letter stating we were in compliance with the French tax system.

Our own version of *The Great Race* began. We drove twenty minutes to a popular and inexpensive translator in the French Quarter, only to find we were at the end of a line that was at least thirty people long. We didn't have that much time.

We U-turned and headed back to Marigot with the hope that our French accountant, Marie-Dominque, would be in and available. Cyndi dropped me off outside her office while she headed to the Chamber to inquire about the *Kabis*. The *Kabis* is evidence of our business license, but when issued is only valid for ninety days. We didn't know why we needed to keep applying for an updated *Kabis* but didn't have time to question.

Marie-Dominique translated what was needed and claimed she would have the required letter in regard to our French tax status ready to go in thirty minutes. I then half-ran, half-walked the mile and a half to our insurance agent's office to get a copy of our policy; the original was in Texas. All was moving forward as I waited for a call from Cyndi at the Chamber. Last year her friend at the Chamber, introduced to her by Paul and Carol, had assisted in quickly receiving the *Kabis* from Guadeloupe via fax. We were hoping luck would be on our side this year, too.

But Cyndi had discovered that her friend was off work for a few days, and the receptionist was unaware of how to expedite the request.

It would take weeks to receive it. Game over. We would have to fly back to St. Martin in a month, at considerable cost in both money and vacation time. I trudged the eighteen blocks back to Marie-Dominique to get the tax letter and give her the bad news. I caught her as she was leaving for a late luncheon.

A few hours later Cyndi and I were commiserating when my cell phone rang. It was Marie-Dominique. "I have your *Kabis* in my office."

"What did you say?" Even though I had heard her, I simply couldn't believe it.

"I have your *Kabis* in my office. Can you come by and pick it up?"

"But how did you get that? That's unbelievable."

"I told you I had a luncheon. What I didn't tell you was that it was a lunch with my friend visiting from Guadeloupe. She works in the business office there and called and had your *Kabis* faxed to my office."

Cyndi and I dropped our mope-fest and charged out the door to drive to Marie-Dominique's after making a quick stop at the nearby Jeff de Bruges chocolatier shop. I rushed into Marie-Dominque's, and she offered me a big smile. She was holding our *Kabis*. I gave her a box of chocolates, dropped to my knees, and kissed her extended hand.

Friday morning we arrived at the Prefecture, and our paperwork was accepted. We were good for another year. We had to return in three months to pick up our new card, but that seemed trivial after what we'd just been through. I silently offered a prayer of thanks.

The process for residency on the island was and remains complicated, tedious, and painful. And because we were flying back and forth it was also costly. Americans are quick to complain about a foreign process, but we stopped complaining after hearing of horror stories far worse in the United States for those from other countries applying for U.S. residential status. In the end, it is what it is. We just had to chalk it up as part of the price we would pay for fulfilling our dreams.

CHAPTER 10

SHIPPING AND STORAGE, THE LANGUAGE BARRIER, AND OTHER CHALLENGES

It didn't take long for us to realize that doing business on an island requires a good relationship with a reputable shipper. Utilizing ships as opposed to airlines was slower, but much more affordable.

Given all the supplies we'd regularly need to import for Tijon, we wanted to make sure we established shipping procedures. Although we were able to distill and utilize some local ingredients, other oils, chemicals, packaging, and equipment had to be imported. We initially ordered and staged the deliveries in our three-car garage in Texas and started with a twenty-foot container load to St. Martin. After that we shipped by pallet or package.

Full-container shipping was remarkably efficient. We would call the shipper and secure a price and date for delivery of the container that was to be dropped off at our residential garage. We hired a few big, young boys from church and loaded the goods in time for the truck to return and pick up the container for delivery to the nearby port of Houston. A week or so later the container was delivered to our business in Grand Case. The entire cost, before insurance, was about $3,500.

For smaller items the process was similarly simple. We would order and have it delivered to our shipper's Miami address, where it would then be loaded on the next weekly ship departing for St. Martin. The goods would arrive at the shipper's island office a few days later, and the shipper would then deliver the goods directly to our business. There were neither customs to clear nor taxes to be paid on this duty-free, friendly island.

Figuring out what to do for letters and smaller parcels was the difficult part. We had to consider how to handle our U.S. tax returns, my bar licenses, life insurance bills, birthday cards, and the like.

We always wondered which address to provide. Getting mail from the States at our actual address in St. Martin took weeks, assuming we received it at all. Our daughter's address in California worked, but she was busy, so we didn't care to list it too often. We also had a Miami mailbox address that was secure but a bit expensive, as the hosting company would fly it weekly to their St. Martin office for pickup. This was particularly proven true when my sister mailed us some pancake mix and wild rice soup mix to that mailbox. It cost us $69 to pick up the package in St. Martin, likely more than the cost of the contents. They were the most delicious and expensive pancakes we ever ate. We also had the problem of trying to remember to whom we gave what address.

Shipping in can be problematic at times, but it works. Outbound shipping is considerably more complicated and expensive. The same shipping agents won't ship anything less than a few pallet loads to the States because of the paperwork and hassles of U.S. customs.

That left us with three options for shipping smaller quantities. We could use FedEx, the Dutch post office, or the French post office. However, only FedEx would accept perfumes to ship, and then only two bottles max. Anything more required extensive paperwork and a label of "hazardous material" due to the alcohol in the perfumes. But FedEx is prohibitively expensive, with one perfume bottle costing over sixty dollars. And it still takes a few days to arrive. Again, the shipping would cost more than the goods themselves.

For goods other than perfumes, we found the Dutch post office to be the least expensive of the three, but it's a long, cross-island drive. Despite that, we utilized their services until December 2010, when they posted a sign declaring they couldn't accept any packages until December 8. Wanting to mail a purse and two wine glasses to a friend in the States, we stopped back on December 15 and again on December 20, only to discover they still weren't accepting packages despite the out-dated sign. We tried again on January 4.

"Hi, I'd like to mail this package to the States," I stated.

"No, we can't accept any packages to the States."

"But the sign says you can after December 8."

"We can't accept any packages until American Airlines gives us the okay," the postal worker explained.

"Do you know when the airlines might give you that okay?"

"We have no idea."

"Could you weigh the package and tell me how much it'll cost when you do get the okay?"

"I can't. Our system is down."

I could see that she was bothered by my questions and continued use of her time. I bit my tongue, thanked her, and left. I kept my grumbles silently tossing around in my head. *It's island life, mon.*

Cyndi and I headed back toward home and stopped at the more expensive, euro-based French post office. We arrived at 1:30 p.m. to see a postal worker locking the door. I asked if they would be returning that day. The sign outside listed their hours from 7:30 a.m. to 5:00 p.m., Monday through Friday. The lady said they would be closed and would reopen the next morning. Cyndi and I looked at each other and shrugged. We were going to have to start going with the flow of island time or drive ourselves crazy.

I returned the next morning, and the doors remained locked. There were no signs saying why, or when they'd be open. Needing to deliver this package, I stopped in early Thursday morning and was delighted to see the offices open. That is, until I entered the shop and counted thirty-five people ahead of me for the two postal lines.

During the wait I discovered the reason for the prior closure: solidarity. A sister post office in Baie Nettle, twenty minutes away, was robbed at gunpoint the prior Monday afternoon. Apparently all the postal workers shut down for a day and a half to show support for the postal workers who had faced the robbers. I'm not sure who was supporting the postal customers. One hour and eighteen euros later, I left the post office counter; another thirty-five people were standing in line behind me.

* * * * *

Downsizing a home and its personal properties has generated articles, books, and consultants. It's a growing phenomenon with us baby boomers as we move on in years. Most have a collection of something or another that seemed like a good idea at the time. And we all have the illusion that our children will want these prized possessions, completely abandoning the memories of how we generally shied away from such parental offerings.

You know how it goes. You start out with the occasional "Thank you, Mom, but we don't have room for that," and end up with the more direct "Mom, we just don't want it." Why should our children be any different? We all want to think that our stuff is better, but our children like to remind us that much of it is just old stuff to them.

Making a permanent move to a Caribbean island was more like abandoning than downsizing. We purchased our island villa fully furnished; this was pretty common, since those selling property and moving off the island typically leave most of their stuff behind. After all, nobody wishes to pay more for shipping furniture than it may actually be worth. The same went for us as far as shipping our furnishings to St. Martin.

Cyndi and I had different approaches as to sentimental value. Cyndi hung onto the hope that our children, when they purchased their own homes, would want items with family memories attached, while my consistent response was "toss it."

Regardless of whether people are moving or downsizing, they need determine two things: what to toss or give away, and what to move to the next location. For us, it was a four-fold decision: what to toss; what to ship to our new home in St. Martin; what to ship up to Minnesota where we would spend part of the hurricane season at a lake cabin before visiting our children in San Diego; and what to store. We created four piles; the pile marked "toss/give-away" was the smallest. Uh-oh.

Logic won, however, and we rented a large storage unit in Texas. I complained about the cost of the rental unit, but Cyndi replied with a definitive tone: "You can't put a monetary value on sentiment." I examined a piece of pottery made by our daughter Rachelle who was now an adult. She hadn't the room or the desire to have her piece of fine childhood pottery as a memento. I placed it into the trashcan. Cyndi was furious.

"What's this doing in the trash?"

"Well, honey, it's old and been on our shelf for years. Shelly [Rachelle] could have taken it with her numerous times but never has. I don't think she'll miss it."

"Listen here! This is important to her, and she'll want it. She just doesn't have room in her apartment right now. This is going into storage and that's that."

I moved the item to the correct pile. End of discussion. This gambler still knew when to fold 'em.

We carefully packed boxes, transported them, and stacked them ten feet high into a vast storage wasteland, possibly never to be seen again—much like the Ark of the Covenant in the government warehouse at the end of *Raiders of the Lost Ark*. Later, while in Texas looking for one particular item from storage for Cyndi to bring to St. Martin, I didn't have the strength or the days to attempt its retrieval. The manager of the storage facility was honest in admitting to me that most renters paid more in storage fees than the items inside were worth. We would be no exception. But I was reminded of the old saying, "If Mama's happy, we're all happy."

* * * * *

It's reported there are over a hundred nationalities on the island with various common languages, in addition to English, French, Dutch, Spanish, Creole, and Papiamentu.

The French term *Creole* is represented in Spanish as *Criollo*, and in Portuguese as *Crier*. All of these derive from the Latin, *creare*. It was originally coined to indicate the language of those born in the colonies, meant to distinguish them from the upperclass, European-born colonists. Really, Creole is any language that began as pidgin but was later adopted as the mother tongue by mixing with a European language.

Papiamentu is a Creole language influenced over the centuries by African slaves, Spanish and Portuguese merchants, and the Dutch. It's spoken by about 250,000 people, and that makes it the official and most widely spoken language on the Dutch-Caribbean islands of Aruba,

Bonaire, and Curaçao. But unlike many other spoken Creoles, it shows signs of vibrancy and official acceptance. For example, most of Curaçao's newspapers and even their legislative debate are in Papiamentu.

Opening a business on the French side of St. Martin without understanding the primary language, French, was difficult at best. Knowing certain key phrases, at least, would help us assist customers in addition to understanding legal documents and other items retrieved from the daily mail.

We needed to learn the language, and until that time came, we'd just have to make do with translation assistance. We had trusted our French advisors with the real estate, insurance, and remodel contracts, because we preferred not to pay the excessive costs for official translations. As Steve Martin once noted, "Boy, those French! They have a different word for everything."

We decided to hire a translator when we needed a number of informational posters in the parfumerie translated into French. I searched online and hired a live translator. The first question was whether we wanted "Canadian" French or "French" French. Since that was the first moment I realized there were differences, I opted for the latter. The translations with this service were speedy, but costly.

Subsequently, I found a number of free translation websites where I could click a text in English and, by pushing the "translate" button, see it in French. By cutting and pasting, I used this free method for brochures and rack cards. Computers were astonishing, and free had to be better, right?

It wasn't until our grand opening in December 2008 that Barbara Warren, an islander with both a Californian and French heritage, informed us that some of our translations were either incoherent or offensive. Naturally, where we used a human translator the language was dead-on.

One example involved our beautiful Arawak Dog postcard detailing the history of this legend in English and French. One line revealed how the islanders had a history of having dogs. Apparently, our free French translation implied that all islanders were dogs. We threw away boxes of postcards. Thankfully Cyndi didn't put me in the doghouse!

Similarly, we had a sign made for our perfume organ, using the computer translation site, which read *"Organe de Parfum."* Barbara expressed concern, indicating it could refer to the male organ, and offered to review any of our future documents. After going back to a human translator, we discovered the correct wording was *"Orgue à parfums."* We trashed the free computer site and decided to hire human translators, even if online, with the dream of someday knowing the language sufficiently.

According to Wikipedia, French is a Romance language spoken around the world by ninety million people as a first language, by 190 million as a second language, and by about another 200 million people as an acquired foreign language. It's an official language in twenty-nine countries, most of which form what is called *La Francophonie,* the community of French-speaking nations.

St. Martin represented one of those twenty-nine countries. We sought to become two of the 200 million people acquiring it as a foreign language. It's reported that approximately 40 percent of the English language is derived from French. How hard could it be . . . even if I couldn't recognize any words to be similar?

Cyndi had a head start because of two years of French in school many years prior, but I teased her for remembering so little. I had foolishly taken four years of German in school and remembered far less of what I'd learned than Cyndi, but I enjoyed boasting that I was fluent in four languages: American, English, Canadian, and Australian. *Danke schoen.* The Berglund children were of no immediate help; Rachelle had fulfilled her schooling requirements by tackling German, and T.J. had taken two years of Spanish.

Back in the days when we were in Atlanta and still in the dreaming stage of our Caribbean lifestyle, we enrolled in an evening community French class, despite our conflict with T. J.'s high school basketball. The class had only one other enrollee, who dropped out after the first session, presumably not to further face our demanding and impolite instructor, whom I shall call Madame French.

This mad instructor was a frumpy older woman with long, pulled-back, grey hair, and tiny reading glasses pinching her nose. Skilled in techniques to intimidate and apparently having no life of her own, her joy was to make others miserable. By the third class, Cyndi had to take

T. J. to basketball, and I was forced to sit alone and receive the defensive evil eye from the treacherous Madame.

That evening, a few classes into my French experience, Madame demanded that a volunteer approach the blackboard to demonstrate proficiency in the homework assignment. Gee, who would be the volunteer? I looked around and was brutally reminded that the class consisted of me. I slowly rose and approached the largest black wall in the history of mankind. My daunting task wasn't made easier by the fact that I had been busy at work and too exhausted at home to open the assignment book.

There I was, a grown man with a chemistry education and a license to practice law in three states, and I was unable to respond to a basic language quiz because of an inability to understand the question. I wasn't even certain the questions were in French. Had there been a dunce cap, I would have received it.

Cyndi demonstrated greater intelligence, having opted to skip class to attend to her motherly duties. I thought transporting my son to his sporting event was a fatherly duty, but Cyndi knew otherwise. Not wishing to be the absentee parent, I volunteered during the next French class to assist Cyndi, and it so happened that neither of us was available to attend any more classes. Madame haunts me until this very day.

We rationalized our failure and class dropout by visiting the local bookstore and loading up on French dictionaries and self-help books. French could be learned at home, and what more appropriate book to start with than *French for Dummies*? I believe you've heard me reference this book before.

Attempting to be self-taught reminded us why we had initially enrolled in the class. We lacked both the discipline to study at home and the required learning capacity to succeed without assistance. As I've mentioned, we picked up a Rosetta Stone course while on the island as a gift from our American expatriate friend, Paul, who had failed in his attempts. We discovered we could leave the audio on all night while sleeping and absorb . . . nothing.

On the island, everybody from government workers to salespeople stressed how important it was for us to learn the language. One sales rep from a local print company stopped in our shop with a brochure of services. He asked if I spoke French, and I said, "I'm sorry, I don't." He then incredulously began lecturing me that I had to learn their language. His tone was condescending and arrogant. I understood his message, but from a salesman trying to sell me something? After he left, I dumped his brochure in the trash.

Other French nationals were more tactful and kind, reminding us French is a hard language to learn. Amen. In English we say, "The car is red." In French, they say, "Red is the car." Even if I got the basics down, what's with the lines above letters, such as é, è, ê? Or the prefixes, *l*, *la*, and *le*? Yes, one is for feminine nouns and one is for masculine, but how do I tell the difference when applied to generic terms? The desire to learn French must bring out the inquisitive nature in a person; the language demands it.

One weekend we desperately needed charcoal lighter, so off Cyndi went to the large French market a mile away. She came home with a strange looking can, labeled in French. I opened it, and it didn't smell right.

"Honey, this smells like furniture polish."

"It was right next to the charcoal. It looks like lighter fluid."

"Did you ask anyone at the store?"

"Couldn't find anyone who would help me."

"I'll run there and see what I can find."

Hunting through the store, I grabbed another can of Cyndi's purchase, finally found a clerk who spoke some English, and asked what this can was for. She pointed to the floor and said, "For wood, to clean." I asked her where the lighter fluid was and she pointed to another row of cans nearby.

An amenable islander named Wayne, working at the Nissan service shop in the French-side neighborhood of Sandy Ground, spoke fluent French and English when he politely asked me, "How can you live on the French side without speaking French?"

Sometimes wondering the same, I responded, "I'm trying to learn, but not doing well."

"You know how best to learn French?" he offered with a smile.

"No, how?" I was all ears.

"Get a French girlfriend."

I laughed and told him, "I'd have to check with my wife on that one."

In summer 2009, before our final and permanent move to St. Martin, we found yet another teacher, Erin Overstreet, who was married to a colleague and taught French at a local high school. She was a tremendous teacher. In a relatively short time we actually learned a few words and phrases and developed a better understanding of the language structure. She was enthusiastic and patient; Cyndi and I definitely needed that.

She also told funny stories about living in France. One sweltering day she told someone she was hot, which technically would be "*J'ai chaud.*" Her phrase, however, was "*Je suis chaud*," which she later discovered meant, "I'm horny." On another occasion she was embarrassed when answering the telephone at her host's home. The correct answering was "*Allô,*" the French version of our "hello," or "*Salut,*" with the "t" silent. Inadvertently crossing the two, she answered, "*Sallo,*" which translates phonetically to "bastard." She would have appreciated the mishap with our postcards and signs more than we did at the time.

We made copious notes of what phrases not to say. Our language skills remain a work-in-progress and, until then, as Cyndi has yet to give me permission for a French girlfriend, we contented ourselves with our ability to utter a few phrases and hire a translator. We've learned the typical greetings: *Bonjour*—hello, *Bonsoir*—good evening, *Au revoir*—goodbye, *Bonne journée*—have a good day, and *Merci*—thank you. We've also learned *Ça va?*—How are you? This is a nice one, as you can answer "*Ça va?*" with another "*ça va,*" meaning, "I'm fine, how are you? It goes something like this:

Ça va?—How are you?

Ça va. Et vous?—I'm good, and you?

Ça va—I'm good, too.

I wish the entire French language was that easy; it's not. Some other common phrases we've adapted to include:

Je parle un peu Français—I speak a little French.

Je voudrais du ti punch avec glaçons—I would like a ti punch with ice. (This one was important.)

L'addition, s'il vous plaît—The check, please.

C'est la vie—That's life.

Très chic—That's nice, trendy.

I've joined the evening dinner Rotary Club where the meetings are conducted in French. I sit quietly and enjoy the wine. My Rotarian friend, Etienne, who runs the St. Martin harbor, is fluent in French and English even though he is from Belgium. He once told me he speaks every language but Chinese. I was impressed and told him so but then saw a sparkle in his eye and, knowing he was a jokester, asked, "How about German?"

He responded with a smile, "Sounds like Chinese to me."

* * * * *

In my previous corporate life I had managed trade and professional associations. I have a strong belief that belonging to organizations relevant to one's career is important. Organizations consisting of like-minded people provide education, support, and strength while affording opportunities to give back to the profession and community. With that mindset, I discovered the existence of the American Society of Perfumers (ASP).

I was now a perfumer. Cyndi and I had created perfumes and had invested over fifteen years of life and life savings to create our ten signature scents, skin care products, and sun care lines. They were all offered for sale at our shop in St. Martin. However, I was also American and believed in the value of some of these structured business organizations. I'd seen them help various professions achieve their goals and directives my entire professional career.

I excitedly reviewed the ASP website and e-mailed an inquiry on the qualifications and fees for membership. There were no existing license requirements for perfume makers, so there is a bit of subjectivity involved in determining qualifications. A senior sales coordinator for Robertet Fragrances, perhaps volunteering her time to assist the small organization or instructed to do so at her employer's bequest, quickly and professionally responded, outlining dues at $200 annually and stating:

> *Thank you for your interest in the American Society of Perfumers. Potential*
> *members gain membership to our society when they are sponsored by an active*

member. The apprentice member must be working directly under the sponsor. If you work for a company for whom an ASP member perfumer works, you can ask that member to sponsor you. If you are a member of another perfumers' society (for example, the French Perfumers Society) you can apply to become a member of our society. If you still feel you are qualified, but do not meet either of the above criteria, you can write a letter outlining your qualifications. We would then review your letter at the next Board of Director's Meeting and would get back to you. Please feel free to contact me if you need further clarification.

I was excited and promptly e-mailed a generous thank-you and quickly submitted a letter of qualification dated February 2, 2009, with a copy e-mailed to our newfound contact at Robertet. Knowing associations, particularly those that may be managed by volunteers, I didn't expect a quick reply. Their letter indicated it would go to the board, which likely convened infrequently.

June came and I still had heard nothing about my application. I sent a follow-up e-mail to my trusty contact at Robertet, noting, "Hi, I am just checking in as I have heard nothing after submitting my request for membership. Could you kindly advise? Thank you."

The computer verified a successful transmission. It seemed like my follow-up was being successfully transmitted—right into a black hole. There was no reply. On June 30 I delivered a certified letter to the ASP address, simply stating I had heard no response to my request and included a copy of my February 2 letter. The next communication was not until September 25, when I called their listed telephone number, politely leaving a recorded message stating that I had submitted an application and only wanted to know its status, if accepted or declined.

I was getting annoyed. I still received *nada*, nothing, no response. Hello, was anybody home? Was the organization bankrupt and inoperative? That seemed like a valid question until I received my answer in an article in the September 2009 issue of *Beauty Fashion*, a trade publication: ASP was alive and well.

The article was titled "Anchors Aweigh with the American Society of Perfumers." The section, complete with photos, referenced their enjoyable July 27 dinner cruise out of Weehawken, New Jersey, "for a delightful evening of convivial conversation while enjoying a cocktail reception and buffet."

A keynote speaker from Givaudan shared with the cruise participants, "The consumer is demanding, but experimental." *Who was more experimental, if not crazier, in creating products than I?* I regretfully concluded the ASP was an organization that didn't want individuals like me as members. I wasn't disappointed at being excluded. Rather, my disappointment lay in their lack of courtesy or aloofness in not providing a simple response as promised. Perhaps they were too busy cruising.

PART IV

OPERATING A BUSINESS IN A THIRD-WORLD PARADISE

PERFUME FACT

Do perfumes last shorter
or longer on blondes?
Shorter; as a general rule,
blondes have drier skin.
Perfume is an oil, and on
drier skin it evaporates
more quickly.

CHAPTER 11

PULLING THE TRIGGER: BECOMING EXPATRIATES

Our metaphorical gun presented not one, but two triggers. We pulled the first in August 2004 when we made our successful offer to buy two side-by-side properties in St. Martin. The second trigger was in September 2009 when I, after providing lengthy advance notice, officially left my corporate day job. Prior to that I had been traveling back and forth assisting Cyndi, who had opened the shop part-time beginning two seasons prior.

I had been laboring at corporate life for thirty years, always fortunate enough to have benefits and insurance. Parting with my dependable corporate paycheck at age fifty-five, in the midst of the worst economic recession in recent decades, proved nerve-wracking. In fact, the Associated Press, in a September 10, 2009, lead article, stated, "The Great Recession and Americans' retreat into thriftiness are teaching retailers a new lesson: how to survive when consumers are focused on needs rather than wants."

That was just two months before my official retirement. Why would anyone leave such comfortable corporate confines during the Great Recession to manufacture and open a retail shop delivering nothing but wants?

I had provided my departure notice during a healthy economy, one year earlier and at the peak of my professional career. A few months before, I had been placed on the cover of a trade publication, named the most powerful person in my industry. The economy crashed while the search was on for my successor. Let's just say, no matter how much we may prepare for some things, we can never truly gauge our reaction when it happens.

But it was too late to turn back. The finality of the gunshot echoed through our minds.

In preparation for our permanent departure to a Third World island, we were motivated to visit doctors and utilize our soon-to-expire insurance. Within a two-month time frame we had physicals with our family physician, colonoscopies with a gastroenterologist, skin checks by a dermatologist, crowns inserted by our dentist, and lasik surgery in an effort to forever be rid of glasses. Cyndi visited her gynecologist and I my urologist.

We'd be ready for the permanent move—or so we thought, until I received a phone call from Cyndi at my office on the afternoon of September 21, only weeks before my departure.

"Hi, Honey. Are you coming home soon?" she inquired.

"I got caught up in something, will probably be another hour."

"I've got some bad news," Cyndi continued. My thoughts immediately turned to my ninety-four-year-old mother, my ninety-one-year-old aunt, and to Cyndi's mother, who was having heart issues.

"I got a call from the doctor's office a few minutes ago on the colonoscopy report," Cyndi said, "and they found a cancerous tumor. It was small, and they believe they got it, but they've scheduled me for a repeat colonoscopy, and they also want me to make an appointment with an oncologist and a surgeon." She told me it was a type of tumor called carcinoid.

I couldn't respond. I was absolutely speechless and immediately dropped everything to run home. I wanted to console Cyndi and probably needed some consoling myself. The ten-minute drive seemed like eternity. My emotions were surging through me in a way that I'd never experienced before. I had so many questions and no answers.

Hearing the "C" word is life altering, as far too many people know. When I heard Cyndi say it, my heart skipped a beat, my lungs gasped for air, my ears blocked out sound, my eyes became still and wet, my stomach contracted, and then my mind wandered. Cyndi and I had been spoiled, having experienced neither cancer nor a tragic accident among family members. How could this happen now?

I jumped to the next questions in my mind. How do we share the news with family and friends without looking like we're seeking pity? Do we wait for them to hear it from somebody else? What do we do? Eventually, even if we cure the cancer, would the threat of a recurrence linger over our heads for the rest of our days? Considering I didn't really know anything yet, I couldn't turn off the questions in my mind. Cyndi structured a heartfelt message and began the e-mail news chain. It read:

> As you know, John and I have been seeing doctors and taking all the physicals, colonoscopies, and eye exams before we leave for St. Martin. Everything was great until I got a bad pathology result from my colonoscopy.
>
> Yesterday I had a second colonoscopy so that they could remove tissue samples from the area and check to make sure they got it all. I meet with an oncologist on Tuesday. At that point, after a few more tests, they will make their final prognosis. However, the doctor that did our colonoscopy said that I will not be going to St. Martin in November.
>
> If I have surgery I want to have it done in San Diego . . . the follow-up appointments down the line will allow me a fun visit to California and the kids.
>
> We could conclude that the timing is not good, but when is the timing ever good for such news? We prefer to believe that the timing was a blessing in that the cancer was caught early, likely giving us an excellent prognosis.

Cyndi's e-mail was so calm and comforting. Her amazing strength had never shown more brilliantly. Our plans prior to receiving the alarming news had been methodically and strategically made, with air and hotel booked:

- October 25—move out of our apartment. Drive Cyndi's Mustang to San Diego to our children's apartment and visit with them for a week.

- November 1—fly from San Diego to Atlantic City for some meetings that I was contracted for, while having our final container of commercial goods and personal items shipped from Dallas to St. Martin.

- November 14—fly to our new permanent home, St. Martin.

But now our dreams and life plans were placed on temporary hold. Would the business require me to travel alone and abandon Cyndi during her recuperation time? It might, but business be damned! I would stay with Cyndi.

Carcinoid tumors are quite rare; only 5,000 cases are reported annually in the United States. It is a slow-growing type of cancer that is usually, but not always, found in the gastrointestinal tract and rarely causes signs or symptoms. These tumors release hormones into your body that can later have devastating effects on the heart and other organs. They don't respond to chemotherapy. Our gastroenterologist recommended surgery.

We asked our gastroenterologist what surgeon he would personally choose. He referred us to a Dr. Jacobson in Dallas, and we scheduled an appointment for a few days later. Dr. Jacobson concurred that removal of a section of the colon, about ten to twelve inches, was likely the best course of action. Sensitive to our schedule, he could schedule surgery at Baylor Medical Center in Dallas the following week. We agreed.

A few days later Cyndi had her first meeting with an oncologist. They scheduled a CT scan, urinalysis, blood work, and a PET scan. Based on our crazy timetable, the results would be forwarded to the surgeon just hours prior to the operation. We had dinner, planned ahead of time, with our pastor John Foster and his wife, Ruth. A reassuring conversation followed and, after dinner at a nice restaurant, and at our pastor's invitation, we retreated to a public fountain and held hands while he offered a prayer.

Surgery followed without complication or side effects, other than the normal recovery period. A successful prognosis from the doctor and the pathology lab proclaimed, "The cancer has been completely removed." Cyndi and I hugged and cried, offered a prayer of thanks, and opened a bottle of champagne. While a bit off schedule, life would continue and all was good.

Health insurance, of course, was another matter. Anybody with an existing or prior condition understands this. Our insurance from my job was set to expire at the end of December that year. We had the opportunity under COBRA laws to extend the insurance for about $1,000 per month, but hadn't planned on doing so because of its high cost in comparison to what was available on the open market. That market, however, had just tightened considerably, since cancer presented a prior condition.

We elected to continue with COBRA while searching for other U.S. insurance, simultaneously trying to explore the free medical care possibilities offered by our French residency. We had been fortunate not to have needed the free French insurance prior to this, and we were unsure of its exact coverage. The letters explaining the coverage were attached to our health cards and were written in French. Medical specialties and procedures were rare on the island; many traveled to Guadeloupe or France itself for those treatments.

BECOMING EXPATRIATES

We took consolation in not being the only newcomers in our new Third World island paradise. We had local friends as well as French and Dutch nationals and expatriates sharing similar experiences. Most of the latter adhered to the American proverb: "The grass is always greener on the other side of the fence."

Americans, a relatively new breed, are descendents of immigrants, if not first-generation. Three of my grandparents came from Sweden or Germany. My maternal grandfather, August Kelpe, received his U.S. Certificate of Naturalization at age seventy-two in 1943.

The people of our generation could be categorized as either content, beneficiaries of our forefather's sacrifices, or continually restless, carriers of the wanderlust genes. Those in the first category are born, raised, and live their entire lives in the same neighborhood. Others continue their forefathers' ambitions by relocating to new lands for better opportunities, if not for the adventure.

Cyndi, borderline in her perspectives, enjoyed dating her boyfriend (me) in her Minnesota home base when I was back from school in San Diego. The thought of living in California was an attraction to Cyndi that strengthened our relationship.

When I returned to Minnesota after school, marriage and children followed. My wanderlust was partially sated by frequent vacations that took the family to all points in the greater United States.

Like an addict needing more juice, I continually needed to visit new, exotic destinations. We enjoyed Hawaii, but to me it was overdeveloped, trite, and too American.

The Caribbean was a land undiscovered by the traveling Berglunds until our 1996 venture. Each island presented unique cultures, foods, and experiences. Cyndi relished the travels, still playing to my dreams and not realizing that we, too, would soon be expats. Expatriates often fit into one of the following groups, all of which are on the increase:

- Professionals working abroad

- Lifestyle migrants searching for a better life

- Economic migrants searching for a better job

- International students

Friends might claim our category was more specific and unlisted: "illogical idiots who thought it was a good idea at the time." We joined other expats on the island of St. Martin who fit all categories listed above. They included hospitality and infrastructure professionals from all over the world; economic migrants from other Caribbean islands, India, China, and other foreign lands; and international students at the island's medical school.

The general category Cyndi and I were in, lifestyle migrants searching for a better life, included other Americans, Germans, Australians, Swiss, and others. If psychologically examined, we all likely shared similar traits to other American expats in St. Martin and beyond, including a thirst for adventure, a love of beaches, sun, and fun, enjoyment of other cultures, and an ability to let go of roots—family, friends, jobs, and comfortable landmarks.

Expatriates presented a grouping from which to choose friends; a number of Americans and Europeans had second island homes or permanently resided on-island, as we did. Take, for example, two European expats, Richard and Judith, whom we met at Orient Beach one sunny Sunday afternoon in 2009.

Richard was a Dutchman with short, curly black hair who had Antillean-African heritage. His father was born in Curaçao. Richard had served in the Dutch military and was earning a living diving in the North Sea and other exotic locales to fix pipelines and oil rigs. He met Judith, a pretty, young, petite, brunette German, on a boat ride from Saba to St. Martin, and they were married in Europe a short time later. Both are fluent in Dutch, German, and English. They made me look like a linguistic slacker.

We've enjoyed many evenings with this lovely couple. Early on in our budding friendship they had us over for dinner at their home in the French Quarter. It was the only log house on the island, and they had built it. The logs were imported in containers from Russia. They served a home-cooked meal of *stamppot*, a Dutch dish of sausage, carrots, potatoes, and onions. After the delicious food and wine, our full stomachs happily rumbled. There was no need to worry; Judith came to the rescue.

"We have a custom in our locale in Germany to have *Underberg*," Judith proclaimed.

"What's Underberg?" Cyndi asked.

"It's something ya drink after dinner to settle ya stomach," Judith said. She produced four tiny, wrapped bottles containing twenty milliliters each, or about two-thirds of an ounce. The slogan on the bottle wraps read "*Nach gutem Essen,*" or "After a good meal." We unwrapped our concoctions, toasted, and each drank directly from our tiny bottles; the liqueur contained 44 percent alcohol. The taste was an unusual anise flavoring, but flowed easily and surprisingly moderated our full stomachs. Fascinating. I wondered why it wasn't a universally known product.

"Where can I buy more of this stuff?" I asked. I thought of how fun it would be to introduce such a strange after-dinner tradition to our American friends.

"Oh, you only buy this in Germany," Judith responded, "but next time I can buy you a case if you want."

My reflective thoughts on our move into the unknown:

> *The primary difference between young and old:*
> *Young people have dreams,*
> *Old people have memories.*
> *To stay forever young—"dream."*

Keep your belts buckled as the dream roller coaster continues its up-and-down progress.

CHAPTER 12

THE TIJON® LINE OF PERFUMES AND PRODUCTS

Anointing our business with an interesting and marketable name was important. Many ask how we came up with our chosen one, "Tijon." The answer is that it hit me like a lightning bolt after a considerable search, one day as I moped alone in a first-floor Atlanta apartment during a colder than usual winter in 1999. I was pondering our future dream while waiting for my faithful family to join me after my career move from Wisconsin.

We chose Tijon for two reasons. First of all, as I've mentioned, it's a combination of our son's first initial and middle name. He is "Tyler John," but we affectionately call him "T. J." He and his older sister, Rachelle, now both adults living in San Diego, had been part of our family's planning for this business, dating back to our first Caribbean trip in 1996. T. J.—or, rather, "Tijon," (pronounced "Tezhon")—was to be our persona, a Calvin Klein–type person of mystery and allure: the designer behind the brand.

The second reason? It sounded French, and that seemed like a good thing. Not quite as profound as you were thinking, is it?

Now that we had a name, we needed a logo. We created the emblem and soon began to receive comments.

"It's attractive, elegant."

"I like your logo; it's simplistic."

⊄TIJŌN
St. Martin, F.W.I.

"What the heck does P or CP have to do with Tijon?"

For the record, if you examine the symbol closely you should make out the letters T and J. But the confusion with CP is understandable. We adapted our logo from a losing submission to a logo contest for a professional association I was assisting, the Georgia Psychiatric Physicians Associations. What had been a "GP" was changed, or so I thought, to a "TJ". Apparently the change just wasn't as obvious as I had thought.

There's a plaque on the door entering our lab proclaiming "Tijon, an experience worth waiting for." Cyndi gave that to me while we were still in Atlanta, after we had settled on the name, neatly hanging it on the door of my lab in our house. The plaque followed us to our home lab in Texas, and now, finally, it hangs proudly at Tijon in St. Martin. Its significance is a meaningful memory of love: not of my love for Tijon, nor even directed to our customers, but the memory of love and support from my thoughtful partner, Cyndi.

OUR INITIAL PERFUMES

We were determined to create fine fragrances, and settled on baptizing the business with three high-end women's *eaus de parfum,* three women's tropical colognes, and four men's *eaus de toilette.* We believed that most customers could find at least one particularly enjoyable fragrance in the mix.

The final ten fragrances each needed a name and an evocative description that would market and sell the products. We selected many attractive names only to discover, with a quick Google search, that they were already being used for fragrances or other related products.

In the perfume classes we offer, the hardest part for the students is often the naming of their fragrances. It is the same with us; giving our creations a name that appeals is tough. That's why master marketers and idea generators are well paid. As we brainstormed alluring descriptions, each choice was carefully selected, dissected, reviewed, critiqued, and frequently changed. Here are the names and definitive phrases we ultimately chose:

Shallae—Since Tijon was named for our son, Cyndi hounded—I mean, kindly reminded me—that we should include our daughter. So, our first women's perfume created was ultimately a no-brainer.

"How are you describing this fragrance?" Cyndi asked.

"Unique and luxurious," I replied.

"Isn't our daughter unique and luxurious?"

"Yes."

"So let's name this after Shelly," Cyndi insisted.

"But shouldn't it sound more unique, or French?"

"Okay then, what about . . . 'Shallae'?"

"That could work."

This fragrance combined the invigorating freshness of orange flower, grapefruit, and amber with a floral heart of jasmine and rose. Undertones of musk, vanilla, and sandalwood add to its magnetism. It was evocative and alluring, as we think our daughter to be.

LaSavane—This name is derived from a nearby village. It's a sophisticated floral fragrance freshened by cool citrus and offers an expression of adventure and sensuality. Blissful top notes of orange flower, bergamot, and grapefruit open this complex, tropical fragrance of multiple florals that includes jasmine, rose, and tuberose, blossoming into a luminescent base of musk, sandalwood, and vetiver, with subtle hints of spice and amber. It's Cyndi's favorite evening scent and a top seller.

Caye Verte—This is named for an uninhabited small island, known in French as a *caye* ("cay" or "key" in English), and was our first tropical cologne for women. The real Caye Verte juts out from Orient Beach. It literally translates to "Green Cay," and is a soft and sensual fusion of lavender, rose, jasmine, orange, and violets with a hint of musk, sandalwood, and patchouli. It's ideal for relaxing after the beach, providing a *très chic* mood.

Baie Rouge—This name was inspired by a beautiful beach on the French side. It literally means "Red Bay." This fragrance opens with a fresh, aromatic, tropical blend of island citrus and moves to a heart of jasmine, rose, geranium, sweet pea, and davana. It finishes with undertones of angelica seed oil, soothing chamomile, sandalwood, coriander, and musk to fully capture the romance and playfulness of the islands. It's Cyndi's favorite daytime fragrance and typically a favorite with the younger women.

Cliché—It is what it is, and the word is French, so it works for the John and Cyndi marketing team. This scent is a tropical fragrance that exudes passion and pleasure. It's subtle yet seductive, offering mandarin and mango opening to creamy florals of freesia, tuberose, and white peony, which are then added to a variety of spices with hints of vetiver and musk. It's best described as sultry and exotic for tropical nights and, like Shallae, is popular with the island locals.

SXM—This masculine scent was our first fragrance. Its basic design occurred in the late 1990s, in our basement lab in Atlanta. It's named for the St. Martin airport code, also a common nickname for St. Martin. This robust signature scent is refreshing, sensual, and playful, blended with citrus, lavender, blue grass, numerous spices, and a touch of mint, all uniquely aged in a French oak barrel to add a natural woodsy blend. It's inspired by the sun and the sea.

I sensed we had a hit when T. J.'s basketball buddies preferred it in a blind test against the then-popular Tommy cologne. I regularly sprayed fragrance formulas on him and his high school basketball team. They weren't the greatest team in Atlanta, but they were the best smelling.

Eclectique—This was the last of the women's perfumes we developed and, to be honest, we were running out of names. We only had one daughter and had used a number of island images for other fragrances. We picked names out of the air and bounced them off our children and friends, who bounced them back. Eventually we switched them to French-sounding words not already in use. I blurted out, "*Eclectique.*"

"What does that mean, and how do you spell it?" Cyndi asked.

"Sounds like 'eclectic' with a French twist. Not sure what it means in French and have no idea how we should spell it." Simple, honest, and direct answers that were completely true.

The Eclectique fragrance is a light, oriental scent with tropical, sensual undertones. Created from pineapple, peach, and lemon, this fragrance blossoms with rose, magnolia, and hibiscus enriched with vanilla, musk, sandalwood, and hints of ivy, coconut, and spices. It's my personal favorite for women and, perhaps not coincidentally, our best seller.

2.0—Officially, this and the names to follow were chosen to be numerically trendy. Unofficially, we were running out of names. This compelling fragrance possesses a luxurious citrus scent combined with various woods and spice. Its mystery is heightened by top notes of bergamot, lemon, and orange with middle and lower tones of clove, basil, coriander, nutmeg, patchouli, sandalwood, and Peruvian balsam. We recommend this fragrance for romantic wear as a deeply evocative cologne. It's also our best-selling men's fragrance. It could, however, be labeled unisex, as many women have purchased it for themselves. Although SXM was my personal favorite, Cyndi enjoys 2.0 more. So . . . guess which fragrance I wear on date night?

X.2—This inventive scent evokes the travel and romance reminiscent of St. Martin. The bold fragrance offers a blend of bergamot, grapefruit, rosemary, lavender, geranium, and jasmine infused with cinnamon, basil, and fir on a background of moss and sandalwood. It's our most intriguing masculine scent—for the daring and adventurous man.

3.0—This outdoor fragrance opens with citrus scents of lime, lemon, mandarin, orange, and grapefruit while adding a floral combination of jasmine and rose, finishing with patchouli, amber, sandalwood, and musk. It was the final fragrance developed prior to our opening and is Tijon's, meaning our son T. J.'s, personal favorite. Similar to 2.0, it's also unisex in that women sometimes puchase it for personal use.

Since the start of Tijon we've introduced additional fragrances in two collections: a French-Caribbean collection and an Au Natural collection, which focuses on single-note names, despite rather complex formulas, such as Amber Musk, Orange Patchouli, and Lavender Fig.

But our most unusual fragrance, with all due respect to Christian

Dior, is Poison by Tijon. Our Poison is a spicy mixture that includes a centipede in the bottle. And therein lies a story . . .

Centipedes are dark-colored, four-inch-long, fast-moving, worm-looking critters with many legs and a venomous bite. Our friend Robin, living in our smaller unit with her husband Mark, knows first-hand; she had the distinct displeasure of receiving a centipede bite. A large welt formed on her limb, and she developed a low-grade fever that evolved into a numbing sensation in her limb that lasted for weeks. Thankfully, these bites are rarely fatal to humans. It put a scare into all of us, and Cyndi called the bug man to do some spraying.

Shortly after the bug man finished, Mark caught one of these ugly creatures slowly crawling on his kitchen wall, likely affected by the pesticide. Mark grabbed the first thing he could find, Ajax, and sprayed the demon into paralysis. He carefully picked it up and, similar to what a child might do, placed it in a plastic container, screwing on the top. He brought it next door to our perfumery for show-and-tell.

We all recalled that a local bar had placed one of these ugly creatures in a rum bottle. I was motivated by the thought of something different and created a spicy perfume mixture that consisted primarily of cinnamon, clove, and Peru balsam. I bottled it along with the centipede.

I proudly slipped the bottle into Cyndi's hand and was completely delighted with my newly created perfume. She looked at it, screamed, jumped, and almost dropped it. I couldn't wait to show Robin the new bottle that is now part of our Tijon Collection.

ADD-ONS

Classic perfume lines also offer scented lotions, gels, and powders. In exploring fragrance components, we simultaneously researched the manufacture of these natural brand extensions, believing it could be beneficial to enhancing our brand and sales.

We manufactured and tested many variations of these components until we finally settled on the formulas we personally preferred. Our final products included body lotions, gels, powders, deodorants, and fragrant soaps.

Of all things, the simple powder formulation gave us the most problems with the oils. Initially, they kept turning the powder into hard little pellets. After much trial and error, we found it better to mix the oils with magnesium carbonate, a white powder constituting about 5 percent of our entire mixture, and let it stand for twenty-four hours before adding the remaining powders and compounds.

Lip balm presented the unique challenge of exploding Pyrex. We needed to heat beeswax to make the base for the balm. I made large test batches and put the wax in a sixty-four-ounce Pyrex glass-pouring container. After only about four minutes, I heard an explosion. Inside the microwave, the Pyrex had shattered, coating the interior with messy and quickly drying wax. Yuck!

I carefully picked out the glass shards, trying not to cut myself. Then I went about cleaning up the wax. As it hardened, I turned the microwave back on, hoping to re-melt the wax so that the paper towels would to soak it up easier. After thirty seconds the machine shut down. I figured I had to buy another microwave. However, with more cleaning I found wax stuck in the little interior holes that serve as air ducts. More scrubbing, and about an hour later, I had salvaged the machine.

I Googled "exploding Pyrex" to see if it had happened to anyone else and discovered it had, many times. I switched to stainless-steel containers and a stove.

EQUIPMENT

We proudly proclaim that we hand-blend our cosmetics, giving them the personal attention our customers deserve. Of course, lack of money for fancy automated equipment plays a role, but we keep that our little secret. Some equipment, however, was unavoidable. We purchased a large wax melter for our all-natural soy candles, a copper steam distillation plant for creating oils, a large lotion mixer, and others.

We had tubes for suntan lotions, so we needed a tube sealer. Not wanting the tubes to deteriorate from the sunscreen oils, I played it safe by purchasing the extra-thick ones and purchased a tube sealer for $5,000. It didn't take long to discover that if the sealing wasn't performed with exquisite care, the tubes would pop open with a little squeeze. I guess we should have bought the regular tubes.

For body lotion I purchased a hand-pump piston filler for $1,500. Hand pumping wasn't the same as compressed air, resulting in the lotion frequently cluttering and clogging the hoses. Cleaning the hoses took longer than filling the bottles.

I subsequently purchased another pump filler without hoses from India for $1,000 that worked considerably better, but it still took a bit to clean. Plastic cake frosting fillers were slower, but easier to use for our smaller filling runs. There's no denying that some serious ingenuity is a good thing.

CREATING SKIN CARE AND SUN CARE LINES

Encouraged by reading that Estée Lauder started as a young woman by selling lotions her uncle made in their basement, I went to work. Along with developing lotions, powders, and gels for the Tijon brand, I contemplated and pursued a skin care line that was later labeled *L'Esperance*. The name was derived from our street address at Tijon.

Years of meticulous research documented that skin care knowledge included three important realizations:

1. Sunshine and salt water can rejuvenate our souls while damaging our skin.

2. Aging and the effects of aging are diseases that can and should be treated.

3. Tijon, to succeed, needed clinically formulated, ultra-powerful products for skin repair and anti-aging, designed to prepare, rejuvenate, and protect the skin.

Our cells use oxygen to produce energy. In the process they generate free radicals, unstable oxygen molecules created during such basic metabolic functions as circulation and digestion. Free radicals are also produced by sunlight, by toxins such as pesticides, and by cigarette smoke and air pollution. In our bodies, free radicals literally bounce about, attaching themselves to other atoms and molecules, whether they're wanted or not.

Free radicals are the central players in tissue degeneration and the aging process. It's the same process that causes metal to rust. This aging damage is typically inflicted (something that has been done to the skin) as opposed to afflicted (inherited and genetic). Heed the warning: it does matter how we treat our skin.

Antioxidants prevent free-radical damage simply by giving these wildly out-of-control molecules the electron partners they seek. In this way, antioxidants spare important molecules from oxidative damage.

Our final compositions included an anti-wrinkle crème, an eye crème, an exfoliating crème, a shea butter crème, and a penetrating massage oil. After years in development, I was particularly proud of our anti-wrinkle formula, which, similar to all our products, was tested on family and friends.

We named our anti-wrinkle formula *L'Esperance Reparation Tropicale 4/4*. It's the only known age intervention formula with an "antioxidant network" of four proven antioxidants and four regenerating agents that repair and reverse the effects of age and sun damage.

Key active ingredients in our clinical formula include coenzyme Q10, alpha lipoic acid (the master antioxidant), DMAE, and hyluronic acid (the most powerful moisturizing agent available).

Tijon's growing product line-to-be consisted of branded perfumes, lotions, candles, and soaps, with a sub-brand of *L'Esperance* skin care. It only made sense, being located on a sunny island with beautiful beaches, to offer a sun care line. That thought began when I was applying suntan lotion on Cyndi's back while sitting on Orient Beach during an earlier island visit.

"If we can offer perfumes and skin care products, why not offer a suntan line?" I suggested.

"There you go again, mixing business with pleasure. Keep rubbing."

When I got back to the States I went to work, studying sun care lotions and consulting with chemists.

Attitudes toward sunlight have changed over the years. At the turn of the twentieth century, the "pale look" was prized and cultivated. The darker, tanned look equated to day laborers who worked outdoors. In the 1930s a gradual change was accelerated when, as I've already mentioned, my hero, Coco Chanel, returned from a foreign holiday sporting a deep tan. Overnight, the whole Caucasian population desired the new fashion that has persisted to this day.

The sun presents a good news/bad news scenario. The sun offers warmth and natural vitamin synthesis and uplifts the soul. Vitamin D has been labeled the "sunshine vitamin" because it's produced by our body when exposed to the light. It's one of four daily supplements television's Dr. Oz recommends, the others being a multiple vitamin, fish oil, and calcium. Technically, vitamin D is not even a vitamin; it's a steroid hormone.

Ironically, just as researchers are discovering the added importance of vitamin D in fighting heart disease and cancers, Americans are getting less of it. This is in part because we've been told to avoid the sun.

A team of Harvard scientists recently discovered that those with the highest blood levels of vitamin D were the least likely to have heart attacks. Other studies found that this vitamin reduces the risk of colorectal cancer, hip fractures, and other age-related diseases.

Milk doesn't provide enough vitamin D. In fact, milk is fortified because it naturally contains little of this vitamin, and even the fortification is insufficient for most. To equal the vitamin D value of ten minutes' exposure to sunlight, we'd have to consume 150 egg yolks or thirty servings of fortified cereal or thirty cups of fortified orange juice. There are a lot less calories in a little sunlight.

The bad news in regard to the sun is relatively well known. Excessive exposure can create significant skin damage, including cancerous melanomas. The best offense is a good defense, which starts with the use of sunscreens.

Other studies have yielded strong evidence that certain vitamins and antioxidants protect body cells from damage and provide the proper environment for the correction of damage. The sun protection factor (SPF) is a measure of the ability of a sunscreen to protect against erythema (sunburn). The SPF number defines how long we can stay in the sun before getting burnt. If it normally takes us twenty minutes before a burn, an SPF 15 product will let us stay fifteen times longer in the sun (20 minutes x 15 SPF = 300 minutes, or 5 hours).

Most dermatologists agree that SPFs higher than 30 are just marketing tools, and in fact, new labeling requirements won't allow a listing above 50. A 30 SPF blocks 96.7 percent of UVB light.

In consultation with many chemists and physicians, I created our sun care line of lotions and sprays that protect from both UVA and UVB radiation. To add moisturizers I included vitamins and coenzyme Q10, an expensive yet exclusive antioxidant, making our sun products likely the only ones including this powerful ingredient.

We also added a wildly concocted yet successful "after-sun lotion." This mixture contained aloe and six active ingredients, not the least of which was polypodium, extracted from a tropical fern found in Honduras.

Polypodium has been used to treat inflammatory conditions and has been demonstrated to have clinical applications in reducing the severity of sunburn from both UVB rays and phototoxic reactions. That makes this botanical extract one of the best studied of the antioxidants. This ingredient is rarely seen in over-the-counter products because of its high cost. We have female customers who regularly use this after-sun product as their evening anti-wrinkle crème.

It was the sand flies, or "no-see-ums," that drove me to concoct an all-natural mosquito repellent and a suntan lotion extension containing lemon eucalyptus. These blood-sucking midges are technically called *Ceratopogonidae*. They're found on many beaches and hilly areas worldwide. It's typically the female that bites for blood, leaving a localized allergic reaction in the victim. Mosquito spray with the chemical DEET works well, but some customers desire to avoid DEET.

So, the research began, and we concluded that lemon eucalyptus oil worked the best. It emits a strong scent that people either love or walk away from. The *New England Journal of Medicine* reported that lemon eucalyptus is the best natural repellent and as effective as a low concentration of DEET. It simply needed to be reapplied every two hours.

We needed a name and logo for this upstart, sun-care sub-brand, and somewhere out of the blue ocean, Caribe Baie was chosen. Our logo included a palm tree, because our expat island pal, Marie, told us she loved palm trees in her décor and suggested it for our logo. Cyndi and I recalled our appreciation for the palm trees gently swaying in the island breeze.

I created a slogan: "Made in the Caribbean for the Caribbean Sun." We thought it was a good slogan until one customer innocently inquired if the lotion was only good while in the Caribbean. Oh well.

I recollected a conversation with a consulting perfumer with the Atlanta Fragrance Company who counseled me on the direction of my sun lotion scent. Roland Williams told me that years earlier he had created a scent for two young men at a Florida college or just out of college, who had started making suntan lotions in their garage. The scent, along with the lotion, became well known as Hawaiian Tropic. Did I have the next Hawaiian Tropic in me? I hoped so.

Would the island support its own sun-care line? Could a new, small, sun-care line compete against the giants? Those were good questions, and we'd never know the answers until we tried. To have a little fun, we thought of adding a mascot to the line and chose the Arawak Dog.

Man's best friend remains a popular island companion. Archaeological studies have concluded that the Arawak civilization, early inhabitants of St. Martin and other islands from 550 BC until Christopher Columbus's arrival, were accompanied by dogs on their island travels. Our chosen Caribe Baie mascot was a replica of a ceramic Arawak Dog pottery piece that dated back to 550 BC. It had been unearthed in an archeological dig at Hope Estate in our village of Grand Case. The original ceramic piece is housed at the museum in Marigot.

In 1996, France invited its territories to submit a proposal for a postage stamp. St. Martin submitted an illustration of the ceramic Arwark Dog. Subsequently, eight million stamps of the Arawak Dog were sold. In St. Martin it appeared as a first-day issue on February 10, 1996. The Marigot post office sold 33,000 the first two days alone.

Today the island is filled with dogs. The islanders like their dogs and the dogs like the beaches. Perhaps it's a throwback to the Arawak days.

Cyndi added to our product mix by crafting island jewelry from sea glass. The ocean's saltwater and sand, combined with the tides, act like a giant rock tumbler and eventually turn sharp, broken glass into beautifully rounded, frosted jewels that wash up on the shoreline. Our Grand Case beach, mere steps from our shop and home, had the best collection of sea glass on the island. It provided another reason to go to the beach.

PACKAGING

By 2007 our buildings were ready in St. Martin. The cosmetic research, initial formulations, and business plan had been completed. We had our logos. The delay in taking up full residency afforded us valuable time to repay Mom and purchase packaging, displays, and unique gift items. The packaging and display budget for all our categories was $100,000—modest in comparison with the big players, but ambitious for us. We needed to discover a specific look within the confines of a modest budget.

We had initiated our packaging strategy a few years prior. After knocking our heads against the wall we understood the popular definition of insanity: doing something that didn't work over and over, but expecting a different result. We contacted suppliers with attractive packaging concepts. I had projected ten different bottles for our ten fragrance offerings. My initial hope was to purchase a thousand of everything. Seemed like a lot of bottles to us. The suppliers thought differently. Their minimums were more in terms of 10,000 to 50,000 for each unit.

I defaulted to the New York City design team of DuGrenier and Associates who, surprisingly, agreed to work with our small startup. They had an impressive résumé and had assisted both little and large cosmetic companies. We agreed to a fee, and they set a timetable that neither of us followed. They were invaluable for their suggestions, but once the building was finished, I had to finalize our choices.

DuGrenier referred us to an upscale, impressive Italian glass-bottle manufacturer, Luigi Bormioli, who graciously let us purchase 5,000-piece minimums. We reduced our packaging to three bottles for the ten fragrances: one for the three high-end women's *eaus de parfume*, one for the three women's colognes, and one for the men's *eaus de toilette*.

Their recommendations, however, for the fragrance components of sprayers and caps were unable to meet the minimums. I had three fragrance bottles at a quantity of 5,000 each. I ordered three pump sprayers for the bottles at a similar quantity of 5,000 each and selected three attractive caps from yet another supplier with a required minimum of 10,000 each. The caps and sprayers surprised us in costing more than the bottle.

The result: we were the proud owners of 15,000 bottles, 15,000 sprayers, and 30,000 caps for a business pro forma optimistically projecting 500 unit sales during our first partial year. The minimum purchase requirements increased our costs, our need for storage, and our financial risk.

Later I discovered that some of the items we needed could be purchased in China at a considerably lesser cost. For example, one of my early frustrations was trying to locate paper bags with our logo, only to discover my average cost for four sizes was close to a dollar per bag.

I turned to China and found a manufacturer, after considerable research, who would sell me the bags at about eleven cents each. I had to pay for shipping, which took months by boat and about another five to ten cents each, and I had to order 5,000 bags instead of 1,000, but the total cost was still considerably less.

Similarly, the perfume boxes that I had purchased from Canada at $2 per box could be obtained in China, at a larger quantity, for about fifteen cents, shipping included. With all that being said, and while being pro–Jobs USA, it was difficult to resist the temptation to do business with China because of the gigantic price differential.

On the other hand, the difficulty of communicating with China and the shipping delays from that region were also typical. It saved money, but it wasn't an easy process. For example, I decided to place a second order with one manufacturer for organza-type bags. After wiring the money and placing the order, I heard no response for six weeks. Previously, the company had started the delivery process in four weeks. Upon inquiry I received this e-mail back, misspellings and all:

> Dear John,
> We're so sorry about the delay! Goods have been ready on Jun 23th, but the

transporter lost our goods on the road. After picking up our goods, he drove his
truck to other companies to get the goods. When he arrived Shang hai, he cannot
find our goods.

So i have to arrange the production again. And because now is our heavy time,
it took a long time for goods production. But we have tried our best to proceed the
goods.

And goods will be ready within next week.

We are very very sorry for any trouble caused!

Thanks.

I had a similar problem when ordering a sample duffel bag with our logo embroidered on it. The manufacturer wanted $140 for payment of the sample and shipping by air. I wired the money on August 15 and on September 13 was told the sample was ready and would be shipped. Then to my surprise, I received this e-mail from the manufacturer on September 21:

Dear John,

Sorry, now we cannot find as our duffel bag #737 flower. Pls. kindly find attached
our another client to order flower duffel bag, pls. kindly check if you want. If you
want, we will add your logo to embroidery on it. Hope will received your new info.!
Best Regards!

Complimentary brand enhancements and unique gift items were needed for the soon-to-be opening store shelves of Tijon, but the obscene quantities required to achieve any pricing advantage were posing a big problem. We felt like the pig who told the chicken, talking about a ham and egg breakfast, "With you, it's a donation; for me, it's a total commitment." We were committed.

Packaging isn't just pretty; it also involves labels and bar codes, and we had neither of those. These were the final pieces to the packaging puzzle that was more jigsaw than crossword. About a hundred products needed an attractive front label and a back label listing ingredients along with a bar code. We had more work ahead of us, and it wasn't necessarily the enjoyable part of the process.

Ingredient labeling wasn't just a listing of the formulation but also a required cross-referencing of products to a recognized universal code called INCI, or International Nomenclature of Cosmetic Ingredients. Coconut oil, for example, is *Cocos Nucifera (Coconut) Oil*. Rosemary oil is *Oleresin Rosmarinus Officinalis*.

Finding no services to assist with the cross-referencing of this scientific language, I set aside the unopened *French for Dummies* and became an INCI aficionado. It was a foreign language unto itself.

On to bar codes. We knew they were on labels and why they were there but had no idea how they got there. I discovered that I could purchase the right to use these codes with annual license fees.

Like many items needed, this wasn't in the initial budget. The money door was revolving wildly, with money going out and none coming in. Fortunately, Mother Bank remained open, and I signed a contract extension on my day job in 2006, hoping Cyndi and I could permanently move to the island before one of us needed a walker. Cyndi had to open the business seasonally in 2007 without me.

After compiling the names, ingredient listings, and bar codes for our numerous formulas in differing sizes, I contracted with a label designer and printing firm. The minimum run for a label was 500, which meant our initial purchase, considering there were often two labels per bottle, was in excess of 74,000 labels. I could only imagine the challenge of keeping those labels organized.

Cosmetic formulation had been a challenge met successfully, but manufacturing was tougher than anticipated. But being "all in," we trudged forward. We were proud, even though wildly over budget, as we rolled out the Tijon line in December 2007. As with any line of products, lessons would be learned and refinements would occur. We were no longer a dream; we were a full-fledged reality.

CHAPTER 13

SELLING PERFUME

Creating and manufacturing perfume had proven to be quite a task in itself, but we soon learned it wasn't the most difficult or demanding. The real challenge reared its head when it came to selling the juice. Ever been to a close-out store? You'll discover many unheard-of, yet decent-smelling perfume brands. Why? Because marketing and selling perfumes is a science all its own.

My perfume-manufacturing dream didn't envision securing shelf space opposite multimillion-dollar brands. Our strategy was to guarantee sales space at a retail outlet—ours. We would be comparable to a boutique California winery where the vino is available on-site or via the Internet.

To enjoy success beyond product creation and in-house retail display, we needed to do much to make ourselves stand apart. Branding, marketing, advertising, and public relations were just a few of the things we needed to embrace in order to sell and distribute our products.

BRANDING

A brand is the proprietary visual, emotional, rational, and cultural image that we associate with a company or product. When I think of Volvo, for example, I might think of safety. Brand identity includes the name, logo, positioning, brand associations, and brand personality.

We had already selected Tijon as our brand. Now, I wanted Tijon to also connote French-Caribbean elegance. As mentioned before, we portrayed Tijon as an individual designer akin to Calvin Klein or Ralph Lauren. Those industry behemoths outsourced the fragrance manufacturing and, like them, Tijon also outsourced . . . but to a bit closer source: Tijon used his dad.

We needed a persona for our "Tijon." We determined, per the Dos Equis man, that Tijon is a man on a mission. There's an air of mystery about him as he searches the world for natural beauty in whatever form it may take. Along the way, he inspires others to create things of beauty that use and celebrate nature's splendid gifts.

"Tijon has some wanderlust, so we don't see him in St. Martin as much as we'd like," our opening press release declared. "But he's always thinking of new and better ways to do whatever he sets his heart on, and that includes finding ways for the rest of us to enjoy life as much and as fully as he does." All this was easily said at the time, considering T. J. was finishing college and enjoying student life more than the studies themselves. The press release continued:

> Never one to put on airs nor make grand appearances, Tijon is an occasional visitor to St. Martin, where he's always warmly welcomed. He's been spotted taking a morning run on the beach or dining at one of the many restaurants in Grand Case. But regardless of where he's seen, there's one undeniable truth when he leaves. Everyone wonders who that man was and what *was* that alluring fragrance he was wearing? Enjoy each day. Eat good foods. An amazing fragrance can make such a difference in the course of one's day. Enjoy life!
> —From a recent note Tijon reportedly left in St. Martin."

We had a name and a persona. We started to add our displays and products to provide the support to our brand. Gift items carried a Tijon or Caribe Baie logo. There was something for everybody. We had beach bags, coffee mugs, drink coasters, clothing, and gold or diamond necklaces. Every item that was for sale was about the brand.

MARKETING

In my business plan I projected a small percentage of island tourists stopping into our parfumerie because of an interest in either the fragrances or locally produced products. I was partially correct. A small percent of the island tourists "who had heard about us" stopped in our shop. There's a big difference, and a huge gap, between the two.

Tourists are moving targets on a tropical island; they come and go every week. Word of mouth, other than Internet reviews, was limited and not something we could rely on.

What I've found to be more practical and affordable was the advice that a marketing guru once gave me. He said the best marketing is to shake hands, look a person in the eye, and give him or her your business card. That was the perfect justification for our daily afternoon trips to the beach.

Our new business needed to communicate what our products and their benefits were. Our target market was twofold. We had locals (those who lived on the island) and transients (those who were spending a holiday in paradise). The latter could be found in hotels, time-shares, condos, and as cruise passengers. Some were first-time island visitors, while others arrived annually.

It had taken us until March 2008 to secure our business license. We had quietly opened the prior December, but held off on any marketing or advertising until the next high season, which began in December 2008. At that time Cyndi would once again tend the shop alone for a few months. I'd be in Texas completing my contractual obligations.

Our objective for the 2009 season was to throw a few marketing strategies and ads against the proverbial wall to see what might stick. We created some rack cards and transitioned into the new evolution of electronic marketing. We created and rolled out www.tijon.com and later added an online newsletter and Facebook page.

Our most enjoyable marketing occurs on weekends at Orient Beach. We drive to L'String, similar to television's Cheers bar, where everybody is starting to know our name. We locate comfortably padded beach chairs, say hi to the owners and staff, enjoy the drinks that appear without our ordering, slather on our Caribe Baie lotion, kick back, and bring out our books, preferring novels set in St. Martin such as *Gone Bamboo* by Anthony Bourdain or *Island Ice* by B. D. Anderson. We'd be hard-pressed to have more fun marketing anything.

After reading a couple of pages, we invariably bump into friends or make new friends by initiating conversations with our beaching neighbors. If we haven't eaten, we'll order lunch, then take a dip in the water, followed by a walk on the beach. Periodically we'll wander over to the Aloha beach bar to say hi to the vivacious and energetic owner, Natalie, or to Bikini for edamame and lunch.

Our dear friend and server, Jean Henri, invariably brings us another drink whether ordered or not. Typically we get offered a taste of his homemade flavored rum *du jour*. Sunday at Orient is considered local day. We'll find groups of French families and friends enjoying a large afternoon lunch on the beach, complete with bottles of champagne or a nice French rosé. Between the relaxing, drinks, and swimming, we have an opportunity to meet people and promote our products. We market while we indulge in our daily dip into paradise.

ADVERTISING

Advertising is an absolute necessity for a startup like ours. Similar to our marketing efforts, we would learn by trial and error what advertising media didn't work for us.

There are four competing annual tourist publications that are provided free on the island. We hoped we could afford to advertise in one or two of them. Only one listed an island address, on the French side, so we stopped there first. *Discover* magazine is a beautiful publication with captions in both English and French. They offered a full-page ad with a cost in excess of $10,000. Catching our breath, we suggested our budget was more beer than champagne, needing a smaller ad. We learned that any ad less than a full page was available only to restaurants. We passed.

Interestingly, *Discover* approached us for the 2010 season, during the economic crash that started in 2009, to say they would accept a smaller ad. By that time our budget was committed to other efforts.

Next I contacted *Destination* magazine. This was an attractive option, because it was distributed to passengers boarding American Airline, US Airways, and other flights to St. Martin. Simultaneously I went online to consider an ad with *Experience* magazine. Our first thought was to buy a small ad in both until convinced by an old marketing hand in the States that we'd be better off spending our limited ad dollars for a larger ad with only one of those publications.

Destination's editor, Christine de la Cruz, was sincerely delighted that she had a new business category to include other than jewelry stores and restaurants. She surprised me by immediately offering a free, one-page editorial about the new parfumerie to accompany the ad, and I readily accepted. She also worked with *Gastronomy* magazine, which highlighted menus from participating restaurants and offered us an extremely discounted price for the last remaining ad. It was an offer I couldn't refuse.

Our first official season as a licensed St. Martin business began on December 1, 2008. We had a website, two ads, and one rack card placement at the airport.

For roughly $2,000 per year, we could place our rack card at the airport's baggage claim. I was a big fan of perusing brochures and flyers at these locations, so I jumped on this and created a card that promoted a free gift for simply stopping in. This was a no-brainer, I thought. We printed thousands of rack cards and ordered 2,000 free promotional gifts: nice tote bags. We also contracted for ads on a few websites. We were ready for the onslaught of new Tijon fans.

At the end of our first official season in 2009 we were able to analyze what had "stuck" in our advertising efforts. The number-one reason customers stopped in was proximity; they were staying at the nearby Grand Case Beach Club or L'Esplanade Hotel and walked by. *Destination* magazine came in second, with a travel website resulting in a distant third. My brainstorm of a rack card at the airport brought precisely two customers to the shop. That's $1,000 of ad dollars per customer. Plus, we had a lot of tote bags in storage. My bad.

The airport rack cards got cut from our 2010 marketing plans in favor of a weekly ad in the island's edition of the *Miami Herald* and an ad in *Experience* magazine. Those ads coincided with our second year in *Destination* magazine, an attractive two-page spread complete with photos. We also included a few other websites. Christine hired one of the island's best photographers, Alexandre Julien, a young French native who had relocated to St. Martin in 2002, to take pictures at one of our perfume classes in 2009 for the 2010 edition of *Destination*.

Dana Sprout, our *Experience* magazine contact at the time, had a house on the island and in the States. Similar to Christine, she was a marketing whiz and knew everyone and everything on the island. Visiting with Christine and Dana separately to brainstorm their marketing ideas was worth the price of the ads alone. They were incredibly insightful and their knowledge was a tremendous help.

The yearly contract to advertise every Monday in the *Miami Herald* island edition seemed like a smart choice, since it was given out free at many of the resorts. I knew I was in trouble, however, when I included the "free gift" incentive. In the first two weeks we had only one taker for our offer. For whatever reason, this otherwise outstanding newspaper didn't work for us as an advertiser.

In summary, the year 2010 changed our marketing results to: *Destination* magazine (first place), www.tripadvisor.com (second place), and walk-bys from the Grand Case Beach Club and L'Esplanade Hotel (third place). We were lucky if the rest paid for the cost of the ads themselves.

TripAdvisor.com was amazing and soon became our number-one advertising resource. In December 2009 we had two sisters-in-law, Renee and Michelle, stop in after reading the article in *Destination* magazine. We talked them into taking the perfume class. They loved it and suggested we get listed on TripAdvisor, which they frequented. They promised to write a nice review if we got listed. We did and they did.

Many wonderful reviews followed, and within months we were surprised to be ranked as the number-one non-water activity on the island. To make it even more amazing for us, we discovered in January 2011 that we became the island's number-one overall activity/attraction listed on this user review site. We pinched ourselves; TripAdvisor had become our best referral source. We were humbled and grateful to all the many people who wrote such nice reviews. Many customers resulted, and best of all, it was free!

PUBLIC RELATIONS

This form of communications is primarily directed toward gaining public understanding and acceptance and gaining publicity that doesn't necessitate payment in a wide variety of media and is often placed as news or items of public interest. Because PR communications are placed in this manner, they offer a legitimacy that advertising does not, since advertising is publicity that's typically paid for.

Marketing gurus often characterize public relations as "earning media," and note that it often isn't truly free. The best media spots often are placed by professional PR agents on behalf of their clients. I acutely understood this, having previously spent an annual six-figure retainer with a PR firm in New York City for a corporate client. Basically you want to look like you're getting free exposure, even if you're paying a price for it. It seems complicated, but it's manageable.

Of course, we had zero available funds to hire a PR firm to help Tijon get this type of media coverage. We were reminded of a chance encounter on St. Martin during the spring of 2007, when we were making a trip to check up on our remodeling.

During that trip we took a break from the project and traveled across the island to Mary's Boon, a lovely small boutique resort and restaurant on the ocean near the airport on the Dutch side of the island. We had heard stories of their unusual happy hour. It was an honor bar where we could step behind the bar, make our own drinks, and report the number of drinks we enjoyed upon leaving so we could square up our bill. That sounded like fun and, in case you can't tell, Cyndi and I love to have fun!

We arrived during the bewitching hour, confirmed the honor process, and walked into a bar that was completely empty. We were staring at a multitude of liquors, mixes, and garnishes. I gleefully let my inner bartender go wild. I began creating exotic, strong mixtures adorned with an abundance of fancy fruits.

I remembered our young bartender friend, Colin, sharing the knowledge that the island alcohol was cheaper than most mixers. I wanted to help the house. Cyndi brought out the camera, and right around that time a young American woman entered the bar area. She had a broad smile and gave us a big hello. She could sense our fun mood and bellied up to the bar to participate.

"Hi, I'm John the bartender, and my first customer over there is my wife, Cyndi. What can I get for you?"

"Do you have a glass of chardonnay?" she asked. She tried to sound conservative and proper. I think she was questioning my mixology mastery.

"Let me check . . . ya mon, we have that. Coming right up. And you are?"

"I'm Janet, from Columbus, Ohio. My husband is on the beach taking a run. We missed our plane today because of traffic, so we're staying here for the night and flying home tomorrow."

"What a nice place to be stuck for the night. And what do you do in Ohio?"

"My husband and I own a PR firm. And where are you from?"

"We're from Texas, but are in the process of soon opening a parfumerie in Grand Case. Do you give good PR, and can we afford you?"

Conversation flowed as easily as the drinks. Janet's husband, Brad, entered the bar. He'd just returned from his beach run in a bare-chested sweat. Before he exited for a shower, we all connected and exchanged cards.

I called them months later, and they agreed to a small fee in addition to a trade-out on our rental villa. Their experience, guidance, and visions were invaluable in helping formulate our brand, website, and product positioning. They also assisted with our official grand opening event in December 2008, both in spreading the word as well as last-minute bag stuffing. They created our press kit and remain good friends and PR mentors to this day.

So, when many people think it's hard to find what you need on a small island, they have to realize that you need to talk and think outside the box. The islands summon people of all talents and skills. Cyndi and I have always been fortunate enough to cross their paths when we needed them most.

SELLING AND DISTRIBUTING

Initially we decided to offer our products for in-store sale only. Our target market was American tourists, since we had been tourists previously and had a certain understanding of their buying habits. To motivate locals and French nationals to buy, we needed a broader understanding. That was more challenging.

A group of islanders attended our first in-house party back in December 2007, the month we unofficially opened. Our dear friend Derryck Jack of KFC invited twenty friends and staff members to our shop. They attended for pre-holiday beverages, appetizers, and shopping.

We were delighted with their feedback, ranging from encouraging words of support to downright purchases. One lady had a small inn and wanted us to contact her when we started making hotel-sized lotions and shampoos. It was an exciting day and was the rejuvenation we needed for feeling great about what Tijon could become.

We found that word of Tijon traveled down the local pipeline. There were some wonderful articles on Tijon in the island's *Daily Herald*.

We loved it when we introduced ourselves to shop employees in the island's big town of Phillipsburg, and they would say, "We've heard of it, have heard good things, and have been meaning to stop by." Conversely, we had taxi drivers and some shop employees a few blocks away who didn't know where we were located, even three years after our opening. We've learned to never assume that anybody, local or tourist, will know how to find us.

Cyndi had an interesting encounter one morning prior to Valentine's Day 2010. A local man dropped into the shop and went on a rather intensive (even by Cyndi's standards) smelling spree of all the women's fragrances. Finally he turned to Cyndi and proclaimed, "I like this one, and I want to buy a bottle of this [LaSavane] perfume for my girlfriend."

Cyndi smiled, and, trying to be helpful, offered another suggestion. "That's an excellent choice, and my personal favorite for evening wear, but perfume is personal. If you'd rather purchase a gift certificate, your girlfriend could come in here and pick out the perfume she likes best."

"No, I like this perfume. If my girlfriend doesn't like it," he laughed, "I give it to my wife."

Cyndi blushed, having no idea if the gentleman was serious or joking. She just rang up the sale and didn't inquire further. We hope that whoever ended up with the perfume enjoyed it immensely. We couldn't help but laugh with the realization that the intimacy of perfume had many levels for some people.

The French nationals proved more difficult to market to. We had the obvious language barrier to deal with. If we had been able to afford a French-speaking employee, sales would have surely increased. Some French customers were openly perturbed that we didn't speak their language. Cyndi and I had differing opinions.

"We're trying to learn French and it's been tough, but most of the French coming in can speak some English. Yet they still get upset that we don't speak French," Cyndi reasoned.

"But, honey, think if we were in the States and we went into a boutique and the shopkeeper spoke no English. Not only would we be unable to communicate, we might be upset that he lived in America and had no apparent desire to learn English. That's probably how the French feel here. After all, we're in their country."

"English is the international language for business," Cyndi reminded me. She had a most exceptional memory when it came to reminding me of things I've said in the past for various reasons.

"That's certainly true in our case," I agreed.

Our thoughts on the subject didn't matter. The French are a discerning bunch. American fast food is offered on the Dutch side, with old standbys like KFC, Pizza Hut, Burger King, McDonald's, Dominos, and Subway. The French side has only one, a Subway. They predominately prefer their French-style foods.

Perfume falls into the same category as food. French people favor French perfumes. More than one person of French persuasion has stopped in to ask if we sold French perfumes. Initially we said no, but now we say, "Of course."

Our perfumes are not only made with French traditional methods, but are made in France, since St. Martin is a part of the mother country. Despite our response, some French shoppers suspiciously sniff a few perfumes and walk out. When we do conclude a sale to a French national, we always jump for joy.

Tours and discussions on creating perfume play an important part in attracting customers and sales. We met with hotel concierges and placed our fragrances and lotions in some nearby restaurants. We worked with the tourism and hospitality departments on both sides of the island and provided gift bags to their VIP guests. Trying to broaden our horizons, I met early on with two island perfume retailers, seeking to have our brand included in their inventory. Both graciously declined with similar explanations: tourists were hurriedly looking for name-brand designer perfume at a duty-free discount. Our brand was neither name brand nor discounted.

We decided to look beyond the borders of the island. We kicked off sales at our Internet site in March 2009 and arranged it to coincide with our first online newsletter. We had four sales that first week and were delighted. We couldn't help but wonder if we'd hit the jackpot. Unfortunately, we had time; the fifth Internet order arrived three months later. No jackpot, yet.

The first worldwide distribution began quite by accident in spring 2009. I was on an American Airlines flight returning from St. Martin to Miami. A conversation ensued with the passenger next to me, who identified herself as Debbie Danielson. Debbie and her husband Dana hadn't particularly enjoyed their first trip to paradise. They were disappointed with the retail experience and found the island a bit too third world, which it certainly was in many ways. I inquired if they had gone to this or that location and they hadn't, claiming they wished they'd had such info prior to their trip.

"What do you and Dana do in the DC area?" I inquired.

"Dana is a contractor, and I have an upscale dress shop and boutique near the Capitol," Debbie replied.

"What's the name and how is it doing?"

"It's called Forecast, and we've had it for over ten years, but this is the worst it's done, with people not spending. Instead of cutting employees, I took a pay cut, and we're keeping our staff intact."

That was a quick flight and about the fastest two and a half hours I'd ever spent on a plane. Debbie had inquired as to the Tijon distribution plan. I honestly replied there was no plan, and she expressed interest in selling a few products if they passed the smell test of her and her staff. I promptly ordered a package of various scents and merchandise to be forwarded to her. They passed the sniff test, and she placed an initial order, with reorders following.

Our efforts to get our products known on the island were best served by two chance encounters that happened in late 2009. The first encounter was with a tour operator, Mary-Beth, with Lagoon and Rising Sun Tours, who contacted me for a tour of our parfumerie. Mary-Beth had walked a similar path as mine; she had lived the corporate life and now chose to semi-retire in St. Martin.

Their first visit turned into two wonderful things for Cyndi and me: a lasting friendship and considerable business. Mary-Beth is one of the most organized and detailed people I've met, and that lends her the ability to be a most outstanding group organizer. She has many corporate clients, and they often choose to provide welcome bags to their conference guests. You guessed it: we're fortunate that often our suntan products and lip balms are included. Some groups offer our perfume class as a side tour. One group even invited us out to their hotel, LaSamana, to provide a class to twenty-five spouses.

Mary-Beth would later introduce us to Ali, the owner of Rising Sun Tours, who had worked for a Middle-Eastern prince in his younger life. Ali had been on St. Martin for years and knew everyone who was anyone.

The other encounter was suggested by our artist friend Asif. We were talking one day about growing our respective businesses.

"You should go to some hotel orientations," Asif suggested.

"What goes on at those things?"

"Mostly it's the time-shares. They have get-togethers to welcome the guests. There are some beverages served, and sometimes local vendors are allowed to come and speak or present their wares."

"How many do you go to and when are they?"

"Oh, I go to three or four a week, but mostly I just go and set up my paintings for sale."

"What's one of your favorites to go to?" I inquired.

"Well, the Oyster Bay Beach resort usually works out well. They allow me to set up during an evening, but I think their orientation is Sunday mornings."

"Whom should I see at the resort?"

"Go see Ingrid. She runs it. Tell her I suggested it."

A few days later I went with a few sample products in a gift bag and met the beautiful and personable Ingrid. She listened to what our business offered and invited me to come to their Sunday morning orientation. I thanked her and said I'd see her Sunday.

Over time I tried different resort orientations. None have proven to be as productive as the busy Oyster Bay Beach Resort. As our business has grown and my schedule has gotten busier, it's remained the orientation I choose to attend.

A few months after I'd started going to Oyster Bay weekly, Ingrid stopped in our parfumerie and became a big fan of our business model and boutique. She knew merchandising and complimented Cyndi on her skills. Sometimes I'm remiss in telling Cyndi what a wonderful job she does, and I could tell it meant much to her to hear it from a reputable and skilled woman like Ingrid.

Some restaurateurs told us that hotel staff wanted (read: demanded) cash rebates or nice gifts for referrals. I broached the subject tactfully with Ingrid and discovered that her only goal was the complete satisfaction of her guests. If we were to do anything, we should give free gifts or discounts to her guests, she said. There was no doubt that Ingrid was a remarkable lady who could likely have a position at any resort on the island.

REPOSITIONING

Grand Case is often referred to as the Gourmet Capital of the Caribbean. It has a unique concentration of intimate restaurants that offer fine dining, all within a few blocks of our shop. That means that our evenings are busy with car and foot traffic. We know this well, because for a time we watched them drive or walk by our shop every evening.

They hardly gave us a glance, despite the rather large OPEN banner that hung across our porch poles. We had positioned Tijon as an upscale shop and were concerned that we had misjudged the audience.

"Big car," Cyndi said, on one occasion. A big car did indeed drive by, but didn't stop.

"Six people," I surveyed. Cyndi was fidgety and started to dust the shelves for something to do. I got excited as I saw a car park on the street out front. Four people got out and started walking our way. I anxiously went to the door, only to see them walking right past our building. "Maybe we need a lighted sign out front," I offered to Cyndi.

"We have a big sign on our building. How can they not see it?" Cyndi replied. "But there's a lot going on here: tourists looking at the mountains and down the road at the fabulous restaurants. I don't think they notice us. Remember when we first came here? We were the same way." I hoped my assurance that a better sign would solve the problem was the truth. Cyndi remained unconvinced.

Since we were closed on weekends, we enjoyed a happy-hour sunset one particular Saturday at nearby Grand Case Beach Club. We ended up chatting with a lovely couple who were new to the island. They were celebrating the last night of their weeklong stay.

When it came time to tell what we were doing on the island, they knew exactly where our building was, as they had walked by numerous times. Further discussion revealed their perception that we were simply another duty-free shop selling name-brand perfumes.

Ahhhh . . . a much-needed awareness immediately came to us. When we explained what we actually did, they expressed surprise and regret for not stopping in.

That enlightening conversation convinced us to reposition our marketing efforts. We needed to educate would-be consumers that Tijon manufactured its own unique fragrances and lotions on-site. It wasn't simply a store selling perfumes.

Cyndi finally allowed me to order two signs. One was lighted and read, TIJON, LOCALLY MADE FRAGRANCES and the other read, TIJON, ST. MARTIN'S ONLY WORKING PARFUMERIE: FREE TOURS / FREE SAMPLES.

The tours were the easy part of that sign; we'd been offering those from day one. Some opted for the tour; others preferred to simply browse.

For the tour we enlighten guests on how we make perfumes, starting with the gathering of essential oils. We explain how we manufacture some oils from island flowers through steam distillation. We also demonstrate the labor-intensive extraction used years ago in Grasse, France, called *enfleurage*. We would point to some artifacts in our museum and conclude our tour at the perfume organ, explaining how we mix and match top, middle, and base notes among the hundreds of oils.

The free samples were the hard part. Yes, we offered in-store sampling from the perfume bottle, but that didn't make the cut for a free sample. What we really needed was a little gift bag for those who initially took our tour, later to be replaced by an offer of free fragrance samples. We had to find a way to make their enjoyment lead to the best kind of advertising, word of mouth.

I reflected upon some of the favorite tours I'd taken in my twenties: brewery tours. At the end of the tour I always received a nice tasting of the products. Why couldn't we do the same?

The gift bags that we used for tourism events and various island VIPs wouldn't work for this. They were quite expensive and not planned well for a sampling-type gift bag. We needed to locate and purchase sample-size containers with a card or letter explaining the item. It also needed to promote the product. Our estimated initial quantity was between one and two thousand bags. That number was based on foot traffic and included a few hundred bags that went out to various promotional events throughout the island.

The initial bag contained a small, 2-milliliter plastic perfume spray vial of a chosen fragrance; a 4-milliliter plastic pump with lotion; a 2-ounce bar of soap; a 1-ounce sample of moisturizing massage lotion; a 1-ounce sample of SPF 8 suntan lotion; and a 4-milliliter plastic jar of lip balm. We didn't want our gift bag to look chintzy. However, keeping the cost of the bag, products, and promotional materials affordable was challenging.

We had to purchase some of the packaging products in considerable bulk (5,000-piece quantity) to get per-item pricing that made sense. We also decided to distribute the sample spray perfume vial outside the store. Although it was a greater outpouring of funds, we both knew marketing was an essential part of making Tijon a part of the island attractions.

ADDING A MUSEUM

What could we add to our marketing repertoire to attract customers to the boutique itself? We had always visited and seen businesses with their individual gimmicks. We recollected some of our favorites to form our own plan. Wall Drug in South Dakota, for example, kicked off their business eons ago by offering free ice water. Others had attractive, if not garish attention-getting monuments in front of their shop. Some destinations advertised the fact that they provided free tourist information.

Several nice jewelry stores in Phillipsburg provided guests with beer or wine while shopping. This wasn't to lure customers, but to reduce inhibitions. It has also proven a useful trick in casinos.

Being born and bred in Minneapolis, Cyndi and I were familiar with the tourist mecca, Wisconsin Dells. We'd made plenty of those four-hour treks there as children. One of our favorite travel stops was an Indian trading post on the main four-lane highway east of downtown. It was basically a large, cheap souvenir shop. It always had a sign outside that proudly displayed the words "free museum."

The sign lured customers and never disappointed our family. I enjoyed looking at the artifacts while Cyndi and the kids surveyed the souvenir toys. To this day, I believe I got the better end of that deal. The more we chatted about those days in the Dells, the more ideas started to run. Cyndi hit the nail on the head when she said, "Why don't we have a museum at our shop?"

The rich history of perfume making was evident when we visited the Molinard and Fraginard parfumeries in Grasse. They had antique bottles, machinery, and knick-knacks on display. Tijon, however, wasn't so ancient. One thing I always recalled, though, was how certain displays drew larger crowds than others. We started to brainstorm what we could add and where we could purchase it.

This began our international quest as curators of antique perfume bottles. Collecting these bottles is popular enough to warrant a Perfume Bottle Association. We joined that association and they gladly accepted us, unlike a certain other one I won't mention again.

If one considers fragrance a creation, these bottles are the art. Many books outline their history and the reasoning behind the multitude of designs. Our collection began modestly, but now includes over one hundred rare and unique pieces. One of our favorites is a Mary Dunhill "Flowers of Devonshire" clear glass bottle and stopper.

We purchased bottles at antique stores but hit the jackpot when we attended the annual convention of the Perfume Bottle Association. By coincidence, it was being held that year just a few miles from our home in Dallas.

The convention offered an annual auction, run by a professional auction house, with many prized and beautiful historical bottles. Wine was free, so we toasted our then-future dream and had the best time bidding on many items, securing about forty unique bottles with history attached.

Later, I found a museum store online and purchased our prized centerpiece, a bronze perfume vial from the ancient region of Bactria, located in parts of the modern countries of Afghanistan, Pakistan, and Tajikistan. Certified as originating between the third and first centuries BC, it has a bird-shaped stopper and is in superb condition. It is only 85 millimeters tall, with a stopper and three legs attached to a bulbous base. The midsection is decorated with a single circular rib and another on the lower neck.

While we loved our collection, we knew our museum needed more than polished old bottles. We found a vintage box of Molinard Paris solid perfumes in their individual, tiny hand-painted jars. We also located an antique distiller and glass enfleurage chassis used to extract fragrant oils from flowers. We added a 1914 original lithograph art nouveau poster of a nude woman in a garden of butterflies that was used to promote the French perfume Fleurs de Mousse.

We augmented our collection with Victorian perfume buttons. Originally made in the mid-1800s, these buttons have an underlay of velvet fabric with an ornate, pieced brass overlay. Most perfumes of the Victorian Era were oil-based, unlike the alcohol-based mixtures of today. That meant they could soil a woman's clothing. The buttons were designed so that women could dab their perfume on the velvet of the button, thus protecting their clothing and carrying the scent for a long time.

During the Civil War, women would give such a button, scented with their perfume, to a husband or lover going off to war. He would stitch it under his uniform collar as a reminder of the love he left behind.

An educational component of the museum was to showcase raw materials before their conversion to oils. One of the more unusual pieces we located was ambergris, a solid, waxy substance that is dull grey to blackish in color. It occurs as part of the natural biliary secretion from the intestine of the sperm whale. We found our piece on the beaches of North Carolina after Hurricane Katrina. Today ambergris has been replaced by synthetics, mostly because of cost and the challenges in retrieving it, in addition to protecting the whales.

A recent addition to our museum was a Rosoli bottle of Eau de Cologne. Yes, Eau de Cologne was and still is a brand, even though it's now used generically, as Kleenex is used for tissues. Introduced in 1709 by Giovanni Farina, an Italian living in Cologne, Germany, this unisex perfume soon became the hit of Europe. The alcohol- and water-based formula was composed primarily of neroli, bergamot, rosemary, and lemon. The perfumer wrote a letter to his brother, demonstrating that his marketing skills were as good as his fragrant compositions:

> I have created a perfume which is reminiscent of a spring morning following a soft shower, where fragrances of wild narcissi combine with that of sweet orange flowers. This perfume refreshes me and stimulates both my senses and imagination.

Eau de Cologne wasn't initially intended solely for exterior use; Farina also described it as "good for dental hygiene and to ward off infectious diseases." History reports that Napoleon himself may have used up to four bottles of Eau de Cologne per day. He used it to mask bodily odors while in the field and to help with medicinal needs, similar to what some might call snake oil. The Farina descendants still manufacture the original Eau de Cologne at their perfumery in Cologne.

Additional odds and ends, such as the original 1923 edition of W. A. Poucher's *Perfumes and Cosmetics*, rounded out our museum. Our space wasn't large or fancy, but the museum added an interesting historical perspective to Tijon and to the customer experience. It's particularly fun to see customers gather around the artifacts and call to their friends nearby, "Come here, you've got to see this."

BUS TOURS

Watching buses full of tourists, usually cruise passengers, pass by on the way to wherever they were going, figuratively brought tears to our eyes. When we first inspected the property for purchase, we noticed buses driving by and thought we had the right location. However, getting the buses to stop proved to be another story.

One cruise ship operator told us to contact a local tour operator to solicit bus stops. I called immediately and left a message and repeated this every few days. I never received a return call, and after a few weeks I stopped in her shop, hoping to catch her. She was in, but too busy to see me. I saw her assistant, left information, and never heard back. Did I happen to mention the phrase "island life, mon" before?

One week, Ingrid, the fabulous director at the Oyster Bay Beach Resort, asked if we were interested in being a part of their weekly Sunday bus tour. I gave an emphatic yes. Cyndi thought I was nuts and had lots of questions on the details. "How will we get fifty people in our small shop and a large bus in our lot?" We did manage, and it gave us the confidence to reapproach the cruise ships for tours.

Aqua Mania, an island activity-booking group, recently included us on their Monday bus stop, and as of October 2011 we are included in an island tour promoted by Royal Caribbean Cruise Line. I continue to believe that someday a local tour operator who has been too busy to see us will take notice.

CHAPTER 14

OFFERING PERFUME CLASSES: "INVENT YOUR SCENT"

We opened the shop offering our island-made creations in combination with unique, branded gifts. That didn't stop some customers from wandering to our perfume organ and inquiring if we could design a perfume for them, or if they could create a perfume themselves.

While surfing the web during that first year of the shop being open, I ran across a special class on creating perfume in New York City. It was a one-time event and, if I enrolled, I could choose from thirty oils in making my fragrance. I was in Texas at the time and Cyndi was in St. Martin. I was instantly excited and Skyped Cyndi quickly.

"Hi, honey, want to run an idea by you," I started.

"Okay, shoot."

"What would you think if we offered a 'make your own perfume' class?"

"How would you do it?"

"Not sure yet, but do you think people would be interested? Would it draw people into the shop?"

"Well it's certainly different, and some are asking for it. Don't know anywhere else it's done, so it might work."

"Thanks, let me do some research and I'll put some thoughts together."

I've always enjoyed lecturing and knew that it would be enjoyable to share some of the acquired knowledge of fragrance with others in a fun environment. I also love trivia so I constructed a little history of perfume, including how oils were extracted and utilized. I included information on the importance of our sense of smell and instructions on how to make perfume.

The final piece would be entering the lab to create one's own signature fragrance. I envisioned providing lab coats for an extra fun touch, explaining that if the lab coats were too warm, they didn't have to be worn, but that they were highly recommended for two reasons: if you spill oils on your clothes it could ruin them; and second, it makes you look professional.

St. Martin is an inviting tourist destination with beaches, blue seas, water activities, fine dining, tropical drinks, and duty-free shopping. Historical attractions and educational outings, however, were few and far between. Would an indoor perfume class in a tropical destination boom—or bust?

I conducted an experimental class for Cyndi and our T. J., then in college. I went through a rough draft of my routine, passed out a newly created workbook, and pushed them into the lab. Cyndi was fascinated throughout and created a simple but elegant fragrance heavy on gardenia. T. J., with a lesser attention span, participated, but appeared happy to have it over. However, his fragrance wasn't bad, meaning even the less interested could possibly succeed.

The next class we provided was a complimentary to our visiting San Diego friends, Mark and Robin. They enjoyed it, while offering valuable feedback and suggested changes, such as making the lecture more interactive. In 2009 we were ready to open our perfume class to the public.

Predictably and by design, classes started filling at a snail's pace. We did receive encouraging reviews from the early attendees, who enjoyed the information and the multitude of oil ingredients to choose from. We asked for and received constructive feedback, much of which we've incorporated into our evolving class routine. Our class was a work in progress and showed definite potential.

Students, in creating their signature scent, could choose from over three hundred oils on the perfume organ. We think, but are not sure, that Tijon is likely the only place in the world where participants can choose from so many oils in making their own perfume.

We had to make sure that we set up expectations properly. Those thinking they could invent a classical scent in two to three hours would likely leave disappointed. What took weeks, if not months or years to create could simply not be done by students in a matter of hours.

One woman brought her husband's favorite fragrance, intending to duplicate it. To identify its precise ingredients required an expensive gas chromatography machine that I didn't own. The nose had to guess the synthetic ingredients and transfer those to natural oils on our perfume organ. This proves next to impossible in such a short time frame, for even those with seasoned sniffers.

Needing to clarify the class as one of education and enjoyment, with a chance to leave with an exclusive, if not unusual fragrance, we set out to market the event accordingly, while retaining its flavor as an informative and interactive workshop. In addition to the history of perfume, attendees would discover the reasons our sense of smell is our most acute sense; what raw materials are utilized and how the oils are extracted; perfume classifications; and how to compose a perfume by mixing top, middle, and base notes. The unique balancing act in the mixture of these notes, the *accord*, is what gives a fragrance its distinct personality.

As part of the class we ask the students to write a few words describing each of our initial ten perfumes and colognes offered for sale. We ask this for three reasons: to awaken their sense of smell; to think of descriptive words, which we ask them to use for the perfume they'll soon create; and to select their favorite Tijon perfume, since a free bottle is given to them in their departing gift bag.

Recalling the fun and challenges of creating our initial perfume descriptions, we weren't disappointed in the wide range of descriptions that resulted. Most describe our fragrances using terms such as "floral," "fresh," "light," "sweet," "exotic," "island," and "French."

One local man circled our X.2 fragrance as his favorite, but his wife described it with a simple phrase: "It stinks." When I told the husband his wife didn't like the cologne he'd chosen for his gift, in case he wished to reconsider, he went against the studies that claim most men purchase perfume their wives or girlfriends like when he said, "No, I like that one, and that's the one I want." I knew who wore the pants in that family—the question was whether those pants ever came off, if you take my meaning.

Periodically we get a few attendees who seriously dislike a few of our fragrances before locating one they admire. Their descriptions of the discards have included, "sickly sweet, smells like rotten flowers"; "smells like bug spray"; "soapy"; "Yuck, strong, spices"; "medicinal"; "hate it"; "too smelly sweet, offensive"; "old lady"; "dull"; and "burns my nose." Conversely, we have students on occasion who love them all. One teenage student who loved each of them described her free perfume gift as "candy."

Our most popular woman's *eau de parfum* to date has been *Eclectique*. This fine fragrance has been described by our perfume students in a range of words including "sensual," "sexy, flowery," "baby powder," "vanilla-naughty," "yummy-warm," "stinks," "edible," "floral," "fruity," "sweet like honey," "youthful," "grandma flower," "pineapple," "coconut," "cherry like," and "smells like Mom."

Are they really smelling the same fragrance? This is further evidence that everybody experiences scent differently. It would be easy to take personal offense from some of those non-favorable descriptions, but not all scents are everything to everyone, and complete honesty is required for truly valuable feedback.

In fact, this type of uncertainty about how an individual will process a scent is what makes it fun and exciting. And it's why there are so many perfumes.

Participants take our classes for a variety of reasons. Most come to create a signature scent, some yearn for the learning process, and others simply enjoy the hands-on interaction. After teaching over eight hundred students how to make perfume, we discovered a new motive. Elizabeth, a cute, petite fifth-grader, participated in the class with her mother while proclaiming her intent of creating a "stinky" perfume. I asked why.

"There's this boy in my school who I think is going to ask me to a dance, and I don't want to go, so I want to create a stinky perfume," she replied with a devilish smile.

She ended up making two beakers, a nice fragrance and a stinky one heavy on capsicum oil. We bottled her nice one as part of the class, and I bottled the stinky one as my gift to her—or was it my gift from one parent to another?

The greatest difficulty for many students is selecting a name for their signature scent. Cyndi and I understand that hurdle. Attendees come prepared to learn and create but have given little or no thought to the naming rights for their finished product. Many ultimately choose references to their own names, the island, or French words. From personal experience, I think that perhaps if I served rum punch drinks it would become easier.

Product names can be as unique as the scents themselves. Our first couple, friends Mark and Robin, chose "Rocco" for him and "Bambi" for her, resulting in a good laugh about their sexual fantasies.

Other names were equally fascinating. One New Yorker, working in Manhattan for Calvin Klein's clothing division, named hers "SXM [the island airport code] in the City." One thoughtful honeymooner made a perfume for his mother and gleefully named it "Mommy's Little Monster." A retired divorce attorney from California, attending with his wife, named his "The Things I Do." A favorite was "Sandy Polished Toes" from a woman who walked in with sand on her feet. Another favorite was from a beautiful young opera singer from Manhattan named Victoria, who named hers "In Love on the Beach." One lovely grandmother named Dot creatively called her fragrance "Dot.Com."

Other class perfume names of interest have included "Romeo No. 5," "Sexy Orchid," "Too Sexy," "Sex Island," "*Besa Me*"("kiss me" in Spanish), "*Volim*" ("love" in Croatian), "*Moana*" ("ocean" in the Hawaiian language), "*Bon Bini*" ("welcome" or "hello" in Papiamentu), "Virgo Queen," "Morning-After Kiss," "Toots," "*Dieu de Manche*," "*Citrus sans Sucre*," "Wired," "*Eau de L'Eau*," "Glitterazzi," "*Giglio*," "*Spuisito*," "Barefoot," and "Luscious."

Christina was a most interesting student, originally from San Diego but now studying veterinary medicine at Ross University on the island of St. Kitts. She named her perfume "Now." When I inquired as to the meaning, she replied, "I felt it appropriate to label my perfume as a nod to enjoying and embracing life in the moment and appreciating everything that brought me to this point." Her source of inspiration was a quote by author Asha Tyson.

Similarly motivated, one perfume student named Stacy called her fragrance "Phenomenal" after Maya Angelou's poem "Phenomenal Woman," which every woman should read. Sonia from Chicago named her fragrance "Atia's Dream" in honor of her three-year-old niece, who had just finished chemotherapy for leukemia.

After eliciting a name, we boldly ask our new perfumers to describe their concoction. Typical responses include "soft citrus with floral undertones," or vice versa. One beautiful island lady who manages the front desk at a popular hotel named her perfume "Delight" and sensuously described it as "something I would spray all over my body for my husband to deliciously lick and eat." I may have blushed.

Other enticing descriptions were by Stacie, studying nursing in Boston, who named her perfume "*Belle á la Plage*" and described it as, "The way you should smell fresh out of the shower after a day at the beach: clean, light, with a lingering hint of sunscreen."

Sarah, a dance instructor in Dallas who named her perfume "*Pas de Deux*," a ballet term for a duet dance, described her scent as "a bold array of strength and femininity, mixing wood, floral, and vanilla notes into one symphony of smells. Inhale deep. The nostrils will rejoice."

My favorite description came, surprisingly, from a ninth grader, Julia, off a cruise ship with her mother. Naming her favorite concoction "The Asian Vampire," she described her complex formula of twenty-five mixed oils as a scent reminiscent of "walking into a coffee shop, smelling fruit, caramel, and a mixture of randomness, with a hint of sunscreen and old people." I suggested she consider becoming a writer. Descriptions like that took me right to the scene and drew me in.

One participant, Linda from La Jolla, California, paid particular attention when listening to the intro revealing that scientific studies have proven the top combination of scents enhancing male sexual arousal were lavender and pumpkin pie. Naturally, she made a perfume focusing on those two oils. Bumping into her a few days later, we inquired as to the perfume's effectiveness and were treated to a warm smile and approving nod. It was her fortieth wedding anniversary, and the fragrance had proven itself to be quite magical.

A younger lady visiting with her brother from Dublin, Ireland, similarly made a concoction with pumpkin and lavender she named "*Deoch Suin,*" hoping to attract a coworker at her bank employer back home. She e-mailed us upon returning that her coworker had left the bank's employ while she was enjoying St. Martin, but she nevertheless enjoyed her fragrance.

Judith, our friend from Germany, now living on the island, created a most delightful perfume with numerous ingredients. However, she had forgotten the perfumer's cardinal rule: to keep copious notes of each ingredient and the amount added. This fine creation would never be replicated. For many that might be fine, but for somebody who lived nearby and could easily recreate it, it was a tough lesson learned.

Phyllis, from Washington DC, where she worked in international affairs, was so enthused by her creation that she suggested, and initiated at our perfumery, a plan where we could take the student's recipe and bottle as many as requested. This inventive student was to give her family and friends the best island souvenir, a bottle of perfume she had personally concocted.

Psychologists would have a field day studying the behaviors of those creating perfumes in our classes. Some students have a primal need for ingredient suggestions and verbal reinforcement of their final mixture, while others outright reject any assistance, and if a suggestion is given, take the opposite path.

We sometimes are asked who the best students are. Without a doubt, honeymooners. They're in love, and everything tastes and smells good. One bride even named her fragrant formula "Honeymoon." Here's the typical honeymooners dialogue:

"Honey, what do you think of this one?" the man asks his new bride.

"Oh yes, I like it. It smells nice," she invariably responds, smiling. Probably pats his hand. "What do you think of mine?"

"I love it."

Perfume-making classes proved to be a fabulous way to create new "couple" memories. One young, good-looking duo from California stopped in at the appointed time of their reservation. Turned out the husband had planned a surprise for his new bride, who thought they were headed out on a boat trip that evening and had been drinking

Presidente beers before arrival. When the class turned to identifying ten single oils, the new bride laughed and said, "I can't smell any of these oils. But I could smell a Bud Light a mile away." Nevertheless, she created a wonderful fragrance and appropriately named it "Lush."

While some students in the perfume class are easy to work with, others can be quite difficult. I understand the latter, because I would be one of those. These tougher students are the perfectionists, especially when they desire a spicy or earthy scent, either of which is considerably more difficult to make in a short time frame than fresh, floral, or citrus scents.

These students experiment with multiple oils, believing their combination is always one away from perfection. Ultimately, they find a barely acceptable fragrance, or simply tire and conclude, "Let's bottle this one."

One difficulty for all students is including oils they may not particularly find appealing but that may help round out their new creation.

In smelling oils from the perfume organ, students naturally want to add only those oils that smell good individually, not fully sensing that they're trying to steer their formula in a certain direction. Some want a spicy note, but don't particularly like the smell of clove, cinnamon, or other spice oils offered. We encourage them to experiment and dig deeper than their initial response to the scent.

I tell struggling students that to become a perfumer, it's not about smelling like one, it's about learning to think like one: envisioning the combination of oils rather than thinking of individual scents.

Music plays in the lab and impacts the creativity of students. How and when it impacts them is a science I don't understand. We offer two types of music on our lab CD player: soft piano music from our friend Danny Wright, and jazzy, French bistro music. If I find students struggling during their creations, I simply mix it up and switch to the other style of music. Amazingly, it seems to help.

Class participants have ranged from ages seven to eighty-seven and come from all walks of life, including students, teachers, pharmacists, business people, and Avon and Mary Kay sales associates. Surprisingly, about 10 percent of our students come from the health-care industry, with half of that group being doctors. I asked one to speculate on why so many take the class. He responded, "We like to learn things, and we're not real good at sitting on the beach for long periods."

Our physician students typically have one trait in common: they typically elect not to wear our lab coats, which likely remind them of work. This category has included family physicians, internists, radiologists, gastroenterologists, urologists, anesthesiologists, emergency room doctors, and even a retired neurosurgeon.

The last, Dr. Claude Bordelon, was a fascinating individual who became a good friend. His knowledge and experiences were most engaging, and he annually volunteers his time and skills in Iraq and Afghanistan to the American troops. He and a colleague have received a federal grant and are in the process of studying the effect, if any, of essential oils on comatose patients and their recovery.

Not surprisingly, another 5–10 percent come from the food industry: chefs, restaurant owners and servers, both on-island and from around the world. This is understandable when one considers their creativity and the sense of smell that accompanies fine dining.

In fact, we've had the enjoyment of many local participants who own, manage, or are the chefs for various restaurants or wine shops we love, including locally from Le Ti Provençal, Bistrot Caraibes, Sunset Beach Café, Bel Mar, Vinissimo, and L'Estaminet, to name a few. When I went through the routine of showing off a fragrance oil called "baked bread" from the perfume organ, Ina, the chef owner from L'Estaminet, in her cute French accent, frowned and accurately stated, "*Non*, that's not baked bread. 'Tis *buttered* baked bread."

To date we've had participants from most every state in the United States and thirty-three countries. We inquire about their homelands and receive wonderful stories, with invitations to visit. Two guys from Uruguay took the class and later e-mailed us photos of their country, attached to this note:

> We would like to thank you for providing us such an incredible experience during the class. Eduardo and I agree that our visit to Tijon was the best thing we did in St. Martin. . . .
>
> If you ever decide to visit Uruguay, we will be very pleased to be your tour guides. . . .
>
> Sergio.

One January day in 2011 we had a group of nine taking our class—a bit larger than we generally allow, but they eagerly agreed, understanding that quarters might be a bit cramped. While in the lab, a family of four from São Paulo, Brazil, stopped in with a daughter aged ten and a son a bit younger. The beautiful young daughter, Beatriz, had wanted to take the perfume class but was unable because we were full. She started crying, though trying to be brave and hide her tears. Cyndi tried to console her, giving her a gift bag containing some of our sample products and telling the family that if they stopped back at 1:00 p.m., we had another class, the shorter, one-hour version. The father didn't think that was possible, but thanked us and left. As she exited, Beatriz's tears resumed. It broke our hearts.

We were surprised and delighted to see the family return at 1:00 p.m. Beatriz took the class as her mom interpreted. Seeing the look on her face when she reentered the shop sent electricity through our hearts. That day had nothing to do with money; it was about providing an opportunity for enjoyment and accomplishment. Her mother e-mailed us when they returned home:

> Dear Cyndi and John,
>
> Thank you for your kindness and for receiving us so warmly! We love the magical moments in St. Martin. . . . Undoubtedly one of the highlights was the visit to Tijon, where Beatriz held her dream of creating her own perfume. We were all excited to provide this time to her. . . .
>
> Hugs from Brazil,
>
> Beatriz, Caio, Vaqner, and Claudia.

One weekday in early November, two cute young sisters, Isabella and Juliana, ages nine and seven, from New Jersey, were dropped off by their father, who had made a reservation for them to create their own fragrances. They were on a cruise ship and were visiting St. Martin. Both sported long, dark Italian hair. Their father went to explore our village while the girls went to work.

I quizzed the youngest, "Do you have a good older sister?" She looked down, and slowly shook her head no.

I asked the older girl, "Do you have a good younger sister?"

"No, oh, maybe sometimes," she replied. They both looked at each other and smiled.

"Who likes perfume the best?" I inquired further.

They both enthusiastically raised their hands, whereupon the oldest scolded the youngest, "You don't wear perfume."

The youngest replied, "That's because you don't let me."

They got busy, shared oils and ideas as would good friends, and made delightful fragrances. One was named "Tropical Essence," and had a citrus bent, and the other was named "Calm," despite a nice touch of butterscotch. They returned home with a prideful sense of accomplishment.

Creating perfume can also prove therapeutic. Jean Rich, a highly regarded cancer researcher in the States and now an expat who had been on the island for over twenty years, has taken the class with different friends, eight times to date. After her most recent encounter she e-mailed us:

> Another magical afternoon—all the gals are raving about their first or -nth Tijon experience. . . .Whatever my demons of the week, they waft away on the alizés [trade winds] and are replaced by delicious scents. . . .

It's particularly rewarding when others find our calling an inspiration. One such person, Celia, called us from the nearby island of Tortola in the British Virgin Islands. She'd seen an article on our classes and scheduled a fly-in for the sole purpose of participating. She was a well-educated native Trinidadian, having lived and done business on Tortola for over twenty years. She sold Avon, among other things, in her shop, and was looking for education and ideas. She enjoyed her class greatly, and we received a heartwarming e-mail after the class that read in part:

> Dear Cyndi and John:
> Thank you for a wonderfully mystical encounter on Saturday. . . .Your shop was indeed an experience and inspiration to me. . . .You've also inspired me to start my own line of T-shirts and kitchen towels with imprints of butterflies, metaphysical musings, and butterfly-related thoughts. . . .

No two classes are ever the same, and there are always comments we've never heard before. When I explain where musk originally came from (the anal glands of the male musk deer) one student, David from Montreal, expressed to the class, "I wish my anal glands smelled as good."

With one student, what began as a challenging experience transcended into a fun and memorable afternoon. Peggy, from Indiana, had a discerning nose. She was an avid perfume collector, and we're talking expensive, actual perfumes, not bottles, *eaus de parfume*, or colognes. She had with her a typed list of her collection, sourced from points all over the world. It was most impressive. We visited, and she decided to create her own perfume.

After many mixtures, Peggy wasn't finding any of the fragrances acceptable and was getting a bit frustrated. But she persisted and with more time created what I regarded as a beautiful floral scent that she named "Summer Breeze" and described as "summer flower scents wafting through a meadow."

She claimed she liked it, but to what extent I couldn't be sure. Her oils primarily included top and middle notes of tulips, green tea, anise, black pepper, clove bud, and cedar leaf, with base notes of vanilla, teakwood, musk, and frankincense.

About a month later, during a slow post-holiday morning at the shop, my spirits lifted when a package arrived containing a hardcover edition of *Perfumes, the Guide* by the renowned Luca Turin and Tania Sanchez. It was a fun read and remains a useful reference. Accompanying the package was a nice note from Peggy.

> Dear Cyndi and John,
> I wanted you know how very much I'm enjoying the "Summer Breeze" you helped me create in your lab at Tijon. . . .
> Congratulations for having established such a fine perfumery on St. Martin, and my sincere thanks for making the complete experience available to me.
> Peggy

While many local islanders and repeat tourists to this day have never heard of Tijon, we've been fortunate to receive the most beautiful comments on TripAdvisor.com. This definitely bolsters our belief in our unusual concept. Here are a few favorite comments we've received:

> "The Perfume 101 course at Tijon is a must for any vacation. You will leave with the memory of a magical event."

"The highlight of our trip, the best thing we did the whole cruise."

"The shop is beautiful and their products are such great quality. Even if you can't attend the perfume class, you'll definitely want to stop in."

"Absolutely magical experience, really enjoyed designing our own perfumes, everyone was having so much fun we didn't want to leave!"

"I'm a foodie and love to cook and this is as much fun as putting together a gourmet meal . . . without the calories!"

"I just happen to LOVE my new scent, and when people ask what am I wearing, I can tell them, 'oh, this is my exclusive line!'"

The first fifty-three reviews received on TripAdvisor were amazing; all rewarded us five stars. On Monday morning, August 8, 2011, we e-mailed our quarterly newsletter boasting of an award from the website for having received only five-star ratings, added to the fact that for over six months running we were rated the number-one activity on the island. We had to periodically pinch ourselves, but not for long.

Hours later on that fateful day, we received notification of a new TripAdvisor review, our fifty-fourth, that was headlined, "Not our Thing." My heart sank as the three-star rating blasted out at me. I anxiously opened the review and read:

If you have time, you should visit, but the parking lot was really small and we had trouble parking. When we entered, we weren't acknowledged. . . . If you are into perfume and high-class product, this is one place you should not miss. If I was into this type of thing (or my wife), we probably would have given it five stars.

My skin tightened and my emotions ranged from anger to disappointment to devastation. Food that night had no taste. We take pride in greeting all guests, and if we hadn't done so immediately we must have been in the middle of a perfume class. Our five-star run was over forever, in addition to losing our number-one ranking. The bigger you are the harder you fall.

Cyndi consoled me, analogizing it to someone who walks into an Italian restaurant, reads the menu, and leaves because they don't like Italian food. They might say it's a great place and recommend it to others, but would only rate it three stars as opposed to five because they weren't into Italian food.

One month later my spirits lifted as TripAdvisor again elevated us to the number-one activity-attraction on the island. It did remind me that we are in the people business; most are absolutely wonderful, but there are always a few, well . . . people.

One class inspired a Christmas Eve sermon delivered in Arlington, Texas. Our Texas pastor and his wife took the class over Thanksgiving while on the island to officiate at our daughter's wedding, and it inspired his message during the following holiday season. He sent us a copy of his sermon.

December 24, 2010

On the French side of a Caribbean island called St. Martin, there is a parfumerie by the name of Tijon that on one side has a beautiful boutique and on the other side of this glass wall, a full laboratory.

And the reason I know that is because last month Ruth and I had the opportunity to spend a few days on St. Martin with John and Cyndi Berglund, as a part of their daughter's wedding celebration. And one of the highlights was participating in one of the interactive workshops that they offer at their parfumerie. . . .

The real fun begins when you put on your lab coat, then, surrounded by row after row of bottles filled with smells like lemon, mandarin, rosemary, lavender, sage, ginger, rosewood, sandalwood, and hundreds more, you get to use your own set of beakers and droppers and oils to create your own personal fragrance. . . .

And because I used a little frankincense and myrrh and named my scent "Christmas Holiday," I set the fragrance that I created out on a table in the narthex tonight for anyone who might like to give it a try. . . .

And the reason I wanted to share some of that with you this evening is because tonight, as a way of helping us to understand how the power and the hope and the miracle of that first Christmas continues to impact and bless our lives and our world, I'd like you to reflect for a few moments on what that very first Christmas might have smelled like. . . .

For most of us it's pretty easy to forget what barns are really like, with all that dirty straw. And all the rodents and urine and manure.

And though there is absolutely nothing wrong with putting on a little perfume or getting dressed up and working extra hard to make our homes and our church extra beautiful for tonight, it's also important that we not forget or lose touch with the actual conditions that surrounded the birth of our Lord when he came into the world on that very first Christmas. . . .

Classes conclude with a certificate of completion, a champagne toast for the adults, a gift bag to go, photos, and fond farewells. It's rewarding and topped by my little ritual: I apply a mist of each perfume created on part of my body. I love to smell each newly created fragrance.

And what a pleasure when our new perfumers order additional bottles of their fragrant formula or schedule a return engagement to create an entirely new fragrance. We created a Perfume Class 102 for our graduates, allowing them to return and head right into the lab to concoct. Our students touch my heart in the most amazing ways. It starts with the smiles on their proud faces and extends to the beautiful odors of the newly mixed oils and the education of discovering how certain oils mix together.

One of our class champagne toast finales began with my offer of "*sant*é," French for "to your health," and continued with a lady from Manchester, England, offering "cheers," then a couple from Greece proposing "*eviva*," and concluding with a lady from Poland, now living in Colorado, chiming in with "*nostrovia*." What a beautiful ending to another fun-filled, memorable class!

CHAPTER 15

THREE KINDS OF MAGIC: A VENTURE INTO MUSICAL PRODUCTION

Three Kinds of Magic is a north-meets-south, American-meets-Caribbean musical trio that Cyndi and I created because, well, it seemed like a good idea at the time.

Prior to the opening of our parfumerie we were shopping in the Arlington Parks Mall in Texas, enjoying a Starbucks coffee break, and Cyndi eyed a CD on the countertop display by the cashier. She had a certain gleam in her eye. The CD had a Starbucks label on it. I must admit, I couldn't see what the glint was for. It inspired an idea.

I wondered if we'd be able to sell a Tijon brand of local island music. I decided to do some research on the entire idea. Cyndi loved music, and I wasn't sure how private label rights would work for Tijon, but it was worth figuring out. We enjoyed our coffee and chatted about the idea. Cyndi confirmed that it was okay to move forward by simply saying, "Could be fun."

The first step was to locate an island musician on our next visit whose music we would enjoy and who would record for our untested Expatriate label.

Grand Marche is a popular grocery store on the Dutch side, and their Phillipsburg store has a tremendous selection of CDs, including local artists. We purchased a variety and listened closely to analyze the sounds and styles. Some of the CDs were outdated, a few were steel pan bands, and the newer ones consisted of local hip-hop. We were not of an age or interest level for hip-hop so we quickly excluded that.

It was time to regroup at Orient Beach with a rum punch or two to start brainstorming brilliant ideas. A dreadlocked, short, skinny, smiling, bearded man about forty years old broke our concentration. He wore a funny-colored knit hat and walked the beach selling CDs.

He announced his presence in a heavy island accent: "I'm Dread'I." This unusual looking individual turned out to be a Rasta reggae artist hailing from Dominica, now living on the Dutch side. "Rasta," short for "Rastafari," is a portmanteau of *ras*—"head," an Ethiopian title equivalent to "duke"—and *Tafari,* the pre-regnal given name of Haile Selassie, the former Emperor of Ethiopia.

Rastafarianism is a religion that combines Judeo-Christian beliefs with the veneration of Haile Selassie. Adherents worship God, using the name "Jah." It's also a cultural movement that believes in the possibility of social, political, and religious reform.

Observant Rastafarians practice *Ital*, a diet that shuns meat. However, usage of cannabis, or marijuana, is considered a religious sacrament. I thought of college life years ago and smiled at the recollection of many of my friends who didn't even know they were practicing a religion.

"Would yah like to listen to mah music, mon? Feel the vibes, it is een us."

Dread'I had a portable CD player with headphones plugged in, and he extended them toward us. It was clear to see that his music was his life and that he loved to share it for its meaning as much as for the income.

We listened to one of his CDs and were star-struck with the sounds and energy of his soulful reggae. His voice, not well rounded but unique, reminded of us of a Caribbean Rod Stewart. Dread'I had composed and recorded six CDs by the time of this first meeting. The backup musicians mixed nicely, and all his CDs were professionally engineered.

I bought four of his offerings and told him I was looking for a local artist to record. Would he be interested? "Absolutely, mon." We exchanged e-mail addresses.

We returned to the States, and a few months later I e-mailed Dread'I the dates of our next trip to the beach. Acting as the mega producer I wasn't, I suggested he and his people get together for lunch with me and my people. I met him at Mark's Place, a local Creole restaurant connected to Grand Marche. It was just the two of us; our people were apparently busy.

Over juice we struck a deal, and a new record label was born. However, neither of us anticipated the beautiful friendship to follow. Dread'I invited me to a local studio, and I invited him to our perfume shop. Additional, impromptu meetings regularly occurred on his retail stage, Orient Beach. The new CD would be simply called *The Tijon Collection: Tropical Reggae*.

After December 2007, when Cyndi opened the shop part-time while I was still working in Texas, Dread'I would call on her periodically to be sure she was okay. He also would bring us mangos or genips. The latter is a round, green fruit, about the size of a crabapple, that grows in bunches. To eat a genip, you place it in your mouth to chew and suck the thin, gelatinous, and juicy pulp covering the seed. It has a sharp, exotic taste. The seed kernel could be roasted and eaten.

Dread'I may have been a beach-walking, musical Rastafarian, but he was also well-read and a deft teacher of island politics. He awoke at 6:00 every day for his morning run. He didn't drink alcohol or eat meat, but I suspect he did "practice his religion."

Our favorite of many Dread'I sayings is, "everyting is everyting." For example, when I see him, I might say, "How are you today, Dread'I?"

"Well, good; everyting is everyting, yah know."

Or I might ask, "How are the CD sales on the beach?"

"Dey good today, today tis good day. Ah, yah know, everyting is everyting."

One December, a few days before Christmas, we were at Orient when we bumped into our good buddy. "Hey, Dread'I, what's up?"

"Ya mon, all my love, nice to see yah and Ceendi."

"Today is T. J.'s birthday. We were supposed to pick up him and Rachelle at the airport this afternoon, but their plane was cancelled because of the volcanic ash from Montserrat. Can you believe it? They're stuck in Puerto Rico for the night."

"Ya mon, give dem all my best. Everyting is everything. T. J. will always remember Ash Day."

Tijon now had a beautiful island CD for sale. However, we recognized that all customers might not enjoy the energy of reggae. Since we boasted a "collection," we determined *Tropical Reggae* needed a baby brother. Being jazz fans, we thought such an offering might fit nicely.

We asked Dread'I if he knew any local jazz artists, and he referred us to his good friend and local sax master, Connis Vanterpool. Connis was to perform that Saturday evening at Axums Café, an artsy, second-floor setting on Front Street in Phillipsburg. Dread'I promised to call Connis to tell him we were coming.

As we crowded into the small, steamy alcove, the music of Connis on his sax entranced us. Seeing him blowing the sax invoked a sense of familiarity. We were reminded of an experience a few years prior when we had taken our first ferry ride on a Sunday morning from Marigot to Anguilla.

Anguilla is a thirty-five-square-mile, flat, low-lying island of coral and limestone. The population of fifteen thousand constitutes a self-governed British overseas territory. It has beautiful beaches, friendly people, and little development other than a few incredible five-star resorts. Once, a few years earlier, we started a conversation on the ferry with a man who looked to us like a male Whoopi Goldberg. He had long dreadlocks and a big smile. "Are you from Anguilla?" we asked.

"No, mon, I jus' go there each Sunday to play music."

"We've never been to Anguilla. What's fun to do there?"

"Come to Johnno's, mon. It's a beach bar where we play."

"What time do you start?"

"Not till afternoon, maybe two or so, but there's good food and it's a nice beach, mon."

We thanked him, exchanged names, and said we might see him there.

At the ferry landing we hailed a taxi and, trying not to act like tourists looking for a road tour, blurted out "Johnno's" when our driver asked, "Where to?" About ten minutes later we arrived on the other side of the island at a shack painted in multiple bright colors, complete with Anguillans playing dominos on a wooden barrel out front.

An hour or two later we ordered some locally caught fish and patiently waited for the live music. We found our ferry buddy and visited with him until he was beckoned to the stage. We ordered some tropical drinks, propped our feet up, and basked in the entertaining sounds of the jazz band.

The sax player at Axums, although seemingly a little heavier, strongly reminded us of that artist we'd seen at Johnno's years earlier. Connis took a break and we introduced ourselves. We stood out from the local native crowd, and he likely recognized us as Dread'I's friends. We asked if we possibly had met him at Johnno's a few years earlier.

"Ya mon, I go to Johnno's every Sunday," he replied.

"Would you have any interest in putting together a jazz CD for our new record label?" I asked.

"Ya mon, let's do it." We easily struck a deal similar to Dread'I's, giving Tijon a new artist with the subsequent CD simply titled, *The Tijon Collection: Tropical Jazz*. Creative name-givers we were not. Still, we wanted to fill Tijon with what we hoped would be appealing and unique items.

Our relationship with Connis developed as it had with Dread'I. We now were friends with two of the island's best musicians. Since it was a small island, we would bump into each other frequently and periodically get together.

Our new friends reflected our transition to island life. Our peers had gone from being corporate associates in suits and ties to being barefoot buddies born and raised in a Third World paradise.

We loved our new CDs. Both were upbeat, loud, and quite different from the music we'd been listening to in the States. Now, when we decided to play our favorite American CDs, something seemed to be missing. Perhaps it was the energy of the island beat, perhaps it was our relationship with the musicians. All we knew was that everything was everything.

The business plan was to play these CDs at the shop and sell them when customers asked what the good vibes were. After repeated playing, however, Cyndi expressed a bit of concern.

"I love the music, but I'm not sure I can listen to the same loud beat every hour of every day the shop is open," she surmised.

That led us to the conclusion that we needed to add another sound to our Tijon music collection. We researched softer, more romantic music.

A month before our unofficial opening in December 2007, we celebrated my fiftieth year on Mother Earth at a bed and breakfast in the hill country of Fredericksburg, Texas. In the romantically cozy second-floor room was a CD player complete with one CD, titled *Black and White*. We both remembered putting it in, pushing play, and listening to soft piano music by an artist named Danny Wright. We had never heard such an exquisite pianist with such gentle, expressive hands on the keys. We were immediate fans. The music coincided with a beautiful session of intimacy, further adding to the musical memory.

The CD's back cover claimed the artist hailed from Texas. I Googled his website and discovered that he was from Fort Worth and currently lived in a suburb near our Texas home. I contacted him, inquiring if he had any interest in recording for a new, upstart label. We agreed to meet for lunch in Colleyville, near Danny's house. Cyndi was back in St. Martin working at Tijon but was excited about the quest.

I reached out to shake Danny's hand, but it was heavily bandaged. Danny explained that he was to have surgery in a few days as the result of an injury he received while playing a game with his son. He was obviously concerned, since he made his living playing piano. We sat down for a luncheon that started with a bottle of a crisp California chardonnay.

Danny was a child prodigy. One evening, he and his parents had returned from the movie *Dr. Zhivago*, and he sat down at his parents' piano. He started playing the movie's theme song without any sheet music. He was only four years of age. He would later study piano and be selected to be a member of the famed Texas Boys Choir. When we first heard him, he'd sold over four million CDs and had been named as one of the top ten artists in his genre.

As we traded family stories, I discovered that Danny's parents had both recently passed away. Danny, still grieving, was the only child of their union. His life partner, Ed, had previously adopted two youngsters, and Danny enjoyed being a parent to them as well.

Being the dealmaker that I am, I struck an agreement for Danny to join the Tijon label. The new CD would be called *The Tijon Collection: L'Arrangement*. Hey, it sounded French.

When Cyndi returned to Texas in May, we hooked up with Danny and Ed for a delicious dinner at the same restaurant in Colleyville. Graciously, they invited us to their house for an after-dinner drink. Danny had recovered from his surgery and sat at his Steinway grand, giving us an amazing private concert. It was our first time seeing Danny perform live, and we were mesmerized.

I believe the best business partners become friends, and as with Dread'I and Connis before, Danny was no exception. We invited Danny and Ed to our island villa over for the New Year holiday. Together we enjoyed the beaches and fine foods.

During Danny's visit we stopped in the Red Piano one evening, co-owned by our young Canadian friend Colin. It was a busy and fun sing-along bar. During a break by the raucous performer, we encouraged Danny to the piano for a few songs. He sat down, positioned himself, and let his fingers fly. The noisy club quickly calmed and quieted in pleasant shock and awe, listening intently to the impromptu concert. After two songs, Danny took a polite bow to resounding applause and rejoined us. We departed with Danny, proudly feeling part of a celebrity entourage. T. J, usually a hip-hop fan, had joined us at the club, and he immediately became a Danny fan, actually packing his CD for his college apartment in Georgia.

Leaving the Red Piano, we drove to Axums, where Connis would be performing. Dread'I, whom Danny had previously met on the beach, was also part of the crowd. Connis stepped to the stage and invited Dread'I to join him for one song. It was a fabulous experience.

* * * * *

Before we eventually moved to the island full-time, I continued working my day job for the bowling association in Texas. I was helping to plan their 2008 annual convention in Orlando. It was to be a grand celebration, and the conference would close with the exclusive rental of City Walk at Universal Theme Park. I had contracted with a few bands for the different venues, including the Temptations, Diamond Rio, and Frankie Valli as headliners and thought, why not have a little jazz and reggae as one of the opening acts?

Connis and Dread'I readily accepted the gig in return for airfare, hotel costs, and a bit of spending money. Connis had been to the States often, having attended Berklee College of Music in Boston and later working at Gloria Estefan's studio in Miami. He'd also been a part of a band that opened for Spyro Gyra.

Dread'I had never been to the States, and his prior visa attempts had been denied. I investigated and filed an abundance of paperwork for his one-week work permit. Once it was acquired, he had to fly to the closest American embassy, in Barbados, to complete his visa.

As anticipated, the two were big hits at the convention. Their superb performance was matched by their personalities and interaction with the conference attendees. After the big gala at Universal, we rode a shuttle bus back to the hotel with the pair. A couple of young ladies, in high spirits from imbibing spirits, started shouting in a slurred accent, "Dread'I, Dread'I, sing to us, Dread'I!" He complied by taking out his guitar and singing. Connis was just a few rows back, but, impervious to the chants, he lazily dozed off.

In planning that conference, the volunteer leaders of the Bowling Hall of Fame expressed the need for a first-time-ever entertainer during their evening fundraising gala. Because they sought an elegant sound, I asked Danny if he was interested in performing at a discount for a good cause. Danny graciously agreed.

Danny met up with his previous island acquaintances, Dread'I and Connis. The three were becoming friends, bonding through music. While we were all in Orlando, I had a brainstorm: would they be interested in recording a new CD for the growing Tijon Collection? They wholeheartedly agreed, and I flew Danny to St. Martin, where he spent a week in Connis's small but sufficient studio. This promised to be a most unusual trio.

The possibilities for the sound created by such distinct personalities made the blend most unique. The three musicians got along famously as they recorded tracks for the CD. Connis played and, with the assistance of a friend, served as studio engineer. We hired a photographer who snapped beach shots of the trio for the CD cover.

We produced a CD package. I had already planned my last bowling convention in the States: the 2009 convention was to be in Las Vegas. I arranged for the new trio to open for the headliner, comedian Bill

Engvall. The crowds in Orlando in 2008 had loved them individually, and as a threesome they received similar accolades in Las Vegas.

We waited to officially release their CD at a first-ever "all-four-island-club" Rotary fundraiser at the Dutch-side Westin hotel in November 2010. The trio donated their time and played to a packed house.

The show began with Danny opening with "Lara's Theme" from *Dr. Zhivago*, the same song that inspired him as a four-year-old. He moved to "Amazing Grace," then played a few songs he'd arranged or composed, including two that had been used for a winning Olympic ice-dancing competition.

As orchestrated, Connis interrupted Danny from the back of the room, walking to the stage while playing to Danny's version of "Dueling Banjos," with the piano and sax going at it. A few songs later Dread'I walked onstage to his song "Sons and Daughters," then went into "Summertime" and "The Girl from Ipanema." After intermission, Danny opened with an incredible rendition of "Carol of the Bells" with Connis and Dread'I returning to the stage for a few songs.

The event concluded with another group, Remo and his band Barbed Wire, who sang one original and one Bob Marley tune. The initial trio returned, joining Remo to sing the evening's final song, Marley's classic "One Love." A lengthy standing ovation followed. The proceeds, over $30,000, benefited the children on both sides of the island.

Remo, like Dread'I, was originally from Dominica. He was an amazingly talented reggae musician who composed his own songs and performed around the island. Typically, he would strip down to a tank top, showcasing his muscular build. With his high forehead and long, braided hair pulled back, he reminded me of Stevie Wonder.

Remo, who had once toured in Europe, asked if I would help him with contracts for his local bookings. I was happy to help to the extent of my limited abilities. Of course, having no real experience in the entertainment industry, I never charged him. He returned the favor by periodically grilling fish for Cyndi, me, and his wife, Jerri, and by teaching me the basics of cricket.

* * * * *

The Tijon Collection began with a desire to simply produce and sell CDs. It ended with the creation of a new trio with a brilliantly distinct sound. The music remains a popular choice for customers at Tijon and is also offered for sale by the artists, on the Internet, and at other shops in St. Martin and the States. Our goal was three-fold: to have a CD collection for sale that was exclusive to our brand, to befriend local musicians, and to have fun. We've been hitting a triple, and the experience has been wonderful.

CHAPTER 16

HOURS, HOLIDAYS, AND SALES

The French enjoy life and are proud of it; we learned this early on. During one of our visits to a French restaurant in Grand Case we anxiously, but politely, asked the waiter how much longer our food would take. It had been about forty-five minutes since we'd ordered.

"You hurry? Enjoy life! It come soon," he said with a broad smile.

We were surprised by the comment and took some time to ponder both his words and his attitude. When the food, in its glorious presentation, finally arrived and we took our first bite, we looked at each other and smiled. It was all worthwhile. Not just the food, but the ambiance and relaxed setting. We discovered that on this French island, food is cooked slowly, eaten slowly, and meant to be enjoyed at a slow pace. It even takes time to get *l'addition*, the check, because the table is yours for the evening. How un-American—but how nice!

The workday on the French side is interrupted by a two-and-a-half hour lunch break. Pretty shocking when we plan a trip to Marigot and arrive around 1:00 p.m. only to find that all the stores, other than restaurants, are shuttered.

The Spanish term their midday break a *siesta*: a short nap taken in the early afternoon, often after the midday meal. Most of the French islanders don't have time for such a nap, being too busy wining, dining, and visiting—that is, enjoying life. They celebrate this philosophy through taking a leisurely lunch or a beach break. Admittedly, it didn't take me long to master the local custom.

Remember that French traditions were an important part of the equation that drew us to St. Martin in the first place. Actually, we opened Tijon by one-upping the French: our posted shop hours totaled only twenty-five per week. We were determined to work hard, enjoy life—and to go to the beach.

In addition to the limited workweek, the island celebrates more holidays than even Hallmark has created. Our accountant explained that the French have twelve holidays in addition to the eight holidays exclusive to the French West Indies. That makes twenty days, and on occasion that can be difficult for employers. Also, that didn't include official time off for Carnivale and other obscure holidays.

One such holiday celebrated by banks and many businesses on the French side was *Mi-Carême*, or Mid-Lent. This is traditionally the time when people dress in disguise and go to houses, singing, dancing, and asking for treats. Today, it's valued more as a day off work.

Many of the same holidays we find in the States and Canada are celebrated, except that in the Caribbean they come with more time off. They include Christmas, Easter, New Year's Day, a Labor Day on May 1, Good Friday, Ascension Day, Boxing Day (December 26), Bastille Day, All Saints Day, and other holidays too arcane to note.

Often the locals themselves have no idea about the reason behind the holiday, but they're happy to celebrate it. Once, we were listening to a French-side radio station that was actually having a discussion in English. The DJ was asking callers when All Saints Day would be celebrated this year, the Monday or Tuesday after the Sunday Halloween. Half the callers said Monday, half said Tuesday. Turns out the government was closed on Monday, with other businesses playing it safe and closing both days.

Shops are required by law to close on many holidays. As a consumer, I found it frustrating to drive to the grocery, hardware store, or bank, only to find it closed. It made little sense to me as an entrepreneur. Don't get me wrong: as shop owners living in a tropical paradise with no debt or rent, life was good. Problem was, we were never sure what holidays were when, and if we had to be closed.

One Monday morning, I drove to Marigot to drop some papers off at our accountants only to discover . . . easy parking. Something was wrong. I should have known: it was a holiday. Not only was her door locked, but all the shops surrounding her office were closed up tightly. Oops, our shop was open.

A car drove by with the window down. I immediately recognized the older man as one of my Rotary buddies.

"Hi, Justin," I said. "Hey, is today a holiday?"

"Oh yes, 'tis Pentacost. All shops are closed, and 'tis a holiday Thursday also."

I thanked him and returned home to discover that Pentecost was a holiday celebrated only on the French side; Dutch-side shops were open. Not sure what the upcoming Thursday celebration was, I decided to investigate a bit. I asked a local school-age girl.

She asked, "Were you open Monday?"

"Yes, we didn't know it was a holiday."

"Thursday is holiday, too," she added.

"I heard that. Do you have school that day?"

"No, it's holiday."

"What's the holiday for?"

She thought for a moment, put her hand to her face, and gave her honest reply: "Because people aren't working."

That night we were at a tourism event and cornered one of our favorite persons, Terttu, a Finnish woman married to a Frenchman, Maurice. He was the long-standing general manager of the Hotel Beach Plaza.

"Terttu, tomorrow is a holiday, correct?"

"Yes."

"What's the holiday for?"

She thought a few moments, then apologized. "I don't know how to say it in English."

Naturally, that made us curious. We opened our doors on Thursday, figuring if we didn't know what holiday it was, we might as well be open.

Olivier, a local jewelry vendor originally from France, drove by and dropped in. He gave us the answer: it was Abolition Day, the day slavery ended in 1848 on the French side, a glorious day diminished by the fact that so few knew its origins, including our young friend who was a descendent of those so terribly oppressed.

If holidays were abundant under French laws, sale offerings were rare and unique by those same laws. Not only does French law dictate that all prices must be in euros, which is understandable, but the law is also very specific on when and how businesses can offer sales.

Fortunately, the island government, although a territory of France, understood that 80 percent of its revenues were from tourism and worked to accommodate the struggling and/or carefree shop owners. We discovered that enforcement of these strict interpretations was rare.

Our sales at the boutique were typically markdowns of slow-moving items or inducements on items for which we were overstocked. One of our first post-holiday markdowns was our handpainted Christmas ornaments bearing our logo; we marked them down from eighteen euros to ten.

This was a particularly good sale, because two people on a bus tour purchased one each. We completely forgot about the discount and inadvertently charged them full price. They either hadn't seen the markdown or weren't paying attention at the cash register. We felt terrible, not realizing what we had done until the bus had left. As we grew older, would we need to put a disclaimer on our discounted tags: "Sale price valid only if you remind the forgetful clerks at checkout"?

Some items needing a sale could be labeled our "clunkers." Sometimes we win, sometimes we don't. We suspect most retail shops purchase a few such pieces now and then. I thought of my father, who opened a liquor store in later life, ordering ten cases of some unheard-of California wine on sale. The wine was at a cheap price for a reason; it didn't taste particularly good and, as a no-brand, was a tough sale. Some things resell, some things don't.

Thinking of the Hawaiian Tropic swimsuit models, I wanted to compete by adding a women's custom swimsuit for our new Caribe Baie line of sun care products. I meticulously sent off my design to a plant in Thailand and, after final approval via pictures on the Internet, ordered a number of red bikinis in various sizes. The final look was an attractive bikini-v bottom with an athletic, over-one-shoulder top. The logo Caribe Baie logo was strategically plastered across the chest.

Cyndi, although liking the look, expressed doubts as to any consumer demand for such an unfamiliar brand. What did she know? I had to know more about woman's swimsuit fashions, right? And then . . .

Upon receipt, the tops looked beautiful, and the bottoms were cute—but surprisingly tiny. The units labeled "large" would at best be a U.S. "small." The smalls couldn't be for adults. We ordered substitute matching bottoms from a U.S. manufacturer. I was proud of the brand apparel and neatly placed it on a mannequin in our shop, with a retail price of sixty euros.

Cyndi simultaneously discovered some lower sitting, nicely folding, yellow nylon beach chairs that could have our Caribe Baie logo imprinted on them. Negotiating a good price, she ordered a hundred units, despite my concerns about both storage and resale value to tourists, who arrive and depart by airplane.

Cyndi reasoned there were many Americans with condos and time-shares who should be interested in a good-looking, compact, light-weight beach chair. The nicely displayed chair retailed at fifty euros.

Our first brief season in winter of 2008 brought sporadic activity to our shop, with most items receiving at least one sale. The forlorn bikinis and beach chairs, however, went untouched. A contest naturally developed in our second season as to who would be the first to sell one of their prized purchases. Cyndi was her own worst enemy. As the boutique manager, she smartly placed the bikinis on a half-price sale of thirty euros each. She believed the chairs retained their value and didn't need such a gimmick. Guess what happened?

At the end of our part-time 2009 season, the scorecard ran five to zero: five reduced-price bikinis sold with *nada* as far as any chairs moving out the door. Each bikini sale resulted in little profit but did deliver to me the satisfaction of winning our little contest. I gave Cyndi my best little celebration dance and said, "I told you they'd sell." Even if we didn't profit from them, they were being worn by beautiful bodies on the beach (unless they all frequented the clothing-optional section at Orient).

In a sarcastic effort to assist Cyndi's chair sales, I suggested a promotion whereby every customer purchasing an eight-euro bottle of our suntan lotion would get a free chair. Cyndi glared, and I dropped it. Years of marriage make me wise up quickly.

In 2010, our first full season, we did sell one chair to a local French person and immediately wanted to know more about this purchaser. But the language barrier prevented that. We now offer our friends and renters "free" chair usage during their stay. The good news is that both items remain for sale in our shop, and it has cost us nothing to replenish the unending inventory. The glass-half-full theory proves to be extra helpful at times.

PART V

LIVING LIFE AS AN ISLANDER

PERFUME FACT

Where should one apply
perfume? According to
Coco Chanel, "Wherever
one wants to be kissed."

CHAPTER 17

WELCOME TO A NEW CULTURE!

One starry, starry night not so long ago, I finally joined Cyndi permanently on the island. It was November 2009, and we decided to take a leisurely stroll down our narrow village beach road lined with small, intimate restaurants. First we stopped across the street to chat with the local security guard. A hundred yards later we ran into neighbors walking home, said hi, and chatted for a bit. Another two blocks down we stopped and waved to a shopkeeper friend and had a short visit. We were in our new home and starting to slow down life so we could get to know our island friends better.

Communication is an important aspect of cross-cultural competence. As expatriates, we need to communicate with a multitude of ethnicities, and it begins with the greeting.

In the United States, as in other countries, looking someone in the eye and giving a firm handshake is the recognized greeting norm. There's conflicting debate whether a woman should initiate the handshake with a man. Men may quickly kiss the cheek of a woman.

All of these things are acceptable in some cultures and not in others. In India, women would never initiate the handshake and will only shake hands with other women, but never with men. In China the greeting is usually a slight nod and bow. Italians enjoy long handshakes often extending to warm hugs with frequent kisses.

How to best greet others in French St. Martin? When in Rome, do as the Romans do, so they say. Men greet men with a handshake. That's easy, but men greet women and women greet each other with the custom known as *faire la bise,* "air-kissing" one another on both cheeks to say hello and goodbye. It's common and so quick it can hardly be described as a kiss; it's more like a touching of cheeks.

During the swine flu pandemic threat in the fall of 2009, there was a French declaration discouraging these pecks. Some French schools, companies, and a health ministry hotline were telling students and employees to avoid the ritual for fear that the pandemic could make it the kiss of death, or at least illness, as winter approached.

In Dutch St. Martin the greeting escalates to three kisses, alternating cheeks. Go figure. That begged the question: how do we greet a Dutch national visiting on the French side? Would something like baseball's interleague rules on the designated hitter apply, where the home field determines the policy?

Suddenly a friendly greeting became considerably more complicated than a simple hello. Greeting other visitors or tourists generally begins with the typical handshake. And if we meet them once, odds are we'll meet them again on the island. As I've mentioned before, a good thing about the island is that it's like a small town where everyone knows everyone else, and meeting tourists means we'll bump into them three or four more times. Of course, the bad thing about the island is that it's like a small town where . . . everyone knows everyone else.

One of our earliest greetings while on the island searching for property involved meeting an American couple at a beach bar where a TV was broadcasting a Sunday Minnesota Vikings game. Being die-hard Vikes fans, we were compelled to watch, only to learn that the woman next to us also had origins in Minnesota.

We introduced ourselves in the Minnesota way, by shaking hands and saying "hi" and "you betcha." Our new friend, Kathy, told us she was married to Randy Moss. That caught our attention. "You mean the Viking wide-out Randy Moss?" Not him, she told us, but the Randy Moss who enjoyed his own fame as an ESPN horse racing analyst. Kathy was a beautiful, petite blonde, while Randy looked like Trapper John, MD, without the beard. The couple now called Tulsa home.

After invariably bumping into them a few more times, including giving them a ride back to the boat on a day trip we both happened to take to St. Barts, they invited us to dinner at their rented villa, high up the hill in the neighborhood of Pointe Blanche. The owner was their friend and was looking to sell. We had friends visiting who were looking to buy.

We have made friends of many American visitors like Kathy and Randy Moss. They enjoy our story of wanderlust, while we enjoy talking "American." We relish retelling how we went on an adventure and kept coming back for the delicious foods, and we've stayed because of the many friendships, local and otherwise. That's what this book is about as well: a celebration of all those things and a declaration that you can do something different with your life if you wish to, despite how challenging it may seem at times.

CHAPTER 18

REPAIRS AND MAINTENANCE IN A THIRD-WORLD PARADISE

In certain ancient philosophies everything balances; for each good occurrence, something bad happens and vice versa. That's what creates the harmonious energies of life.

Living in the Caribbean is good. It's paradise. Trying to maintain and repair property is bad. It's Third World. It balances. Parts are often unavailable, and labor runs the gamut from an exceedingly expensive contractor who insures his work to an undocumented local person.

Regardless, when the repairman says he's coming, it's similar to the cable guy in the States: if he says he'll be there at 1:00 p.m., expect 2:00–3:00 p.m., if at all, and if he doesn't come, never expect a call. If you're not sure what I mean, let me share a few island experiences that clearly illustrate the difficulties.

CISTERN REPAIR

Most island buildings have cisterns to collect rainwater for daily usage. Water is a precious commodity on islands such as St. Martin. That's because the island is derived from volcanic rock and has no rivers. Lack of rivers, however, does present one positive effect: the beaches stay clean and, without river water flowing, mud and debris aren't deposited into the bays. City water from desalination plants is available and quite drinkable, but costly.

The villa was superbly designed for the cistern to pump water to our outdoor faucets and water heater. All other water arrived via the desalination plant. If city water was lost, say, to a hurricane or temporary shutdown, the system was designed to pump cistern water to all faucets. Of course, electricity was needed for the pump, which might pose a problem after a tropical storm.

During Christmas 2008 some good friends from Minneapolis came to visit. Mark and Connie Andrew stayed in one of our rentals and mentioned the water wasn't working. I checked the meter at the street and realized somebody had turned our city water off. I promptly turned the handle and saw water spurting out of a pipe. Obviously, a Good Samaritan had passed by, noticed water leaking, and shut off the valve to save us money. Our cistern had kicked in for all faucets, including drinking water, and was now drained. Apparently some time had passed. What's most fascinating is that neither the Andrews nor we noticed any difference between the filtered cistern water and the good city water.

We promptly called our plumber to fix the meter leak and filled the cistern with our hose. This task took all day and was costly. The cistern was located underneath our porch, but it's quite big. We estimate it to be about ten feet by thirty feet and nine feet high. It was the size of a recreational pool.

We thought life had returned to normal—that is, until we discovered the cistern was dry a week later. That seemed impossible, since we hadn't used that much from the outside faucet or the water heater.

Our cistern had developed a crack after it first ran dry. A tree root had worked its way inside, looking for water. Now we needed a cistern repairman, and there was only one listed on the island. We called and the owner promptly came over to inspect. He discovered the tree roots and announced he could fix it for only $4,500 USD with a five-year warranty.

What? We knew this contractor had a monopoly on cistern repair. City water was expensive, but it would take years to recover that repair bill utilizing cistern water.

We decided to put off the repair and told the contractor that we'd get back to him. I came up with my own plan to board up the cistern. I proceeded to do just that to prevent it from caving in, forcing us to become exclusive city water users.

A few days later Cyndi got a surprise. There were two young men with a ladder in our dry, muddy-bottomed cistern. Naturally she asked what they were doing, and they responded that the contractor had sent them to start working on the repairs. She immediately called the contractor and explained that we hadn't authorized a repair and couldn't afford it. He offered to knock off a few hundred bucks. Thanks, but no thanks.

I had arrived on the scene by this time and introduced myself to the young guys. The older of the two said his name was Roger and asked, "How much were you quoted?"

"$4,500. I can't afford that."

"That's crazy, mon. I do all the work in two days and get thirty-five dollars a day. I fix it much cheaper on my time off."

"Really, how much?"

"You buy supplies and pay me something."

"How much are supplies?

"Around $300."

"How about if I pay the supplies and give you $500?"

"I do it this weekend, but I need a ride."

"Okay, where do you live?"

"Do you know the gas station in French Quarter?"

"Yep."

"Keep going past. You see car wash, take right after, go up road and through gate. I'm there."

I drove Roger to the hardware store, where he directed me in purchasing the necessary supplies. We drove back to the home and he went to work. I later discovered he was on the island illegally, so he didn't drive much, because he didn't want to be stopped and asked for papers that he didn't have.

By Monday afternoon the cistern appeared brand new. It had a sparkling coat of waterproof paint and the cracks were filled in. "Roger, it looks beautiful, brand new. You do great work."

"Thanks, mon."

"How long should it hold up? Your boss offered a five-year warranty."

He smiled and said, "I give you a lifetime guarantee, mon."

Cyndi and I couldn't help but wonder if Roger was being taken advantage of by his boss. Another young lady who lived illegally nearby told us that before having children she used to work at a souvenir shop in Phillipsburg and was paid twenty euros a day. If it were a Sunday or holiday she would get twenty-five dollars a day. It was an eight-hour workday with an added half-hour lunch break, but she had to eat her lunch in the store.

I suggested the shop owner was being unfair, and she responded, "It's more money than I would make in my homeland of Guyana." That issue apparently is a matter of perspective and could be debated for years.

CAR REPAIR

The first car we purchased on the island was a 2000 Nissan Xterra. We wanted a smaller SUV to haul equipment and packages. We found one that would work nicely and purchased it from a car-leasing agency on the island that assisted many of the island's medical students with their transportation needs.

The good news with the Xterra was that it was a fairly uncommon make on the island and so would be unlikely to be stolen for car parts. The bad news was the Nissan dealer stocked few of our needed parts, needing to get them from Puerto Rico or direct from Japan. Ordering and receiving parts could take two to six weeks.

Since one of the reasons we purchased an SUV was to haul packages and equipment, it could be challenging to wait for repairs. Constructing an island lab requires certain items. Some were shipped from the States, and the remainder were purchased on the island.

St. Martin has an outstanding restaurant supply house called PDG, with vast inventory at relatively decent prices in either Dutch-side (U.S.) or French electrical voltage. We purchased our stainless steel tables, hand mixers, and other items non-specific to a chemical lab from

PDG. We also needed commercial equipment to mix our lotions and crèmes. At PDG I found a good buy on a ten-quart pizza dough mixer with French plugs. They offered to deliver it, but I proudly pointed to the SUV and simply said, "Load it up."

The three-hundred-pound load fit into the back of the Xterra with minimal concern. I figured that three-hundred pounds couldn't easily move. Stupid me to not realize that most of the weight was in the motor of the mixer, located at the top end of the unit.

As I made my way home I steered the car left around a curve near Columbier. This made the top end of the crate veer right . . . through the backside window. The rest of my journey was at a slower pace, since I had the top end of the crate sticking out the window.

I arrived home and found some assistance to help me unload the mixer. Then I did what all people do in a car-window emergency: I bandaged it with duct tape. I was thankful that the mixer motor worked fine and hadn't had any issues as a result of my lack of foresight. I didn't know about any car glass shops on the island and immediately drove the thirty minutes it took to get to the island's only Nissan dealer, located on the French side.

I arrived at 11:30 a.m., and the nice service attendant said they could help, but to come back after their 12:00–2:00 p.m. lunch break; then they would fix it. I arrived back promptly at 2:00 p.m. The friendly service manager computerized our information and reviewed the car title to confirm ownership. He was fluent in French and English.

Around 3:00 p.m., with the car in the shop and the remainder of the glass and duct tape removed, the nice man informed me they didn't have the glass; it needed to be specially ordered from the mainland. I was unaware if mainland meant the United States or France, but it didn't much matter. I was told it would be on-island in two weeks.

I'll admit that I was a bit perturbed. This information could have been relayed sooner, but I was happy it could be fixed. I asked them to re-tape the window and left a deposit for the special-order glass. They said they'd call when it arrived.

By now I had learned not to seriously expect a call back in situations like this. I found it difficult to call them because of their French voice-mail system. One day Cyndi stopped in the dealership to follow up. It had been about three weeks, and she discovered the glass was in. They told her to make an appointment.

Cyndi arrived later that day for her appointment, and the car was driven into the shop shortly after. After sitting there about an hour Cyndi was told they had received the wrong glass and would need to reorder it. They apologized and said they would call.

This time the dealership actually did call two weeks later when the glass arrived. We made our third appointment. Cyndi took the car in at 2:00 p.m. that day. After it was in the shop for an hour she received word that they couldn't find the special-order glass. They weren't sure if it had arrived or if they simply couldn't find it, claiming the person who had called us was off for the day. They apologized sincerely and proactively brought the general manager over. They said they would call us when they located the glass.

I had to start wondering if this crème mixer was getting more expensive than it was worth. And when I wasn't wondering, Cyndi would remind me. To think it all started with turning down free delivery from the wholesaler.

The dealership called one week later with the glass in, and we scheduled our fourth appointment. This time, I picked the small straw; I'd be dealing with the dealership that day. The service manager remained sincere and apologetic, and the window was finally fixed. In getting the invoice I asked if there was any discount for the delays. He checked with the general manager and knocked off 10 percent. *C'est la vie.*

PROPERTY MAINTENANCE

Our final trip to the island, two years after opening Tijon but before relocating permanently to St. Martin, gave us a real reminder of the good, the bad, and the ugly of island life. We departed Texas in August 2009 for a week in St. Martin to collect our one-year residency card, which had been approved the previous June. We had to pick it up prior to August 23 but were warned to wait until closer to the deadline to be sure the cards were ready.

The bad came in the form of maintenance issues. Everybody who owns a second home knows how frustrating and difficult they can be. Plus, issues seem to invariably pop up while we're away and, of course, that means we have no way of knowing.

We arrived late in the day on Saturday evening, August 15. We immediately discovered that our refrigerator wasn't working, and we swiftly removed all of the smelly stuff that had been purchased as food. The Sunday morning sunshine brought a new day as well as our twenty-ninth wedding anniversary. We walked the six or so blocks to our favorite bakery for *pain de chocolat* and coffee, knowing we could overcome the icebox failure.

Returning to our villa, we noticed that our toilet leaked when flushed, telling us the seal was shot. Unlike the fridge, I could fix that with a trip to Ace Hardware.

Before leaving for our errand runs, Cyndi checked the villa upstairs, only to find water on the kitchen floor. This had resulted from a cracked plastic pipe located by the shutoff valve. Cyndi put a bucket under the drip and brought out the mops. I'd be lying if I didn't say that Cyndi and I were nervous about checking on our Tijon building next door. Luck didn't seem to be going our way at that particular moment.

Sure enough, we discovered something classified as bad when we entered Tijon. A few roof chunks had fallen in, and water was on the floor. Two-thirds of the building had a flat roof, newly remodeled a few years earlier, and now it had a leak. We got more buckets and the mop and started to clean up.

It didn't take long to start feeling the excessive warmth inside the building. We both looked at each other and neither of us wanted to say it. We knew it, though: the air conditioners weren't running, representing a threat to our lab and chemicals. We were fortunate enough to get the air conditioners back on and later discovered that our brand of air conditioner didn't automatically turn back on after a power outage. There are frequent power outages in St. Martin, so from that moment on we knew that we'd have to ask Jackie to stop by the building on a frequent basis to check things out when we were off-island.

We put together a list and started tackling one issue at a time. First, we would go to Ace Hardware to get a toilet seal. I retrieved the car battery, hooked it up, and amazingly, the engine started. We zipped the windows down for our thirty-minute drive to go get the toilet seal. Halfway there we passed through a light rain, requiring us to close the windows—only the windows didn't move upwards or anywhere else. Now we were hitting the ugly phase.

The ugly continued when we returned to our villa and it took two hours for Cyndi and me to repair a toilet that should have taken just a few minutes to fix. As Oliver Hardy proudly informed Stan Laurel, "Stan, our two minds are equal to one."

We believed it useless to try and call any repairmen on Sunday, so we did what they were likely doing: we headed to the beach for a late afternoon break. The beach never let us down and was the most low-maintenance place we knew; sunscreen and drinks covered it.

The next day Cyndi drove to Phillipsburg, where we had purchased the refrigerator. They gave us the phone number of their repairman, but said he was off-island on holiday for a month.

I called our Tijon architect Jym about our roof, and he said he would get the roofers who installed it to come back out. It was under warranty.

We drove our Xterra to the Nissan dealer, who manually raised the windows and determined that the switch was shot. The €170 part wasn't in stock and would take a few weeks to be shipped in. The car air conditioner had gone out, needing a switch that also wasn't stocked. It was a hot week, tooling around the island with no A/C. When I reflect back on my dreams, I had been happy my car didn't need a heater. It did indeed need an air conditioner.

Eventually yin will meet yang and all will balance out. We called our repair buddies, who were friends of Jack and Jackie Jack. Erickson the plumber arrived Monday morning to fix the water leak upstairs; Keith the electrician came shortly after, located a bad defrost switch on the fridge, and returned Tuesday with the part in hand.

Also on Tuesday, the roofers came out and in a few hours had found three holes in the plastic sheathing, which they fixed at no cost to us. Jack said he would get the plastering and painting inside finished after we left. He was true to his word and did just that.

Finally, it was time for the initial purpose of our trip. We arrived at the Prefecture on Wednesday around 11:00 a.m., simply needing to pick up our residency cards, or so we thought. We were duly informed by an angry, older male worker we hadn't seen before, and who spoke little English, that we had to return the following day at 8:00 a.m. and stand in the general line.

We followed his instructions, returning Thursday around 7:30 a.m. to count twenty-five people in front of us. Our turn at the window came around 9:15 a.m. They took our names and said they would call us at noon over the loudspeaker. We left and returned a few hours later to successfully retrieve our cards.

During our usual morning stroll to the bakery the next day for our *pain de chocolat,* we shouted *bonjour* to our usual locals along the street. We bumped into our friends Stephanie, who ran the Sexy Fruits shop on Orient Beach; Mike and Marilyn, the retired American expats who lived near the bakery; and Julie, our Tijon model, who was in the car while her boyfriend Nick was picking up baguettes. We said hello to Arnold, better known as Kela, a local who liked to talk NFL football. He was an avid New York Giants fan.

It was this sense of community that we missed when not in St. Martin, and it reminded us of just how much we still wanted this life, problems and all. It was a good feeling after a few hectic days of unplanned business.

We fled the island exhausted, but claiming success. We had fixed all our unexpected problems and knew that, when we went back, problems wouldn't be as stressful if they came up. Our next trip was to be our last "trip." We'd be on the island permanently to live the "island life, mon" approach to unexpected situations that came our way.

TELEPHONE REPAIR

Electrical blackouts and water stoppages had become commonplace to us on the island. It was a first, and hopefully last, when our business line went out during the high season in April 2010.

This was one of the few repairs that hadn't been our fault or responsibility to fix. All we needed to do was notify the telephone company that it wasn't working. With anxiety over losing business, we did that promptly. We had wanted to use our cell phones for everything, but our bank wouldn't give us a wireless device for processing credit cards. They only had a certain number available, and the beach bars were the recipients of those.

We headed to France Telecom in Marigot to stand in line and hope we'd get Jessica, the nice lady who set us up with the line, to help us fix it. It would be much easier to stand in line for this than to try and navigate the French phone system. She promptly put our repair paperwork through. We were unable to accept credit cards during this time but were able to take advantage of our neighbor's kindness to help us with certain manual transactions. Some of them still had working phone lines, but not many.

One week passed, and no phone service. Knowing that we weren't alone wasn't that comforting, since they couldn't find the problem or troubleshoot it in our area. Eventually several weeks had gone by without any real resolution. Cyndi made a plea for a wireless credit card machine at the bank, and I went to visit Jessica again for an update.

On April 28, 2010, I stopped by France Telecom because we had now been without phone service for over three weeks. There was no end in sight, and Jessica knew exactly why I was there.

"Hi, Jessica. Any news for me on the phone fix?"

She got on her phone and called the regional office in Guadeloupe, spoke in French, and after a few minutes said the correct person wasn't there, so she had no updates.

"Jessica, do I have to pay for service when the phones aren't working?" I didn't want to ask, but I had to.

"Oh, yes, because you have a subscription."

"Yes, I have a subscription for phone service, but the service isn't working."

"This is not like the United States. The French policy is that you pay if you have the subscription. You can cancel the subscription, but until you do, you have to pay. But you'll have no charges for making calls."

"But, Jessica, isn't that because I *can't* make any calls? The phone doesn't work."

"Yes."

There was nothing to do but bring out my island smile and thank Jessica. Even though it was frustrating, I knew the broken line and the archaic French policy weren't her doing. Coincidentally and miraculously, a few days after our visit to Jessica, our phone was back up and running. Yahoo!

Generally, utility service on the island requires a good sense of humor. Locals claim the island has four utilities, but that it's seldom they all work at the same time. The electric company on the Dutch side is named GEBE. Locals claim it stands for "Generating Everything But Electricity."

SNAKE IN THE HOLE

Many people wouldn't realize it, but St. Martin's has a plethora of snakes and Rhinos. I would take on a Rhino any day over a snake. You see, a Rhino is an inflatable boat that visitors operate on the most popular island tours. The snakes, however, are something different.

I discovered the devious ways of the plumbing snake when we arrived back on the island after our visit to the States in autumn 2010. I flushed our upstairs toilets in the villa only to hear a gurgling sound. I flushed again and still they gurgled. I Googled the problem and discovered there must be something trapped in our air vent. This was something I could handle. I was fully confident that it wouldn't take the same number of hours that the toilet seal had taken previously.

I went to Ace to buy a plumbing snake, wanting a twenty-five-foot, manual model, but naturally they were out. So I purchased the more expensive twenty-five-foot model that could be hooked up to a power drill. I climbed onto our roof with a hammer in one pocket, a flashlight strapped to the other pocket, and carrying the snake and drill, looking and proudly feeling like "Tim the Tool Man" Taylor.

I carefully fed the snake down the hole about fifteen feet until it seemed to hit pay dirt: a trap, or whatever was clogging the pipe. I smiled, hooked up the drill, and blasted away. Seconds later I observed the last foot of the snake leave the coil, plunging downward into the abyss. I couldn't believe my eyes.

Astounding. The snake hadn't been attached to the coil and was now lying somewhere in our air vent. Our small problem was now a large problem. I climbed down the ladder to tell Cyndi the bad news.

In my casual, trying-not-to-make-a-big-deal-out-of-a-very-big-deal voice, I sprang the news on Cyndi. "Hey, honey, the snake went down the drain. I can't believe it wasn't hooked up to the coil. What were they thinking? I just drilled away and, bam, it was gone."

Cyndi wasn't quite sure she fully comprehended what had just happened. She looked skeptical and went to look for the directions that came with the snake, as if that would help. "Look here, it says right on the directions, in capital letters: 'Important. The snake is not attached to the coil.' Did you even look at the directions?"

"Uh-oh." I hadn't had the patience. I believe directions are just warning labels created by attorneys to protect against product-liability lawsuits. After all, how hard could a snake be?

I didn't argue when the look and tone I was sensing urged me to call Erickson, our plumber. This is the same plumber I didn't bother to call earlier in my do-it-yourself attempts to save money.

"Hello, Erickson, you working today?" It was Saturday.

"Well, I do have some things to do, but I could be working."

"You the man. I've got a new challenge for you, and I know you like challenges," I said as I explained the situation. "When can you pass?"

"I can come this morning about eleven."

He arrived around noon, surveyed the situation, flushed all the toilets, which still gurgled, and said the snake could stay where it was or we could cut through the wall and retrieve it. I told him to leave the snake and asked if he could fix the original problem, the gurgle in the toilet. He said he'd come back and work on it, which he did. While working on the gurgle, taking a lower-unit toilet out, and essentially fishing, lo and behold, he extracted the snake.

We're fortunate to have located good repairmen for most types of work we required. This was mostly thanks to our friend Derryck Jack. Talking with people on the island and making friends has proven to give us the best resources for the work and labor we need. These skilled workers make certain details of island life a bit easier to manage. I'm a fan of easy-to-manage!

CHAPTER 19

ISLAND TAXES

Dreams of an island lifestyle include visions of less regulation and taxes, and to that end we weren't disappointed. There may have been innumerable French regulations, but enforcement was everything but stringent.

France has been appropriately described as a semi-socialistic state with its political roots dating back to the *Fête de la Fédération*, or the storming of the Bastille, on July 14, 1789. The monarchy was abolished and beheaded. The workers, the common people, craved attention and care: easily accomplished, as they were now running the government.

Today, French social services are good: free basic medical care, affordable housing, and retirement income. Everyone wants that in the United States; we just want others to pay for it. The result in France has been quality services and a highly taxed state. The services weren't quite as abundant in St. Martin, thus the taxes were reduced and local government revenues were subsidized.

St. Martin formerly reported to Guadeloupe as a commune within France's regional headquarters. Tax monies were sent to Guadeloupe, and locals believed very little flowed back. A perception of unfairness grew, and the desire to cut out the middleman, as the government in Guadeloupe was seen, grew in popularity. As a result the French-side population appealed to France to become a direct territory in 2003, and their wish was granted by the French Parliament in 2007. The results since then bring to mind the old saying, "Be careful what you wish for."

As St. Martin became a *collectivité*, reporting directly to France, most funds that had formerly gone to Guadeloupe now went to France. Of course, money coming from Guadeloupe similarly disappeared. Whether the French government provides more funding to St. Martin or not I don't know, but clearly the need to establish services on St. Martin that were previously being administered in Guadeloupe cost more than the funding received from the mother country. By 2011 it was fairly obvious to all locals that the collectivité was broke and dependent on France, who shared in the difficulties of the world economy. Taxes would need to increase, or at least be applied uniformly.

Many islanders simply ignored the tax call, despite the collectivité's campaign in late 2010 and early 2011 declaring the obligation of all citizens to pay their fair share. Placing guilt for not paying your share never worked where I came from. Rather, what had impact was the threat of going to jail, courtesy of the Internal Revenue Service. However, if France, and specifically, St. Martin, had such an agency, islanders didn't know it.

According to St. Martin's president, Frantz Gumbs, "The organic law states clearly that the collectivité is responsible for defining the tax system, but that the State [France] is responsible for tax collection and tax audits." This unintentionally allows each to point a finger at the other when the money comes up short.

Recently an official publication stated that of the 16,000 households on the island liable for taxes, only 3,365 were taxed in 2010. The collectivité received €6 million of the €9 million owed from those taxed. The €3 million difference was not collected, despite some four thousand notices being sent to the non-payers. Not exactly a superb collection ratio.

There are roughly four types of taxes affecting everyone in St. Martin—at least, everyone interested in complying, a category that includes expat Americans who have been born and bred for compliance.

INCOME TAX

I don't pretend to understand the French system, which isn't surprising, since I barely understand the American system. Other than CPAs, who does? It does appear, however, that islanders receive a significant break in income tax, possibly as much as a 40 percent reduction, compared to their fellow citizens in the mother country, presumably because the islanders lack sufficient resources and receive fewer benefits.

BUSINESS AND CORPORATE TAX

Businesses formerly paid a flat fee for their licenses, around €300 annually in addition to a corporate tax of 22 percent. Not sure what qualified as deductions before the tax kicked in, I simply knew I hadn't yet paid much in corporate or income tax as of the date of this writing. We were cash-flowing nicely without any debt service but had made a significant investment that apparently served as our tax deduction.

In 2011 the collectivité abolished the flat-fee license tax and replaced it with a tax based on the size of the entity, claiming it wasn't a tax increase. Right. Our prior fee of €300 would soon become €857.

Our buddy, Gilles, who ran ADT Security Systems on the island, suspected that 60 percent of businesses weren't registered to pay taxes. In 2011 the collectivité, in an effort to reduce whatever that percentage was, smartly began requiring stickers to be visibly posted on the front of the premises, demonstrating their registration.

SALES AND USE TAX

Use taxes included those on gasoline, electricity, and other consumable products, similar to that in the U.S. Sales tax didn't exist in St. Martin until August 2010, when the collectivité, needing revenue, instituted a 2-percent turnover tax, akin to a state sales tax. Similar to the United States but unlike the Dutch side, the tax had to be separately shown on invoices. On the Dutch side, this tax, which had been 3 percent but jumped to 5 percent in 2010, had to be included, or hidden, in the price.

REAL ESTATE TAX

We experienced an example of tax collection inefficiencies when we purchased our property. In the States, we wouldn't have received a deed from the county registrar until all outstanding taxes had been paid in full. On the island, that wasn't the case. We bought our real estate only to later receive bills, in the prior owner's name, for the tax owed for the previous year. We sent those bills off to his address in the States, where they likely went in the trash.

Shortly after the closing we met our new island buddy and neighbor, Vic Laurence. He calmed my nerves by explaining that we wouldn't be responsible for the prior owner's tax on our villa. Vic then volunteered island assistance that I readily accepted.

"Vic, when are real estate taxes due?" I inquired, having received no statement.

"Dere due da end of November, or else you get penalized 10 percent."

"But I haven't gotten any tax statement," I said, noting that it was the end of November.

"Dat's not so unusual. You go to da assessor's office in Concordia and get a bill, and den you pay da bill across da street. Do you know where da tax office is?"

"I know where Concordia is, but don't know where the tax office is."

"I can show you, if you'd like."

Vic explained the process, and the next day he personally guided me to the secluded assessor's office. Ahead of me in line was a peculiar older man with short, gray hair and black-rimmed glasses and dressed in handsome tropical attire. Vic introduced me to his younger brother, Ed, now a Florida resident, who was on-island to pay bills for his St. Martin home. Ed's property was just a few doors down from ours.

Ed's turn with the assessor occasioned a fluent and somewhat heated discussion in French. The assessor, a transplanted Parisian, apparently spoke little English. I didn't speak French, and Vic had forgotten most of his.

Thankfully, Ed stuck around and straightened things out with the assessor for both himself and me. I was equally thankful that there was nothing heated about my tax bill–paying experience. While we waited our turn, Ed explained French taxation to me, with less of an island accent than his brother.

"There are two types of taxes on a house under French law. One is for the building and the other is for habitation. If you have a bed or toilet in the house, you pay both. However, most don't pay the habitation tax."

I half-jokingly said, "Count me in the latter group."

Today, the dual tax has been replaced by one unified tax, presumably in an effort to increase collections. The combined real estate tax is about four-tenths of 1 percent of property value, considerably cheaper than our rate in the States.

I successfully paid our taxes and was overcome with a wish to celebrate. Who could have imagined such a reaction in America? Both Vic and Ed were traveling without their wives on this trip to the island. Cyndi and I took advantage of their availability and hosted the knowledgeable brothers for dinner. We gave them their choice of any location, and they unanimously settled on the home-cooked island fare of Carl's Ti Coin Creole. We shared goat, red snapper, and Vic's favorite, johnnycakes, along with a few Heinekens.

The following year the tax statement was actually mailed to us, but not so the year after that. I trekked to the assessor's office, now knowing where it was, thanks to Vic, and after a thirty-minute wait in line, found the notice sitting on the assessor's desk. The year after that, again we didn't receive our tax statement. This was getting to be difficult. Why did I keep going to the tax office? To avoid the late fee of 10 percent.

One year, while standing in line at the tax office I mentioned not receiving the statements and was told they were still adjusting the tax rates and that's why they weren't available. I'm sure St. Martin was like the States in this one thing: tax adjustments never seemed to go down. They said they weren't sure when the invoices would be mailed out.

A month later and still no statement in the mail. I asked a friend if he received his and he had, so I made another trip to the tax office, had another wait in line, and paid the tax. They had no idea where my invoice was, but they found the amount owed in the computer and gave me a receipt. I thought, "It's island life, mon." I could easily see how that phrase came to be used often by the locals. It made everything a bit more acceptable, a convenient, four-word explanation for everything that happened . . . or didn't happen.

CHAPTER 20

TAKING THE PLUNGE: BUYING A BOAT

What's the point of living on a tropical island if you don't enjoy the beach and boating? Cyndi and I absolutely loved both. I never particularly cared for fast, powerful motorboats, but I had taken sailing lessons back in my collegiate days. Cyndi and I also enjoyed canoeing at her family cabin on Lake Vermillion in northern Minnesota.

When both our children were school age, I ventured to a weekend sailing course in the "big boats" on Lake Superior and received my captain's license, allowing me to charter sailboats for personal use. A month later I packed up the family for an extended weekend on board a thirty-one-foot Island Packet that slept up to six. The crew consisted of me, Captain John (with a single weekend's training in a boat of that size), my first mate, Cyndi (who had no sailing experience), and our two young children. My sailors were precious to me, but were we seaworthy?

The charter company rented boats owned by others. I concluded that if I ever owned a boat, I wouldn't lease it to a charter company that would rent to people like me.

One sunny August morning, with the temperature in the rare eighties, the Swede Family Berglund hoisted anchor and sailed away toward Lake Superior's Apostle Islands, part of a national lakeshore consisting of twenty-one mostly uninhabited islands at the northern tip of Wisconsin. They're known for their collection of historic lighthouses, sandstone sea caves, remnants of old-growth forests, and animal habitat.

With a strong wind and a sunny day, we were halfway toward our first island destination when an unbelievable fog quickly rolled in, limiting visibility to about thirty feet. It brought to mind one of George's quotes in *Seinfeld*: "The sea was angry that day, my friends."

Since I was the captain, I looked death in the eye and calmed my crew, simply stating, "No worries." I was a man of few words at that moment. Inside my head, of course, some of the words were a bit more colorful than what was appropriate for the ears of my little ones.

The expensive boat was equipped with radar and sonar. That would have been nice if their use had been covered in captain's class. I had absolutely no idea how to turn them on, much less use them. Locating an old, trusty air horn in the aft compartment, I handed it to little T. J. and demanded that he sit in the bow, blowing the horn every few minutes while watching for ferries or other commercial vessels.

I turned the boat to starboard, toward Madeline Island, not an official part of the Apostles, but a long, narrow island directly across from the mainland. I instructed Cyndi to watch for rocks that would alert us when we were closing in on land. Rachelle, a new teenager, did what most teenage girls would do in such a crisis: read a book in the cabin below, disgusted with her parents' mismanagement of her youth.

After nearly running aground on Madeline, we knew the mainland was a few miles directly across the channel. The now-experienced team resumed positions, I glanced at the compass, and we churned into the foggy abyss under full motor power. Meanwhile, Rachelle started a new chapter in her book.

Locating the mainland, we followed the shore back to the docks, where we elected to spend our first night. The ever-watchful T. J. abandoned his foghorn, jumped onto the dock, and gratefully kissed the ground.

Cyndi and I gathered Rachelle, locked up the boat, and headed with T. J. to the nearest eatery that served strong drink. The following day we ventured out fog-free and enjoyed the remainder of our first family sailing adventure. All was great in the Swede Family Berglund, and our lovely Rachelle's life wasn't ruined, after all.

The following year we chartered the same boat and had a pleasant, uneventful journey. Now I had two notches on my belt and was ready for the island waterways of St. Martin. The time to purchase our vessel had arrived. Of course, by now we had budget restraints, with most all our funds dedicated to the business side of our island dream.

Nevertheless, Cyndi and Rachelle, who was visiting, found the perfect watercraft in our price range: a kayak. They had come to the island to check on our remodel, but during a break at Orient Beach they ran into Rachelle's new friend, Colin, who in turn ran into a buddy who was a water sports vendor. Colin and Rachelle discovered the vendor would sell one of his used kayaks. It was in the right price range, and Cyndi accepted on the spot, not considering how she would transport it back to our villa. Sometimes it's comforting to know that I'm not the only one in our relationship who allows little details to escape in the excitement of the moment.

Cyndi had two options: she could try to fit the kayak on top of our car and lose her sanity in the effort, or she could ask Rachelle and Colin to paddle the kayak from Orient to Grand Case Beach. Those familiar with St. Martin would recognize the challenge presented by the latter option; it was a rather long trek with some rough-water passages. Fortunately Rachelle and Colin were young, healthy, and foolish.

The young duo set off, plowing over, above, and through the surf crashing into Orient Beach. They headed toward Pinel Island in three-foot swells and turned left around the island's north point, heading toward Grand Case. Hours later they rode the surf into Grand Case, safe but exhausted.

Cyndi, anxiously waiting for them at the beach, was relieved to see them and assisted in carrying the boat the final seventy-five steps to our villa. The Berglunds were now both islanders and proud boat owners. A finer first vessel there couldn't have been.

CHAPTER 21

MEETING LOCAL ARTISTS

A smattering of quaint villages across the good ol' USA proudly portray themselves as art colonies. They offer a collection of artists and artisans residing and working in the community, attracting local consumers and traveling tourists alike.

Surprisingly, St. Martin, renowned for beautiful beaches and fine French foods, is an art colony in itself. As the island's Art Lovers Association (*Association d'Artistes*) claims:

> Saint Martin, a little rock emerging in the middle of the Antillean chain, a port of call on the way to the new world, is home to a fabulous enthusiastic community of fifty richly diverse artists. Painters, sculptors, photographers, and ceramic artists, sharing this tiny island, have gathered . . . to offer . . . a vast, colorful, creative panorama; from charming souvenirs to monumental works. Inspiration abounds, influenced by cultural diversity and sparkling sunshine.

What attracts these skilled men and women to the shores of a Caribbean island? Perhaps it's the exotic location, the cultural lifestyle, the multitude of potential customers, or all of the above. Maybe it's the proud French art tradition, which, similar to French passion for the culinary arts, has recorded numerous famous painters, sculptors, and movements in its rich history.

Whatever St. Martin has, it works for the growing international art community that includes incredible talent born and bred on this French-Dutch island. St. Martin's Art Lovers Association annually hosts an event called Artwalk, held during a weekend in April and consisting of open houses by participating members. And when we say open houses, we literally mean that many open up their homes in addition to their galleries.

Many years before purchasing our property, we strolled one evening along Grand Case Boulevard and met a young expat. She was selling her prints along the sidewalk and introduced herself as Frenchy Loeb, a New Yorker who spent considerable time in St. Martin. We ended up purchasing a small painting of Grand Case Bay and exchanged e-mails. When we were getting ready to purchase property, we contacted her for some valuable advice on all the different nuances of island living.

A few days thereafter we ventured into the Minguet gallery on Rambaud Hill, between Grand Case and Marigot, and purchased a framed poster that would hang in our bedroom for years, providing visual motivation for our dream move to paradise. A *Frommer's* review exclaimed, "Yet another highly regarded French expat, Minguet's fluid canvases are influenced by the rich colors of Matisse with the bold, contrasting lines of Dufy."

Over time we slowly learned more about all the island art and artists, an effort that brought us great experiences and some wonderful friendships. We've become friends with Minguet's daughter Catherine, who runs his gallery to this day, even though he has passed on.

We also had the unexpected pleasure of introducing ourselves to one of the most recognized islanders, a man known as the "Father of Caribbean Impressionism," Sir Roland Richardson. Distinguished with knighthood, he is incredibly talented in addition to being a fascinating character who bears a resemblance to Monet and Renoir. He has thinning, long, flowing blackish-grey hair, and an unkempt long beard, wears a floppy straw hat, and goes barefoot as much as possible. He'll never be found in anything more formal than a pair of sandals—and that only if it's absolutely necessary.

Roland's wife and business partner, Laura, is from the States and is his perfect complement. She's a published poet with business experience in running art galleries.

We had first seen Sir Roland after a delicious dinner at Mario's Bistro on the outskirts of Marigot. The restaurant appropriately showcases his paintings on its walls. In walks this man, looking just like the artist, with others for dinner. I kept looking in his direction, much like *Seinfeld*'s Kramer glancing at a person whom he believed was Joe DiMaggio. Upon leaving, and with some hesitation, Cyndi and I walked past his table.

"Are you, ah, Roland, ah, Richardson?" I stammered and sputtered.

"Yes."

"I'm sorry for interrupting, but we love your work," I continued. "We're John and Cyndi Berglund, and we'll be opening a business in Grand Case."

If we were proud at having just met one of the most recognizable persons on the island, we beamed at his polite and generous response.

"Oh, really? Where in Grand Case?"

"At the corner of the French airport road and the beach road," I explained.

"I know where it is: where the remodeling is going on, yes?"

"Exactly. Ah, it's nice meeting you, and ah, again we apologize for interrupting."

Shortly after, while walking to dinner one evening, we had the pleasure of meeting another artist with a small rented storefront along Grand Case Boulevard. Our dining companions, Paul and Carol, introduced us to Asif Hakh, an expat from Guyana who was a most engaging young man. He frequently has one of his two young sons, Adam and Jawhar, with him. In addition to captivating local landscapes, Asif offers amazing displays and framing. His beautiful wife, Natasha, or Asha, also from Guyana, would later paint our perfume bottles and periodically assist in our shop.

There's one controversial island painting that I particularly enjoy. Actually there are many of these paintings. They're all similar and all titled *Nathalie*. They depict a solo woman in different subtle poses and colored backgrounds. She has short hair, a petite mouth, a long neck, and a featureless expression.

The thing that makes the beloved *Nathalie* controversial is my even-more-beloved wife and boss, Cyndi. She doesn't share my appreciation for the paintings. I've chalked this up as evidence that art is indeed in the eye of the beholder. If Cyndi allowed it, I would not just visit *Nathalie* at the gallery; I'd have her displayed on the wall of our home.

Every time we drive by Paul Elliott Thuleau's Tropismes Gallery in Grand Case, I fixate on one of the *Nathalie* paintings. It always appears to be staring at me from its place of honor. Cyndi knows where my eyes wander.

The painting isn't by the artist Paul Elliott, who himself is renowned for painting the colorful facades of Caribbean Creole homes, making the complex simple, with elegance to spare. The controversial painting is by another French artist, Nathalie Lepine, whom I had the pleasure of meeting at the gallery one night while Cyndi was in the States. I didn't dare purchase a painting, but I did purchase her published book of art, showcasing multiple depictions of *Nathalie*. The complex art has been described as showing life's beauty through melancholic stillness, similar, to me anyway, to the *Mona Lisa* . . . a perfectly respectable *Mona Lisa*.

Admittedly, when I drive by the gallery with friends, I don't miss an opportunity to point *Nathalie* out to others. Some develop a fond appreciation after viewing her, and others are more like Cyndi.

It wasn't until our first full year of operation in 2010 that I had the pleasure of meeting another famous locally born artist, Ruby Bute. I delivered some calendars to her at the direction of a friend, Jeff Vanderpool.

Jeff and his wife, Bonnie, operated a small-island business in the States called Island Arts & Treasures. They distributed posters, calendars, and other items featuring designs created by local artists. In exchange for warehousing and distributing some of his items, he gave us a sponsorship on his calendar.

Ruby is a St. Martin treasure and a mentor to many emerging artists. Her painting career spans over thirty years, capturing historical aspects of St. Martin's life and culture. She has also written two volumes of poetry. Her strong images capture the raucous joy of Carnivale and the serenity of old homes and ancestral landscapes. Her gallery is her home, which is on the road to Friar's Bay.

The story of how Jeff secured Ruby's participation on his new calendar for 2011 is delightful, especially as Jeff tells it. It's an encounter that he labels "The Dance," and it is so fascinating that I've asked him to guest-author the next chapter.

CHAPTER 22

THE DANCE

Here's my friend Jeff Vanderpool's fascinating story of how he successfully negotiated an alliance with a genuine island icon, the beloved artist Ruby Bute. In many ways, it captures the essence of the island life, its ethos, and why we love living here so much. Here's how Jeff tells it:

* * * * *

Had we known the respect that Ruby Bute commanded from the entire island population, we may have been dissuaded from ever even approaching her regarding our venture. But our naïveté of her position allowed us to forge ahead.

I initially contacted Ruby by e-mail to see if she had any interest in participating in a project we were producing for Island Art & Treasures: a calendar intended to feature the works of some of St. Martin's talented art community. Having spent a little time on Internet searches and reading the volumes of information available about her, I admit to a certain degree of surprise that Ruby was interested. Having Ruby Bute in our calendar would definitely lend an air of credibility and help ensure commitments from the fence riders.

We made preliminary arrangements via e-mail and exchanged phone numbers prior to our arrival on the island. A couple of brief phone conversations from the States left us excited to meet her face to face, but with an image already beginning to form that this was indeed a special woman and that we were going to be in for a unique and rewarding experience.

Upon our arrival we immediately set about phoning the various artists to establish meeting times and locations. Ruby agreed to meet us at the site of her new home and studio in Friar's Bay.

It must be stated that I'm a textbook Type-A personality: take-charge, somewhat high-strung, goal-oriented, and schedule-driven. This entire trip was a carefully orchestrated schedule of successive meetings. In my career in the States, it was a common business practice to schedule a series of successive meetings on the same day and to eventually pull it off, rarely slipping from the original schedule. Such is not the case with "island time."

In the islands I've found it nearly impossible to schedule a morning meeting, have all parties arrive at the appointed place and at the appointed time, quickly get down to the business matters, and conclude the pertinent discussions in a timely manner. In fact, the schedules nearly always get pushed out, yet no one takes offense, and life goes on.

I'm also accustomed to conducting business dealings on a rather large scale, often amounting to several hundreds of thousands or even millions of dollars, with business partners whom I've virtually no personal or prior knowledge of. The individuals are quite often known only by a phone voice, and the relationship is quite professional. The islander characteristic I've come to accept, and in fact to cherish, is that they want to begin to know and establish a relationship with their business partners. They want to get to know you, who you are, and, in Ruby's case, who your parents were!

Upon our arrival we pulled up to the large painted steel gate and honked, per the posted sign. After a few minutes the gate slowly slid open to allow our passing. Driving onto the yard, we saw her sitting on the front porch of her home as the gate slid shut behind us. We were on the "inside" now. We felt élite, part of a select few allowed briefly to see behind the curtain. We approached with trepidation, wondering how we'd be received.

The meeting went well, though it was far from what I had envisioned. We spent two hours talking about her past, her family, our families, our heritage, and her paintings. We even had a historical discussion of a three-hundred-year-old tree that stood proudly between the home and the studio.

She gave us a grand tour of the entire home and previewed a wide array of her completed works. Numerous attempts on my part to direct us toward the purpose of our visit were rebuffed like a pesky gnat. She treated us as special guests, and her hospitality was humbling.

It should be noted that in 2005, her Majesty, Queen Beatrix of the Netherlands, decorated Ruby, thereby admitting her as an honorable Member of the House of Orange-Nassau. The certificate, sash, and accompanying medal were justifiably displayed in a glass case within her studio.

The aforementioned honor has served to strengthen Ruby's place of honor among the island community. And, in addition, Ruby has a stately physical appearance, which she proudly plays to her advantage. As she sat and engaged us, she positioned herself upright against the back of her straight-backed chair. With her arms outstretched, palms flat against the table before her, her body language fairly shouts, "Court is now in session." Throughout our time together she fussed constantly about the incessant heat and dabbed at the beads of perspiration on her forehead.

At the conclusion of our two-hour "visit," she announced that she'd needed to find out who this man from the States was before she committed to the project. "Now we can talk business," she declared, "but not today." She had another appointment that she had to keep and would have to leave. She invited us to come back the following day to talk business.

In other words, this entire meeting had been held only so that she could see if there would be a need for a second meeting. As we drove off the lawn and back to our resort, we felt a bit jilted by the lack of progress, but still celebrated the fact that we had passed muster. I've not known before or since an island resident so clearly in command of everything that goes on around her. Nothing happens without her knowledge and subsequent approval. To have survived this first test of character was exhilarating and left us in a celebratory mood. We now knew that with Ruby in the stable, the rest of our calendar would fill quite easily.

I returned two days later for our "business" meeting to find Ruby gone, but a houseguest asked me to stay. When Ruby did finally arrive, there was still a considerable amount of small talk needed. Discussions again centered on the characteristic heat and the island traffic.

I'd taken great pains to draft a licensing agreement that was fair to both parties, specifically engineered to give the artists confidence in my intentions and in the protection of their work. I had sent the agreement electronically and also mailed hard copies prior to my arrival.

I started the business discussions with Ruby by pointing to the agreement and started to briefly discuss the merits of each article. Mind you, this was a brief legal document, only two pages in length, but nearly one half of its contents were dedicated to the discussion of royalties, their calculation, and their auditing. As I reached Article Three, Royalties, Ruby stopped me in my tracks.

"Why do we need all this?"

"Well," I explained, "I wanted each of the artists to feel I was being transparent and forthright in my dealings."

"I understand, but I don't want to have to worry about what this Mr. Vanderpool is doing back in the States," she said.

I was beginning to see the picture she was now painting without benefit of brush or knife. "Would you rather have a certain quantity of calendars to sell in your own studio?" I asked.

"Exactly!"

Clearly she was pleased that this stranger from the States had finally caught up with her unspoken directive. All that remained was determining a proper quantity. After a pregnant pause, I finally played right into her hand.

"Did you have a number in mind?"

"Well, whatever you think is fair," she coyly responded.

I quickly make some royalty calculations in my head based upon the projected sales and first-run printing. "How does a hundred or 150 units sound?"

"One-fifty is a good number, but I was thinking of a different number."

I laughed out loud, and she, too, chuckled, both of us realizing we were now entering into the Art of the Deal. The hard part was now settled; she had clearly decided she was going to commit to the project. I was now comfortable, too, realizing that I had a commitment and that, if the final numbers varied a few units one way or the other, I could live with the outcome.

This part of the dance would be played out specifically for the enjoyment of the ride that had brought us here. Each partner was going to enjoy this final waltz, as the orchestra played on.

"I'm guessing it's a bigger number," I said, smiling broadly.

"Um, yeah," she admitted. "How's two hundred sound? That's a good number, don't you think?" Feeling we had finally reached a summit of sorts, I agreed. "Yes, that's a good number." So I placed the two agreements in front of me and began to modify the language to reflect our new settlement. Crossing out all discussions of the royalty left little of the original language intact. In handwritten lettering adjacent to Article Three, Royalty, I penned the words "In lieu of royalty, artist shall receive two hundred units of calendar."

I turned the document around toward her. "There, is that what you were thinking?" By now I was quite proud of my dealings with this island matriarch. The deal was equitable to both parties, so it wasn't a one-sided advantage I was puffed up about. Instead, I felt quite victorious in having pierced the veil and in getting maybe even a better deal than I had at first planned.

She looked at it for a moment, then softly, almost in a whisper, she asked, "Do you know how to make a five?"

Puzzled and completely taken aback, I asked, "What do you mean?"

She restated it as if speaking to a five-year-old: "Do you know how to make the number five?"

"Yes," I stated. At fifty years of age I was now quite proficient in almost all my numeral lettering.

"Well then, make a five," she said, pointing to the pages before me.

"Where do you want me to make it?" I asked.

"Between the two and the zero."

I quickly calculated that there was no way I could cut a deal for 2,500 units, and surely she couldn't be looking for a ten-fold increase. So I completely crossed out the "200" and lettered "250" in its place.

"There, is that what you mean?"

"I think that looks good," she replied, clearly proud that she had outdone this slick businessman from the States.

I then completed the changes for the second copy and set my hand to the signature line. After executing both copies and initialing the changes, I slid them across the table for her to sign.

"Now, Ruby, you sign them, give me one copy for my files, and you keep one for your records."

Drawing a full breath before speaking, she again spoke from her regal position. "You know, in France they have a custom," she stated. "Whenever they sign a legal document in France, they always write above their signature, 'read, and understood.' That way people can't say later that they signed it, but didn't understand what they were signing."

"Hmm," I said. "In the States, if we sign a document, that means we've read it and we're responsible to know what we've signed."

Silence. Ruby just smiles at me from across the table. This rock shall not be budged.

"Do you want me to write that above my name?" I asked.

"Well," Ruby said, smiling wryly, "we are on the French side!"

I added the text, and she happily executed the agreement, adding the same above her name. At long last, the deal was done, the dance completed. As we slowly parted and went our separate ways, the band packed away the instruments, the strings falling silent until the next time. Ruby is a special lady, and I'll always look back fondly upon our meetings and the lessons I learned.

CHAPTER 23

ISLAND FEVER, CULTURAL LINES, AND CRIME

Island fever often connotes a need to get out of the cubicle and into a larger space. But it can also have other meanings, as we learned not long after Cyndi moved to St. Martin for six months in November 2007 for the soft opening of our business. I joined her briefly to unload the twenty-foot container shipped from our home base in Texas.

* * * * *

The day after Thanksgiving, with the paid help of some local islanders, we unloaded the container into our building. Cyndi and I were not only mentally exhausted, but physically worn out. Every muscle ached with a dull, throbbing pain.

The next morning we slowly climbed out of bed. I put one foot on the floor and slowly lowered the next. While we couldn't say for certain, we both pictured we were feeling the way one would feel if hit by a big truck—one carrying a twenty-foot container, to be specific.

As the day wore on we loosened up, went back into the building to move and unload crates, and sipped a little muscle-relaxing rum. We finished a productive day with plans to celebrate a nice dinner. We showered but, as Cyndi finished up, she began to look pale as a ghost, something nearly impossible for beach-loving island goers. She uttered, almost in a whisper, "I'm beat; I don't think I can go out tonight."

"That's okay. I'll be happy to walk to the *lolo* [the local term for informal outdoor barbeque restaurants] and bring home some barbequed ribs and chicken," I said, disappointed, but definitely understanding.

"I don't think I can eat. I think I need to lie down," Cyndi continued, looking a bit confused.

"Can I get you anything?"

"No, I just need to lie down."

I put her to bed, thinking I understood her plight—actually, *our* plight. I was also achy. I slowly ventured out to get some food and returned home twenty minutes later. I found Cyndi sound asleep. She woke up a few hours later and tried to climb out of bed, but she felt worse and now had a fever and nausea to go along with her achy body. I found a thermometer and took her temperature. It was a whopping 104 degrees. I put some ice packs on her forehead and offered water, but she wasn't thirsty.

Cyndi's island fever wasn't the figurative type. She had contracted what's known as dengue, or dengue fever. It's acquired via a bite from the *aedes* mosquito. The symptoms are a high fever and pain in the joints, a most miserable malady that lasts seven to ten days. In certain cases it can cause internal bleeding and even be fatal.

A notable side effect is a lack of appetite, most likely caused by how it impacts the taste buds, giving foods a nasty, metallic taste. The subsequent weight loss, which can be significant, is known locally as the "dengue diet."

The mosquito reportedly is active only during daylight, and St. Martin has now done a better job in spraying in efforts to prevent it. The government also regularly advises citizens to rid pots of standing water, where the mosquitoes breed. But, of course, some of the biggest breeding grounds are in the large potholes aligning the sides of the roads.

Murphy's Law dictates that one will become ill in a foreign country on a Friday night, and Cyndi's malady was no exception. On Sunday I was relaying the news to Ciro, our neighboring owner-chef from Spiga Restaurant. He insisted she see a doctor first thing Monday and mapped the location, two miles away.

Monday morning couldn't arrive quickly enough, and I drove my weakened and extremely ill wife to the doctor's small office, hidden behind a pharmacy on the highway in Grand Case. I maneuvered around thirty people sitting both outside and in the tiny waiting area and gave Cyndi's name to the receptionist. Patients were served in order of arrival.

Two hours later Dr. Chico, who spoke excellent English, examined Cyndi. The good-looking physician had a friendly smile and a tremendous bedside manner. I think he helped me more than Cyndi, though.

Dr. Chico discovered a urinary infection and prescribed one injection a day for five days at a nearby nursing office. He also gave Cyndi some medicine to reduce the fever and instructed her to have blood drawn at the Marigot lab to diagnose dengue. I drove her to the lab, smiled at the receptionist who spoke little English, and submitted the French paperwork.

The doctor telephoned that evening to ask how Cyndi was feeling and said he would call again when he had the test results. He did, and it was dengue.

We had health insurance in the States, but as far as St. Martin was concerned, we were not yet residents, were uninsured, and had to pay cash. The island health care reminded us of our youth: small medical offices in backward buildings with caring medical personal at affordable prices.

The doctor's fee was thirty-five euros, with the medications totaling another hundred euros. It was an additional fifteen euros for five injections by the nurses. It was money well spent. When we achieved French residency we would only have tiny copays, if that.

I was ticketed to leave the island prior to Cyndi's recovery and suggested I delay my flight. Cyndi, however, assured me she was feeling better and insisted I stay on schedule. I departed, guilty feelings and all.

I called the first night away while networking at a business cocktail party in Grand Cayman and discovered that, despite her subsiding fever, Cyndi had supervised an electrician, a plumber, and a handyman, and had traveled to the other side of the island to pay for a sail mast that would serve as an antenna for our Internet installation.

She also experienced the tremors of a 7.4-level earthquake centered in the ocean off the island of Martinique. Other than that, she was doing fine. Meanwhile, the conversation had successfully destroyed any sense of enjoyment I was experiencing during my cocktail reception.

Competitive by nature and rarely outdone, I returned to St. Martin a month later over the Christmas holiday and had the opportunity to visit the same wonderful doctor and confirm my own date with dengue. At least by now we knew the routine.

Researching the disease online, it was good news, bad news. There were four types of dengue, and we would likely never get the same strain twice. However, if we contracted another strain, the chances slightly increased for internal bleeding and lights out. We invested heavily in mosquito spray and developed our own natural repellent with lemon eucalyptus and have had no repeat incidents to date.

* * * * *

American friends have warned us about another meaning of island fever: the need to escape the claustrophobic confines of a small body of land.

The business side of Tijon opened unofficially in December 2007, as I've said. Cyndi received the business license in March and kept the store open until May 1 while I worked fulltime in Texas and periodically visited. We determined that I would stay with my full-time employment for a second year through 2009 for financial needs, retiring at the end of that year. I would schedule longer visits during the next season. Cyndi was alone on the island, running an official business with official hours. Despite wonderful customers and caring neighbors, Cyndi remained essentially alone in a Third World country, managing her life, a new business, and the remodeling of a small carriage house behind our villa.

Unlike Herman Wouk's character in *Don't Stop the Carnival*, we enjoyed island amenities that included American cable TV, Internet, and Skype. Still, on April 30, 2009, after I had been absent from the island for a time, Cyndi's island fever exploded with a tactful but pointed e-mail to me:

> *Hi Honey:*
> *I guess having the wrong hormone pill is not a good thing for me. I'm ready to swim to the U.S. I just am tired after two years of trying to do things on this island.*

Everything is difficult, nothing is easy, and it all takes so much time. Vacationing here is a treat. Living here is another thing. AGHHHHHH!

So okay, I'm hot, tired, sweaty, and frustrated. I'm trying not to cry and be depressed. But I've been here toooooo longgggg!

I'm going home for a cold shower. I'll try to talk to you later. Don't worry, I'm fine. Just needed to vent. . . . I miss home. And you, and the kids, and a normal life of English-speaking people. . . . Sometimes I wonder, what were we thinking?

Time for the shower. Love you,

Cyndi

Love you? I immediately Skyped Cyndi and she courageously put on a happy face. She repeatedly assured me that she was venting and would survive. She missed me, which, while difficult, was always nice to hear.

My next visit was scheduled for a few weeks later, and I armed myself with her correct hormone medication and new tropical drink recipes. I assured Cyndi that, when we lived on the island permanently, we could travel back home to the good ol' USA anytime we needed a break. We'd find a way to deal with "island fever" because it was definitely a part of island life, mon.

* * * * *

Long lines are common on St. Martin and perhaps throughout European countries. Waiting in line becomes a norm that one must accept if one chooses an island life.

Most locals don't have checking accounts because of needed paperwork and European regulations. Just as well, because many businesses don't take checks. Our French accountant wanted us to pay using our French checkbook . . . right. Most of our suppliers were either on the Dutch side or in the States, neither of which easily accept French checks. Tijon has become a cash business by necessity.

Locals typically pay for their utilities with cash, on-site. It doesn't matter whether it's electrical, water, or the telephone company. This means that significant queues are the norm at the offices. The same is true at government offices and banks, known for having few workers and many customers.

We have bank accounts on both the French and Dutch side. On

the Dutch side we stopped to deposit some checks and were looking for their deposit box to avoid standing in a sixty-minute line. Not seeing one, but pretty sure they had one, we asked and were told, "Oh, no, we only have that type of box at our other branch in Cole Bay." Must not have had a room for a box in that branch, which by square meters was actually bigger than their Cole Bay location. So much for consistency.

One afternoon while getting a haircut at Laura's Beauty Salon, a few blocks from our villa, a lady came in needing an appointment the following Monday. Laura told her the shop would be closed, as she needed to pay her monthly bills that day. Islanders understand that this can easily encompass the entire day.

And a line isn't always a line in St. Martin. People arrive at many offices without stanchions and simply sit down or stand by a wall, trying to guess their turn. This creates some, although surprisingly few, on-site arguments.

This style of line, or lack thereof, creates anxiety in us Americans, but to the islanders it's an accepted way of life. Some locals complain, but they are few and far between.

The patience displayed by islanders during these lengthy waits is similarly displayed while driving. Locals are courteous and helpful in allowing parked cars to back up in traffic or pull out in front of them. The horn is used not to criticize, but as a short beep to allow another driver to cut in with the imposing driver giving a short beep back in gratitude. Far different than in the States.

Cultural lines do exist between the two countries sharing the tiny landmass, especially when it comes to nudity and sex. The French side has the "European beaches": it's not only okay for women to be topless, it's the common mode for many European and uninhibited American visitors. And I've already mentioned the clothing-optional beach.

On the Dutch side, however, topless bathing is disallowed and rarely seen. But as for brothels and strip clubs, French culture forbids the former and currently has none of the latter, while Dutch St. Martin licenses and inspects both. So, one culture allows public nudity outdoors and the other allows it only indoors. Maybe it's not a paradox after all.

Island crime presents no paradox. The lack of criminal activity is high on most checklists in choosing a travel destination, retirement, or location to open a business. As I mentioned, it was the check that eliminated St. Thomas from our consideration.

It was important to find out about the crime rate on St. Martin before we committed our life savings. During our investigative years, most reports consisted of car break-ins at the beach, domestic violence, or isolated issues among drug traffickers or youthful gangs, the latter typically occurring after midnight. Tourists were largely immune, provided they didn't showcase valuables in the car.

In the years since we opened Tijon, criminal activity has increased. Tourist blogs began expressing concern despite an overall crime rate significantly below most American cities. A few armed robberies have been reported. The incidents, however, seem relatively isolated, and the authorities take crime seriously; they know that tourism is critical to the island's prosperity.

We've been fortunate in personally experiencing no crime on the island to date and only knowing one visiting couple directly affected. That couple, staying at the nearby Grand Case Beach Club, reported that a car drove past, turned around, came back, and stopped. Two men with guns got out and demanded the man's wallet and grabbed the wife's handbag, slightly injuring her in the process.

Word traveled quickly but quietly. Steve Wright, the resort manager, contacted us to see if our cameras might have caught a glimpse of the car driving by. Before we could check, the gendarmes knew they were after a white Mitsubishi sedan with dark tinted windows; there were only two such vehicles on the island. Within two days the robbers were apprehended and confessed. The victimized couple stopped in the shop, and we had a nice talk and gave them a small gift bag to demonstrate our sincere care and concern. We were delighted and amazed when the couple returned the following year, undeterred by such a frightening incident.

Meanwhile, during this same period, our apartment in Texas was burglarized while I was on a visit to the island, believe it or not.

Crime prevention is something that the two island governments work on closely together. Both sides are planning closed-circuit cameras in strategic locations and increasing their number of police to keep criminal activity as low as possible.

The word on the street claims that much of island crime is perpetrated either by illegal residents or young people. St. Martin's economy is better than most nearby islands, so people want to be here. However, St. Martin, along with the rest of the world, has recently experienced higher unemployment.

Similar to the immigration problem facing the United States, the island experiences a problem with illegal immigration because of the fifteen-year boom in the tourism economy.

In 2010, Alex Vignal, the Director of Social Cohesion for the Solidarity and Family Sector in St. Martin's Collectivité, noted that fifteen thousand people, nearly half the population, are under the age of fifteen.

One evening while enjoying an outdoor barbeque at Sky's the Limit Lolo in Grand Case, the owners Jaqueline and Emille joined us and we discussed crime on the island. Both had been born and raised in Grand Case.

"When we were little, no one eva locked their doors," Emille declared.

"Why is it different now?" I inquired.

"No respect."

"And why is that?"

"Children having children," he said, implying youth issues and crime are resulting from the growing problem of teen pregnancies and one-parent households.

The French-side vice prosecutor, Jaques Louvier, has publically acknowledged the justice system on the island leaves much to be desired and that punishments meted out in Guadeloupe are often "too lenient." The French side doesn't have its own *tribunal correctionelle,* a court with powers including immediate sentencing, nor its own prison, so offenders are transported to Guadeloupe.

To accommodate American and Canadian visitors, the gendarmes staff their LaSavane station with an English-speaking officer. Gendarmes train and work efficiently with the municipal police, though some locals believe they can be a bit harsh in their tactics. They travel together in groups of four or more and are easily recognizable in their blue Toyota Land Cruisers.

But the gendarmes have little time to work on smaller issues presumably left to the *police municipale*, though Cyndi's first interaction was less than impressive. She stopped at a parking lot by the Marigot marina, and a shabby-looking man approached, asking for a few dollars to watch her car.

Cyndi told the guy she lived here and to back off. She completed her errand, jumped in her car, drove a block, and saw a municipal policeman. She reported the guy, concerned less for herself than for tourists. The officer brushed her off, saying, "That guy needs to make money, too."

The Dutch provide their half of the island with their royal police, the Marechaussee, to the chagrin of the local police. Turf issues are common, but good police work nevertheless persists. The bottom line is that the island is not crime free, but if we're vigilant and not out late and inebriated, we're safer here than in most American locales.

CHAPTER 24

ISLAND SHOPPING AND CULTURAL EVENTS

Shopping naturally has differing connotations for tourists and residents. For the latter, shopping is an inconvenient and vexing chore that rarely involves a one-stop outing. It's like the United States pre-1950s: void of large chains, malls, or megastores. This creates a localized feeling and a get-to-know-your-server mentality; it also requires a zigzag approach because of the multiple numbers of drives, stops, and parking searches that Americans haven't experienced for a long time, if ever.

Need groceries? That could be a three-store stop to retrieve the necessary items, despite the stores' large modern displays. Housing both European and U.S. brands, the shelves simply don't have enough space to carry or stock all of our familiar products. They are a cultural delight with the European brands, cheeses, wines, and Caribbean fruits. But sugar-free Kool-Aid or my favorite Pop-Tarts? Forget it. I've learned to survive. You didn't think I was all gourmet, did you?

Need building supplies? That may require two to three stops. Even if a store stocks what we need, the shipment from Puerto Rico or wherever may be late. Kooeyman and Builders Paradise provide excellent service but are no comparison to a Home Depot or Lowe's in the States. Need basic cosmetics? Cyndi buys hers at Ace Hardware in Cole Bay, one of the larger stores on the island.

For tourists, on the other hand, St. Martin is a duty-free buyer's paradise. This type of shopping can also be a fun respite for residents and expatriates. The shopping venues offer differing cultural settings and art galleries throughout the island.

CULTURAL EVENTS

Living in the United States affords the opportunity to attend numerous cultural and sporting events. We most always had an opportunity to go to a Broadway-type play, local theater, ballet, or professional sports venue. Living on an island initially appears to offer beaches, foods, drinks, sunsets, more drinks, and bedtime.

Visitors thinking of island relocation may fear cultural shortcomings. Still, while St. Martin will never compare to the mainland, whether it be the United States or Europe, it's not a black hole. In addition to staged events, there are local clubs for many interests, including a book club, a movie club, a hiking club, a running club, and a bicycling club.

The best cultural island event might be simply driving around town on a Saturday evening, listening to and watching the numerous local gatherings in outdoor restaurants, house patios, or alleys lining the two-lane highway. People get out and play music, socialize, dance, eat and drink, and enjoy life. The parties may be planned or spontaneous. You may hear loud calypso on your left, while reggae booms a few blocks down to your right, both intertwined with some hip-hop. These weekly gatherings are the rhythm of our new community. In other words, in the States we visit culture. In St. Martin we live culture daily.

ART AND MUSIC APPRECIATION

It was great to discover that not only is St. Martin renowned as an art community, but also that it holds celebrations to revel in the arts themselves. For music lovers, there's a series of classical pianists and other performers monthly at the Belair Community Center. Many cafés have live music and bars that feature a variety of styles from reggae to jazz to French minstrels. We never run across a cover charge at these bars, either; we'll only find those in the late-night club scene, which is typically past our bedtime.

SPORTING EVENTS

In addition to water activities, biking, running, and hiking, St. Martin boasts numerous traditional team-sports events. The trick is to locate the venues; most are off the beaten path. We read scores in the local newspaper for local baseball, basketball, soccer, and cricket matches, but to this day aren't sure where many are held.

It was with delight one Sunday afternoon that we discovered, on a leisurely drive to Marigot, a sporting match underway in the field between Grand Case and LaSavane. Cars were parked every which way, temporary tents housed vendors selling food and drink, and spectators stood along the roadside. We found a parking place in deep dirt ruts and joined the crowd around the unfenced, uncontrolled pasture. We quickly ascertained the game was cricket. To this day we're not sure who was playing, but it was fascinating, even if we didn't understand it.

Our buddy Derryck Jack is a big cricket fan and sponsor of matches. He, as well as our musician friend Remo, has tried to teach us the details of the sport. We're challenged with learning French, and now we've found out we're also challenged with understanding the intricacies of cricket.

Whenever the beloved West Indies Cricket team is involved in an international televised match, local service slows down, because workers are glued to their sets. To fit in, I go out of my way to appear interested and ask how *our* team is doing. If they explain action in detail, I nod as if I understand or agree. It's what living in a foreign culture is all about: experiencing, learning, and enjoying—with an added bluff here and there.

PARTIES AND CELEBRATIONS

For those who embrace the party atmosphere, there are not one, but two carnivals. The French side conducts *carnivale* in March, the traditional time of Lent. It includes parades, parties, music, and days off work.

If we're not carnivaled out by April, we can go for more; the Dutch side holds its larger celebration a month later. It includes huge street parades and music competitions at Carnival Village, a uniquely styled outdoor theater.

Special menus are common during carnival season, even at the Dutch-side KFC. They advertise for five dollars a *J'ouvert* (a carnival) special of bullfoot soup or chicken soup, souse, chicken, and johnny-cakes. Tempting, but not quite right for my tastes.

And if these official carnivals aren't enough, the island boasts the annual *Mardi Grand Case,* held every Tuesday evening in our village, January through March. This carnival-like experience shuts down Boulevard de Grand Case and includes tables of vendors, musicians, and parades along the path of gourmet restaurants and Caribbean bars.

There's yet another carnival celebrated by many St. Martiners who travel the short distance across the channel to Anguilla, an island only four miles away and easily traveled by public ferry or private boat. They celebrate "Anguilla Monday," the first Monday of each August, with beach parties and weeklong revelries.

Anguilla Monday, or August Monday as it's known, is the celebration of the freeing of slaves. It has attained worldwide fame as one of the largest annual beach parties. Anguilla Monday is also the wrap-up celebration that concludes a week of daily boat racing. The boats—traditional, open wooden fishing boats with the latest technology and a single mast—race while the revelers wager heavily. Each boat might cram in up to eighteen sailors.

In 2010 we rode the ferry over a week before the official activities and had the pleasure of watching a trial sailboat race. We watched from a variety of vantage points with our St. Martin friend Dr. Victor Gibbs. We drove around to capture the best views of boats jockeying for wind.

Because his mother was an Anguillan, Victor is termed a "belonger," meaning he had the right to own property on Anguilla and was entitled to certain other rights as well. He was also popular as a regular visitor with many friends and cousins. In fact, during our evening on the island, Victor introduced us to many of these "cousins," all of them good-looking young, local women—many of whom, remarkably, didn't seem to recognize each other.

Victor sponsored a boat called *Du Chen*. The prior year it had finished near last in the rankings, but this year optimism prevailed, similar to what Chicago Cubs fans likely feel at the start of spring training.

We watched the beginning of the race from a spot high on South Hill, so called even though it's on the north side of the island. We focused on *Du Chen* as it nosed into the middle of the pack. As they sailed into the distance, we loaded the car and drove to the Viceroy Hotel to check the craft's progress. *Du Chen* was holding its own. Our next stop was Smokey's beach bar, where we witnessed the boat in third of nine places, gaining on the leaders until, right before our eyes, the sail fluttered and the craft slowed because of some broken apparatus. We drove back to the ferry dock, with a stop at the Great House Hotel, located on the beach. From the hotel one could see the boats nearing the finish line. Victor got out of the car to assist our friend in retrieving some forgotten items from the hotel.

"Going to check on your boat, Doc?" Victor's dear friend from childhood, Alexis, jokingly inquired from the back seat of the van. For years, Alexis, a pencil-thin man with glasses and short curly grey hair, had driven his good buddy to house calls when Victor would get a late evening or early morning call.

Victor gruffly retorted, "Heard enough from you."

"We have sympathies for you," Alexis continued, smiling. "It must be difficult getting all those late night calls for your services."

"I need no sympathies from you," Victor countered, looking upset but hiding a smile. This bantering continued for fifteen minutes to the ferry dock.

For the fancy craft boaters, St. Martin hosts the annual Heineken Regatta. The wild, windswept annual event has grown to be the largest sailing regatta in the Caribbean, with over two hundred boats and thousands of sailors, boat handlers, and spectators. It's held the first week of March, celebrating its thirtieth edition in 2010. Observers get the opportunity to watch the impressive display of racing boats from land or by boat and can also participate in the massive parties, with top entertainment at different venues every night.

After watching the Heineken Regatta 2010 from the charter sailboat *Lambada* with our friends Mark and Robin, we agreed we should join the racers and wear team colors the following year. For the 2011 event Mark and Robin produced polo shirts and bikinis all labeled with "Team Tijon 54" logos. We proudly wore them to the regatta with other racing teams looking at us suspiciously.

Believing people might ask us questions about Team Tijon, we strategized our storyline the evening before over rum punches. First we needed titles. I offered the captainship to Mark, preferring to be first mate. We named Robin chief steward and Cyndi the purser.

"Why the purser?" Cyndi asked quizzically.

"Because the purser gets to buy things to provision the boat; it's shopping," Mark and I reasoned.

"Oh, I can do that," Cyndi said, smiling.

If asked other questions, we were ready with our replies, such as:

"How long is your boat?"

"Fifty-four feet, of course."

"What class do you race in?"

We thought we'd reply "no class," but knowing there were bareboat and CSA classes and others for which we had no understanding, we decided we would smartly repy, "The Octa One class."

"What's the Octa One class?"

"It's for the Octa hull boats."

"What's an Octa hull boat?"

"You've heard of mono hulls, cats, and tri hulls? Our boat has eight hulls."

"You mean you have eight hulls across?"

"No, we have four over four."

"Huh . . . how many in your class?"

"We're the only one. Quite unique, and we often win our class."

"Why so many hulls?"

"When we're not racing, we smuggle rum and tobacco."

"Is it racing right now?"

"We were, but sadly our boat capsized and sank."

Obviously, we were drinking too much rum after sniffing too much perfume.

SPECIAL EVENTS

Special events are many on the island and include the Full Moon Party, held just as its name implies, every full moon. Kali's Beach Bar on Friar's Bay has sponsored it for years. Most people claim it to be a memorable time not to be missed; our experiences were a bit different. We arrived around 9:00 p.m., ate a delicious dinner of barbecued ribs with beer, saw the band start setting up around 10:00 p.m., saw the band leave the stage to smoke funny cigarettes, and left exhausted around 10:30 p.m. after discovering the band wouldn't actually be performing for hours. The event is apparently for night owls, and we're day owls.

But we do stay up for the celebration of New Year's. There's no better way to welcome the New Year than by combining a warm Caribbean atmosphere with amazing festivities and fireworks from many points around the island. We've found it a fun adventure to start off at the Boardwalk in Phillipsburg and watch the pre-festivities. After a bit, we shoot off on our way home to Orient Beach for the midnight fireworks, music on the beach, and the local French crowd. We'd be hard-pressed to find a better way to celebrate the New Year than having our feet in the sand, a ti punch in our hands, and fireworks booming directly overhead from a barge located a few feet out in the dark ocean waters.

If we had any thoughts of cultural shortcomings, they've faded away. We've been delightfully surprised with the abundance of various events on the island. These happenings may not be like the symphony at the Met, but they're interesting, inspiring, and memorable.

CHAPTER 25

ISLAND FOODS AND RHUMS

I maintain that people visit St. Martin the first time for the beaches, and if they return, they do so for the fine foods. Those who choose to stay do so because of the people. Unlike other tropical destinations, St. Martin shines with its relatively inexpensive gourmet dining housed in intimate, open-air settings. French, Italian, other European, and Creole culinary contributions are abundant.

The French *savoir vivre* is particularly evident for food and wine. French cuisine parallels the passion of its people. It's been said that everything French, whether weddings, duels, baptisms, burials, or even swindling, is a pretext for a good dinner.

To the French, fast food isn't dining, and anybody who would dare suggest it is had better watch out. That explains why such outlets are virtually nonexistent in French St. Martin. McDonald's, with two outlets on the Dutch side, has frequently been the focus of anti-American sentiment in France and is seen by many to symbolize a threat to their culture and cuisine.

All of these fine meals are accompanied with a large smattering of personality. While walking along the popular Marigot Marina one evening, we strolled past a restaurant where we recognized the maître d' by face, but not by name. We weren't eating there that night, but exchanged pleasantries.

"*Bonsoir*, how are you tonight?" Cyndi inquired.

"Ça va, and you?" he replied.

"Ça va."

"Having dinner tonight?" he asked.

"Yes, we're meeting friends by the waterfront," Cyndi answered. "But we'll be back soon to see you for dinner."

"You're welcome anytime, but not tomorrow."

"Are you closed tomorrow?" Cyndi quizzed. She was gazing at his broad smile.

"No, madam. We're open, but *I* am off tomorrow."

The foods served, rich in butter and cream sauces and accompanied by wines, is both delicious and reminiscent of the *French Paradox*, a term coined by Dr. Serge Renaud, a scientist from Bordeaux University in France, who collaborated with a Boston cardiologist. They observed that French people suffer a relatively low incidence of coronary heart disease compared to Americans, despite having a diet relatively rich in saturated fats. They speculated one or two glasses of red wine, regularly enjoyed by the French, was the difference maker. Once reported on *60 Minutes* in 1991, consumption of red wine increased 44 percent in the States.

Another likely reason for less heart disease may be the lack of chemical preservatives in many of their foods. I believe further, although it wasn't specifically mentioned, that their slower, less stressful lifestyle was a contributing factor.

During a conversation with our French friends over a bottle of Bordeaux, Cyndi and I recounted our life in Wisconsin, famous for cheese. Our local buddy Gilles, originally from the Brittany region in France, looked surprised and inquired in his strong French accent, "What type of cheese do they make een Weesconsin?"

Cyndi replied, "Cheddar cheese is famous, made by ah, ah ... Kraft?"

Gilles's smile broadened as he asked, "So you go to a restaurant, and you're asked, would you like Camembert, Brie, Gouda ... or Chraaft?" We laughed at his not-so-subtle dig.

Gilles further expressed his passion for all things French when someone in the group mentioned California champagne.

"There ees no such thing as zees California champagne," countered

Gilles in an authoritarian tone. "You make sparkling wine. Champagne ees only produced from zee Champagne region in France. When you drink champagne, you're drinking zee dirt, the ground where zee grapes grow."

We updated the French Paradox with an Island Paradox. On St. Martin, we discovered a lifestyle encouraging a healthier diet: few rules but significant results. Heading to any beach motivates one to shed a few pounds to fit into last year's swimsuit. Living on an island and going to the beach weekly has motivated us to rein in the excess.

As I've mentioned, St. Martin is widely recognized as the "Gourmet Capital of the Caribbean." Within the village of Grand Case there are more such restaurants per square mile within walking distance than in any other Caribbean setting. French chefs dominate, and the meals typically begin with a freshly baked, crusty baguette, ending with an island tradition of homemade flavored rum. Nestled between those great things is a devilishly delicious evening of finely prepared foods and wines.

One evening Cyndi and I took Pascal and his wife, Donna, to Bistro Nu for dinner. Pascal, born in France but of Italian heritage, was chef owner of Piazza Pascal's in Grand Case, itself a popular restaurant.

Bistro Nu, a gem hidden in a Marigot alley, is a long-standing, old-fashioned French bistro where Jean Claude has greeted diners for years. I ordered my favorite, *coq au vin*. Cyndi ordered *boeuf bourguignon*, while Donna ordered a fresh-caught fish special. Pascal was delighted to order his entrée of beef tongue, reminding him of his youthful days in France. The size of a small, half-inch thick ribeye, this pinkish meat was surprisingly tender and tasty, but with a slight rubbery texture. Pascal explained that it's boiled a long time. My palate enjoyed the taste, but my mind kept asking, "Beef tongue?"

Not to be overshadowed are the Creole restaurants offering local specialties of goat, oxtail, conch, chicken, freshly caught fish, and the ever-popular johnnycakes (deep fried, similar to a beignet). Goat, like many exotic foods, tastes like chicken; oxtail, if stewed slowly, is similar to the rich-tasting *osso bucco*; and conch is a chewy, almost bland-tasting seafood. The chicken is typically fresh; small coops of birds are for sale on back roads in Grand Case.

Creole cuisine is derived from West African cooking. It's infused with styles and food from the slave trade route to the Caribbean. Most is heavily seasoned with some sort of spicy pepper. The basic ingredient of many Creole dishes is a *roux,* French for "brown sauce." It's a base used for gravies and sauces in this style of cooking, in addition to being a fixture in red beans and rice.

The popular *lolos* are another food attraction. Lolos are shacks where large kettles are used to grill ribs, chicken, fish, and lobster, served with a choice of large helpings of delicious, homemade sides.

The Creole grilling complements the French fare. Why don't the French grill? Their repartee claims, "The snails keep slipping between the bars of the grill." The taste of the lolos' food is surpassed only by their inexpensive pricing. At the Grand Case lolos, as of this writing, we can purchase ribs or chicken and a heaping portion of cole slaw or potato salad along with a beer or ti punch for less than ten dollars U.S.

Other roadside stands or local eateries offer traditional island foods. A typical breakfast might be johnnycakes with eggs from yard fowl, tamarind or guava jams, and bush teas, made naturally from backyard plants like lemongrass, sour sap, mint, and basil. Dinners include grilled or stewed yard fowl, sheep or goat, or other meats corned for preservation such as oxtail, pigtail, and salt fish. Sounds uninviting to American tastebuds, but once tried, it's actually quite tasty.

ISLAND DRINKS

The drinks add to the island dining flavor and include a broad range of offerings: fine French wines, piña coladas, rum punches, and ti punches. The beverage of choice in St. Martin is rum, or *rhum,* as it's spelled on the French side. The Caribbean is the epicenter of world rum production, and it has played an important cultural role. Virtually every major island group produces its own distinct style of rum.

The history of rum parallels the history of sugar. Sugar cane, a tall, thick grass, has its origins in present-day Indonesia in the East Indies. In 1493 Christopher Columbus brought cane cuttings on his second voyage to the Americas and transplanted them to Hispaniola, now known as Haiti and the Dominican Republic. The Caribbean basin has proven itself to be an ideal climate for growing this cane.

Flavoring rum by adding spices and aromatics is a tradition in St. Martin, where consumption of this sweeter, dessert-style liqueur often concludes a fine meal. Many restaurants in French St. Martin continue this tradition by depositing a bottle on the table as an after-dinner treat. The flavored rum is either homemade by the restaurant itself, FDA laws be damned, or purchased from a few locally made commercial brands sold as liquid souvenirs throughout the island.

Our good buddy Jean Henri at Orient Beach enjoys providing a shot of homemade rum to lunch patrons and always has a glass for us, whether we eat or not. One day he approached us in our lounge chair, bottle and glasses in hand, with a big smile. "Here's new one I make. Dis you like."

"Looks good to me." I salivated as he poured Cyndi and me a shot. It went down smoothly with a bit of a spice flavor. "That's great. What's in this stuff?"

He laughed. "*Bois bande*, ees good for you."

"What'd you say?"

"*Bois bande.*"

"How do you spell that?" I asked. I had no clue what *bois bande* was, other than the "good for you" that Jean kept emphasizing.

He wrote it on a piece of paper and laughed again, saying, "Good for you. Ees French Viagra." What could I say? Did he actually mean good for me . . . or good for Cyndi?

That evening I Googled this new phrase and discovered it to be the bark of a tropical tree found in the hills of Caribbean islands. It has potent aphrodisiac qualities and is, as Jean suggested, known as French Viagra.

Our other Jean friend, American expat Jean Rich, told us later of the legend of bois bande. Years ago a sylph-like maiden, in white silk robes, floated through the tropical woods with butterflies circling. A *chevalier*, a knight, came across the sylph and fell instantly in love. The maiden, a woodland spirit, smiled at him as she coyly lifted her robe and scratched her back against a tree. The mesmerized knight was about to propose marriage when, *poof,* she disappeared. The devastated knight couldn't locate his love anywhere. He returned to the woods, cut the tree bark where she rubbed her back, and soaked it in alcohol to preserve it, thus beginning the legend of bois bande.

On our next trip to the open-air market in Marigot we found some sticks of this unusual bark and made our own concoction. Other common additives to sweeten rums include banana, vanilla, coconut, passion fruit, cinnamon, and ginger. We were trying to infuse the island traditions into our life, and rum was certainly a fun way to try.

Guavaberry, the island's national liqueur and most popular flavored rum, is made from imported oak-aged rum, cane sugar, and wild St. Martin guavaberries. This produces a woody, fruity, spicy, bittersweet flavor all its own. Guavaberries, nothing like guavas, are rare and found mostly in the Caribbean, with St. Martin reported to have more than any other country.

Although there's a popular retail outlet for guavaberry on Front Street in Phillipsburg, we didn't understand its festive history until our local friend, Dr. Victor Gibbs, explained it. There is a holiday tradition of going to neighbors' homes around 4:30 a.m. on Christmas Day singing, "Good morning, good morning, I come for me guavaberry." The host or hostess of each house would take the precious bottle from the cabinet and pour a little tot for the serenaders.

These activities equate guavaberry with everything that was unique, special, and quiet about the island only one generation ago. Victor followed up his history lesson with a gift of a guavaberry, produced in a local neighborhood, making it unique and special to us, also.

Popular mixed drinks include piña coladas and rum punches. To be a local on the French side, if not ordering a French rosé or champagne, one would order a ti punch, a pastis, or a crème de menthe and soda water. *Ti* means "little" in Creole, and ti punch is the flagship French-Caribbean beverage, served in a small glass or plastic cup with two-thirds *rhum agricole*, one-third sugar water, and a crushed lime. *Rhum agricole* is made in the French Caribbean, Guadeloupe, or Martinique directly from sugar cane, as opposed to molasses. *Glaçon*, or ice, is for American tourists and, when requested, is often served on the side.

Ti punch is inexpensive and medicinally effective; we've seen many people feel pretty good rather quickly from these rum creations. Our

American friend Mark, a connoisseur of this beverage, compares them to women's breasts: one is not enough, two is perfect, and three are too many.

Pastis (pronounced "pah-STEES") is an anise-flavored French liqueur popularized by Paul Ricard in 1932. One of the most sought-after summer drinks in southern France, it's a cloudy, refreshing drink when diluted with water. Formality requires the server to bring us the glass filled with ice and *pastis* with a pitcher of water on the side. The server adds the water to your glass at the table.

Mixed drinks are to be envied or avoided, depending on perspective. Remember what I've said earlier: alcohol on the island is cheaper than most of the mixes one would use with it.

A TYPICAL DAY IN PARADISE

Our typical day in paradise often begins with a walk to the bakery in Grand Case for a freshly baked, mouth-watering *pain de chocolat* (definitely a delectable substitute for the old Pop-Tart tradition). At that time we purchase a baguette for a late lunch that will be accompanied by various cheeses along with sliced turkey and lettuce. A glass of a crisp, French chardonnay enhances our palate. For dinner we enjoy cooking in or barbequing out when not joining friends at one of the delectable restaurants. We've never had a bad meal on the island.

If you've visited St. Martin or live on-island, you understand that half the fun of dining in Grand Case is walking the eight or ten blocks, reading menus posted outside, peeking inside at the ambience, and choosing your evening delight. Odds are it will be a tremendous choice. *Bon appétit*!

CHAPTER 26

AN ISLAND WEDDING

When our family first visited St. Martin in 1996, our daughter Rachelle was fifteen and our son T. J. was twelve. My, how time flies. At that time we didn't know we'd end up making it our home and opening a business there. Another thing we'd never thought about, by choice, is our daughter growing up and getting married. That time had come for Rachelle, and yet another experience of island life begins.

Rachelle and her boyfriend, Scott, lived in San Diego. They arrived with our son, T. J., on the island to enjoy the 2009 Christmas holiday. We were excited to take a breather from work and enjoy some family-fun activities. Scott stole Rachelle for a sunset walk at the Grand Case Beach Club and dropped to his knees in his proposal of marriage. Naturally, she said yes. Scott and Rachelle chose their proposal site for a destination wedding.

It was to be a week of fun-filled activity, including a Sunday welcome party at the L'String beach bar on Orient, hosted by our good buddy Jean Henri and the owner, Leo. Monday we would enjoy a delightful groom's dinner at Orient's Palm Beach, with the official ceremony at the Grand Case Beach Club on the Tuesday before Thanksgiving 2010.

Seventy people flew in from the States, which limited our island guest list at the reception, due to the kitchen's size and ability, to twenty-five. It was quite challenging to narrow the list.

It had rained unusually hard that Sunday, and the showers continued into Monday. The reception was going to be held under a nearby tent atop the Beach Club that offered cliff-top views of the ocean below and the outline of Anguilla four miles across the sea. The Monday night rehearsal had to be conducted in the reception tent, since it was still raining. The outdoor ceremony was on Tuesday—would it clear by sunset that day? We were keeping faith that the weather would break.

We woke Tuesday to sunshine and strong winds; it looked promising. But during the day, clouds gathered in the skies. At the precise moment our buddy Connis began playing the processional, Pachelbel's *Canon in D*, on the sax, dark storm clouds quickly blew in over the mountaintop, dusting us with a few large drops.

I anxiously scanned the sky to determine if I needed to interrupt the ceremony and move it into the reception tent. The pastor made a casual comment about the unpredictability of weather and calmly continued with the service in the howling wind.

Amazingly, the clouds blew away as quickly as they came, the winds lessened in force, and the skies transitioned into an incredible rainbow overhead. If it wasn't a sign from above, it was certainly a welcome and beautiful sight. Rachelle had selected John Foster, our pastor from Arlington, Texas, to officiate the ceremony. One unique pre-wedding thing the pastor requested was for the bride and groom to write letters to each other, and he read them during the ceremony. A beautiful moment.

Few events in one's life are truly memorable, but the marriage of our only daughter and first-born was truly one of those magical moments. The reception was beautiful, and the rum flowed freely as the guests visited. The traditional champagne toast gave way to a passion-fruit rum toast. The dinner, a choice of grouper or stuffed chicken, was the best wedding food I had eaten; most of the guests agreed.

The restaurant owners, Alex and Chantel, did an exceptional job, along with their incredible staff. The last course, at our healthy daughter's request, was scoops of mango and passion-fruit sorbet presented on a tray piled up like a pyramid aglow in color. Music and dancing followed.

Wednesday, Cyndi and I collectively breathed a sigh of relief; we had made it through. The sun was shining that morning, and we took our American family and friends on a catamaran snorkeling cruise. Thursday we hosted Thanksgiving dinner with two home-cooked tur- keys alongside catered ribs, chicken, rice, and beans from The Sky's the Limit Lolo.

It was all an amazing experience, and we were delighted Rachelle and Scott chose to exchange vows in St. Martin. It was a beautiful start to a beautiful marriage.

A few weeks later we returned to L'String and reminisced with our smiling buddy Jean Henri, who had shared a table at the wedding with a few pregnant ladies. He surprised us when he said, "No more weddings. I got too drunk, and Mary had to drive home. I had four or five rum punch, den dey bring bottle white wine. No one at table drink wine. I drink. Den dey bring red wine, I drink. Den dey have the rum afta dinner. I drink. When T. J. get married, no invite me."

Now, fourteen years after our first island visit, our children have become adults. Rachelle is starting her own family. I was reminded of something my father told me when I was young. He had taken a wild-eyed boy—me—to a 1965 Minnesota Twins World Series game. I proudly told my dad that someday I'd take him to a big game, which I did in 1987. But in 1965, my father replied, "Don't repay me. Do some- thing similar for your children when you have them."

I've tried to follow my father's advice. My children need not take Cyndi and me on an adventurous trip as we did with them to the Carib- bean. Instead, we hope that they'll do something similar for their chil- dren. It's what makes memories; it's what makes the world go around.

CHAPTER 27

FINDING A CHURCH AND GIVING BACK

Being "Luterins" (that's how we say it, according to those from outside Minnesota), we joined similar congregations in our moves to Atlanta and Texas. Cyndi and I had been raised in the Lutheran denomination, but there was nothing similar to it in St. Martin. Having a home church was important to our culture and comfort. Where would we go?

St. Martin offered churches for Roman Catholics, Methodists, Baptists, Anglicans, Seventh Day Adventists, and others. We visited some of those options and started with the beautiful, but relatively small, Catholic parish church nestled along restaurant row in Grand Case. A middle-aged priest spoke eloquently with fire and brimstone, reminiscent, I'm told, of my maternal grandfather, who served as a Lutheran missionary in the United States in the early 1900s.

We were enjoying the service until the sermon, in English, was then repeated in French, as was most of the service. The one-hour intended stay turned into two-plus hours, which we suspected was customary. Not knowing French, we couldn't say for sure. That wasn't to be the church for us. So, onward, Christian soldiers: we continued our search.

During our first island visit in 1996, with our young children in tow, we had attended a Methodist service on Front Street, by the cruise-ship shops in Phillipsburg. The service was beautiful and meaningful. It was a historic wooden church with balconies and open windows. The

congregation couldn't have been more welcoming; however, we preferred not to drive that distance for church every Sunday. The service
had also been quite long and, admittedly, I'm not designed to sit still for
two-plus hours. I can't even do that on the beach.

Methodism is rooted in island history, with its founder John Wes-
ley a staunch abolitionist of slavery. The first Methodists disembarked
on St. Martin in 1819, delivering Christian education to the slaves and
those emancipated. The island governors and plantation owners welcomed these missionaries, who turned slaves away from pagan practices
and polygamy.

We had the opportunity to attend the baptism of our godson at the
Methodist church in French Quarter. Jack and Jackie were his parents
and our dear friends. This church was a newer, large structure built next
door to its old, decrepit predecessor.

The hurricane shutters were opened for the service and a beautiful
breeze passed through. It was the Advent season, and the pastor did a
tremendous job with her sermon and stories, including one that easily
became a favorite, her novel story of the making of the candy cane. We
enjoyed the service, the pastor, and the people, and attended Christmas
service 2009 there with our visiting son.

Problem was, they only offered one Christmas service, as did most
island churches . . . at 5:30 on Christmas morning. Must have been to
attract all the neighborly guavaberry liqueur hunters roaming around
at 4:30, just prior. Believing it would be packed, as Christmas services
always were in the States, we slowly trudged out of bed, stretching our
stiff limbs to get dressed. We arrived at church early, while it was still
pitch black out, to discover that most islanders don't rise and shine on
Christmas. The church was about 20 percent filled.

We had believed that this church would become our church of
choice until I began attending a productive weekly orientation for
new guests at the busy Oyster Bay Beach Resort. Orientation began at
10:00 a.m. and the longer church service ran from 9:30 to almost 11:30,
eliminating it from contention.

Returning to our roots of having coincidentally and conveniently
attended churches that were just a few blocks or minutes from our
home, we gave one more church a try. It was a Methodist church just

two blocks away. We later discovered it was the home church of our island friend, Dr. Gibbs. It was a tiny structure and, if it was full, it might fit forty people. Its size, or lack thereof, had somewhat intimidated us. Cyndi had attended a service a few years earlier but was discouraged when only a handful of people attended, and the service began at 9:30 a.m., though posted to start at 9:00 a.m.

Cyndi gave it another shot the Sunday before our daughter's wedding on Tuesday, along with our Lutheran pastor from Texas; I was off to the resort for orientation. That Sunday was Youth Sunday, when the young people deliver a beautiful service to a crowded church of about twenty-five. During announcements, the man who greeted Cyndi warmly and appeared to be the church patriarch, surprised her by announcing her presence as the kind, neighborly owner of Tijon.

The next Sunday I attended with Cyndi, even though I had to sneak out early to make it to the resort for orientation. The visiting minister preached about the beginning of the Advent season. He abruptly looked around, making a slowly spoken but commanding inquiry: "Where 'tis our Advent candles? I see no candles, 'tis the Advent season."

An older lady responded from her pew, "I been sick dis week so couldn't bring dem, but I bring dem next week."

"Okay then, we have Advent candles for next week."

That next Sunday, sure enough, the Advent wreath and candles sat proudly atop a table near the altar. During the service one of the church sisters—all members are "sisters" and "brothers"—unsuccessfully tried lighting it with one of those fancy, artificial lighters. Cyndi, always prepared for everything, came to the rescue by pulling matches out of her purse. The advent candles were finally lit, and we had contributed in our own small way.

This tiny but sturdy, historic steeple church has become our Sunday morning home when we can attend, often made difficult by the hotel orientation and other early morning, marketing-type meetings; island tourism doesn't rest on Sundays. The general attendance at church is usually around ten to fifteen people. The hurricane shutters are always opened, allowing for the tropical breezes to pass through. We hear the sounds of nearby roosters crowing. It's a comfortable and serene sanctuary surrounded by welcoming families.

* * * * *

We moved to the Caribbean for the lifestyle of fun, sun, and rum. There was another motive: to help people less fortunate. Cyndi and I had been blessed with an education, good families, and careers. Many others never had similar opportunities. We wanted to reach out and give back to these amazing people in this different cultural setting.

When our American expat friend Paul, twenty years my senior, invited me to join Rotary, I readily accepted, despite being from the generation on the heels of the Anti-Anything 1960s. I had been a guest speaker at a Rotary meeting in Minnesota as a twenty-five-year-old prosecutor, but otherwise knew little of this impressive service organization of over one million members in 33,000 clubs worldwide. I've always liked their motto: "Service Above Self." The club I joined holds meetings weekly during a late dinner hour at the Sunset Café in the Grand Case Beach Resort, the same café that so nicely serviced our daughter's wedding.

The food, rich in butter and cream sauces and accompanied by wines, is always delicious. The actual meetings, however, are a different story. They are mostly in French, and as you know by now, I'm not particularly fluent in that language. If the topic is significant, the person seated next to me graciously leans over and translates. Heated discussions often follow the topics. Perhaps this is another French tradition. Big George Gumbs, a loyal Rotarian, smiles as he calmly explains in English to non-French guests after angry debates, "Our discussions are an expression of affection."

The most renowned island Rotarian is the aforementioned Dr. Victor Gibbs, our local St. Martiner and Anguillan boat-racing friend. He'd been a charter member of a French club and a district governor of Rotary. In his seventies and keeping regular office hours, he could easily pass for fifty, being trim and athletic. He plays tennis at 7:00 a.m. three times every week with two of his island buddies, and at his invitation I regularly round out the tennis foursome.

Victor has an amazing story. Born to a father from St. Martin and a mother from Anguilla who both spoke English only, he struggled with French in school and was constantly slapped on the hands for speaking English.

Victor's dream was to be a doctor, but first he would have to go to college, in Guadeloupe. His St. Martin school counselors discouraged his post-secondary education because he wasn't sufficiently fluent in French. His father, the French-side island postmaster, told Victor he couldn't afford to send him to Guadeloupe. Victor asked only for his approval, saying, "Don't worry about the money. If you give me your okay, I'll find a way." His father gave his okay, and Victor hopped on a boat hauling cattle to Guadeloupe, where he lived with some people he'd met in St. Martin.

After his graduation, Victor stayed and taught English for a few years, saving money until he hopped on a banana boat for the ten-day journey from Guadeloupe to Nice, France, to enroll in medical school.

The studies were difficult. Victor met a beautiful blonde nurse, Marie Claude, who would later become his wife. They have two wonderful children, Daniel and Alexandra. Victor succeeded in his goals and has found a way to help so many people because of it.

He not only delivered and tended to many of the locals, he also became president of Semsamar, a corporation 51 percent owned by the French government and 49 percent privately owned. Semsamar receives the contracts for building schools and hospitals in St. Martin and other French islands, making Victor both a wealthy and most generous man. His kindness, sincerity, and intelligence make a difference.

The island Rotarians sponsor concerts and other activities, including a few blood drives every year, which I try to help out at. Our Three Kinds of Magic concert netted over $30,000 for the children of the island. Although I initiated the idea, organized it, and supplied the musicians free of charge, it was the good work of the coordinator Louis, the committee, and all island Rotarians who made it successful. It felt good.

On a beautiful December Saturday in 2010, Cyndi and I volunteered to serve on the traditional Christmas Rotary boat ride for a hundred and fifty seniors from French-side assisted-living homes. These were native islanders who had formed the community and culture we now enjoyed. It was an afternoon sail, taking off promptly at 2:00 p.m. The bar was on the lower level of the two-story boat, and after pushing off, Cyndi and I joined other Rotarians in walking around the boat, taking and filling drink orders.

In true French-Caribbean tradition, drinks included beer, wine, rum punches, and of course, the infamous ti punches. Soft drinks and bottled water were available, but rarely consumed. A delicious buffet of salad, rice and beans, fish, and chicken followed. Each of us would take two plates and approach the buffet line servers, then run the plates to the seated elderly. They enjoyed; we felt good. Those are memories that make us appreciate what we're fortunate enough to have in life.

There was a DJ on board playing island Christmas tunes, and after dinner he cranked up the volume to a noise level my son would have enjoyed. Shockingly, about half of these frail-looking seniors got up to dance, shaking their booties faster and longer than I ever could. There really is something medicinal in that rum!

I looked at Cyndi and we both chuckled, wondering who should have been serving whom. But to see the seniors' faces, their enjoyment and interaction, was truly gratifying. This wasn't Rotary giving money for polio or to Haiti; it was Rotary paying for a boat, drinks, and food, and seeing the results in the faces of those served. We made a mental note to sign up every year for this joyous gathering.

We also receive many opportunities to give back that come directly from contact with area residents. One occurred a few months after our permanent move to the island. It was about 9:00 p.m. and pitch black outside. There was a knock on our door, which, by itself, was quite unusual. I opened the door, and a young, thin, pretty girl was standing there. I knew her; let's say her name was Julia (not her real name). Cyndi was standing behind me. "Hi, what are you doing here?"

"Momma kicked me out. She don' love me and I haf no place to go."

"Come in here and tell us what happened," Cyndi said. This young woman broke down crying, then settled down and explained she had a fight with her mom.

"She gonna send me to live wit her sister in Haiti. She don' love me," Julia continued. "I no go. Can I stay here?"

"Here's the deal," I quickly jumped in. "You can stay here tonight, but I have to tell your mom where you are so she knows you're safe."

"No, Momma don' love me. She no care, but if you see her, she make me come home. She beats me. She don' love me."

"Well, that's the deal," I maintained.

Cyndi gave her some soda and asked if she wanted anything to eat, but Julia replied she was tired and just wanted to sleep. Cyndi put her in the guest bedroom and closed the door. I hopped into the car and drove the few blocks down a narrow, dark, congested road to find her mother. I parked, walked a few yards to the house, and knocked.

"Sorry to stop by so late. I just wanted to let you know your daughter is safe. She came over to our house and wants to spend the night with us."

"She ungrateful. She stole from me, and I send her to Haiti. She stay with my sister dere. She no idea how hard I work for dem. I dere mother. Dey haf no father. Dere father don' care. I'm dere father, too, everyting I do for dem. Dey have no idea how tough I had it. My parents died when I young." She was both angry and in tears.

"I know you're a great mother and you work hard. Your daughter just needs a night alone, then let's all get together tomorrow."

"She don' stay der. I call da gendarmes."

"Listen, I need your help here. I promised she could stay one night. Do this for me, or I look bad. You come over tomorrow morning and pick her up, and we'll help you all we can; you know that."

She calmed down and agreed. The next morning she arrived to pick up her daughter. Julia was in our shop doing some chores upon her request. Mom was still angry, but soon both she and her daughter were in tears.

I was presenting a perfume class, so Cyndi initially mediated in what became a tearfest for all three ladies. The mom maintained her daughter had stolen money needed for gas to go to work. Her daughter maintained her innocence. Cyndi intervened, offering for Julia to help out at Tijon on Wednesday mornings when she didn't have school. She was welcomed to have sleepovers, too, if her mom just needed a little break. They agreed and left for home together.

Having raised children ourselves and seeing many others in similar situations, we understood the natural and common conflicts between a mother and her new teenager and how much more difficult it was for a single parent who was barely subsisting. We didn't need the help at the shop, but our new employee showed up, worked hard, and earned her keep. Her mom remains a good friend.

We look forward to the chance to help others in need. Giving back is important to us, and what we receive as a result is most rewarding. I am reminded of a saying by Winston Churchill: "We make a living by what we get, but we make a life by what we give."

CHAPTER 28

HURRICANE WATCH

The intensity of emotions that go with investing our life savings in a home and business in the Caribbean is extreme. Add in a hurricane season that may threaten to wipe it out, and those emotions become supercharged. Each year we find ourselves on a six-month-long alert.

The official hurricane season is between June 1 and November 30, but July 15 to November 15 is when over 80 percent of these wicked storms occur. Most hurricanes come roaring into town during the months of September and October.

Cyndi and I thought it valuable to purchase hurricane insurance, despite being cynical about any payoff. We are unsure to this day what we purchased; the policy and its fine print are in French, and we elected not to pay to have it translated. After all, it's not like translation to English would allow us to change policy terms.

Our first family visit to the Caribbean in 1996 followed on the heels of Hurricane Luis, the most devastating storm to strike St. Martin in recorded history. The date is well remembered by islanders as September 5, 1995, when the a Category 4 storm—today it would be readjusted to a Category 5—not only struck, but hovered over the island for some thirty-eight hours. The eye passed directly overhead, presenting a brief respite before the tail whipped the island with even greater force. Locals recollect the widespread destruction: buildings, beaches, and boats demolished, thousands of trees downed, and shrubs stripped.

Post-Luis, the land was barren and forsaken. Sixty percent of buildings had been damaged or destroyed, and nine islanders didn't make it through the storm. Electricity and water were lost to some villages for over three months.

The other infamous hurricane to strike St. Martin was "Wrong Way" Lenny on November 17, 1999, so coined because of its unusual approach. It passed south of the island from east to west, then reversed direction to traverse from west to east. It was the first time such a trajectory was witnessed in 113 years of weather observations in the Atlantic/Caribbean basin. It was barely under a Category 5, making it the strongest November hurricane on record in the Atlantic basin.

Boats find safe harbor in Simpson Bay, located on the western side of the island and considered the largest protected bay in the entire Caribbean. Boats flocked into the bay only to be the first hit by Wrong Way Lenny. Hundreds sank, with some still resting on the bottom today.

Like most islanders, Cyndi and I fear that the next big one may be heading our way. The one thing that comforts us is that locals have told us our property has fared well during these storms. Trees were downed, windows were broken, and water flowed in, but all in all, no structural damage. We have some natural protection, being boxed in by the surrounding hills. However, our astute young architect, Jym, told us when we instructed him to make our Tijon building hurricane-proof that "nothing stands if hit directly by a Category 5."

While on the island in late August 2009 we were hoping that a tropical storm named Bill would miss the Caribbean. The storms had been quite active that summer, and schools were often cancelled because of the extreme wind and rain. Sandra, the popular bartender at the Grand Case Beach Club, once offered Cyndi some words of wisdom.

One weekend evening, enjoying happy hour, Cyndi asked, "What's with the wind tonight? Hope it doesn't turn into anything serious."

Sandra's simple but pointed suggestion followed. "Ya hof to pray to the gods of wind."

The 2010 hurricane season gave us particular concern. The water had never cooled below twenty-seven degrees Celsius during the tropical winter that never was. We had hurricane shutters installed on our eighteen villa windows, at a cost of $10,000. If nothing else, it was insurance. After all, when we wash a car, it rains. When we put on hurricane shutters, nice weather follows. Sure enough, there was no significant hurricane that year.

We were proud that our new shutters had given us such fortune until we discovered that Sahara Desert dust was the main reason. One day we woke to a somewhat smoggy morning, something most rare in the tropics. We knew it wasn't pollution but were curious. The newspaper reported it as desert dust from an African storm over the Sahara. The good news, we learned, was that the dust in the atmosphere deterred tropical storm formation.

The following year near the end of August, we met some tourists from New York. They claimed their friends thought them crazy to vacation in the Caribbean during hurricane season. Of course, they were safely visiting our sunny island while Hurricane Irene was approaching New York City.

Island living comes with threats of hurricanes, tropical storms, tropical waves, and a slight chance of a tsunami. Family left behind in Minnesota question how we could live with such an annual risk, but we point to a family building in Minneapolis that sustained over $100,000 of damage due to a May 2011 tornado. Every geographical area has climate events and weather calamities. It's the cycle of life. In the meantime, we pray on hurricane watch. *C'est la vie.*

CHAPTER 29

MISSING THE USA

Our dream consisted of sandy beaches, warm sunshine, and a laid-back lifestyle; we've not been disappointed. Still, that doesn't prevent us from missing the busy modern commotions of the States.

Thomas Wolfe was an acclaimed American novelist who knew a bit about travel. He was born in North Carolina, went to New York City at age twenty-three, and a year later sailed to Europe, traveling from England to France, Italy, and Switzerland.

I've often wondered if this is our haunting American paradox: we're fixed and certain only when we're in movement. At any rate, this is how it seemed to the main character, George Webber, in Wolfe's famed novel, *You Can't Go Home Again*, published in 1940, two years after Wolfe's death.

But Thomas Wolfe never said, "You can't go back to Minnesota," did he? Our solution to episodic homesickness is to hop a plane home and visit family and friends.

In the Caribbean, residents usually take their wonderful geography, climate, and culture for granted. That's similarly true for the conveniences in the States. For example, I traveled to Texas on business for a few days in January 2010 with a lengthy shopping list from Cyndi for items unavailable on the island. I was quickly reminded of the toughest part of re-entering the States: putting on socks and shoes after living life in flip-flops.

I spent an hour at Walmart, filling a large suitcase. I was telling a friend in Texas how we missed the conveniences of the megastores. He astutely observed, "But isn't 'no Walmarts' the reason you're in St. Martin?" How dare he call me out and be right? Cyndi and I had willingly chosen the small-town, island atmosphere, despite the lack of conveniences. Can't have it both ways, but we can still bemoan and reminisce.

Our first trip "home" together after our permanent move occurred toward the end of August 2010. Cyndi and I couldn't agree if we should close the business, since it was slow season, or hire an employee. We compromised by convincing our retired friend Marilyn to work it a few days a week. She was bright and capable, although naturally nervous at returning to work part-time to a business she'd never been involved in. One of her first updates we received via e-mail read,

> Good Morning John,
> This comes under the category of "if it isn't one thing, it's another." Last Saturday at about 8:15 a.m. someone cut, probably with a machete, the main telephone line on the pole across the street from us (the line comes out of the ground and goes up the pole). Of course, that is the pole that provides service to us. So we have no landline or DSL service.
> Until they fix it, or until I work again on Thursday, I will be offline. If you need to reach me, I do have your cell phone on every day from 9:00 a.m. until 8:00 p.m.
> Ahhhh, life in paradise!
> Marilyn

We had flown to Texas for a two-day layover for doctor appointments before our U.S. insurance expired, intending to fly on to California to visit our now-adult children. In San Diego we would pick up our car, take a leisurely drive to Minnesota to visit more family before heading back to Texas to visit doctors, then on to California to drop off our car and fly back to St. Martin.

All those plans changed during our initial layover. Having a sore tooth, I had called my dentist prior to our arrival, asking him if he could see me the afternoon we got in. Three hours later I left his chair after a root canal, with an appointment weeks later during my return trip for a crown.

While sitting in the chair waiting for the Novocain to take effect, I enjoyed a *Sports Illustrated*. I wondered how often I had sat there in prior years checking my Blackberry, never taking the time to leisurely read a magazine. I smiled at the thought; I didn't miss one bit owning a Blackberry. Life was slower, simpler—definitely better.

The next morning I had an appointment with the ophthalmologist who had performed Lasik a year before. My right eye had been blurry with floaters for a few weeks, and I suspected scar tissue. I described my condition to the assistant who began the exam.

She said, "Oh, that doesn't sound good."

"What do you think it is?"

"Well, it's the doctor who should talk to you."

"I understand, but what do *you* think it is?"

"You said you saw a bright light and a bunch of floaties, and now you can't see much?"

"Right."

"Sounds like a detached retina, but you need to have the doctor look at it."

"Is a detached retina bad?"

"Ohhh, it's really bad, but you need to talk to the doctor."

I tried to stay relaxed, but found myself more than a bit anxious. A few minutes later the ophthalmologist confirmed her assistant's diagnosis: a "gigantic" retinal tear that would require emergency surgery the next day. She made an appointment with a retinal specialist for that evening, concerned I might never recover sight in that eye.

The next day a surgeon performed a two-hour surgery at the Arlington hospital to repair the large tear on the upper right retina. During the procedure, the bottom of the retina tore, requiring further patching. The doctor also lasered my good left eye, which showed retinal deterioration, similar to welding the retina as a preventative measure.

I woke from the anesthesia, and Cyndi drove us to the motel. I was equipped with an eye patch, drops, and a gas bubble in my right eye. The gas was to hold my retina in place. We were told the gas should dissolve in about three weeks and, until then, I couldn't fly or drive through mountains, meaning the California trip was postponed. For the first week I had to keep my head down and sleep facedown.

I convalesced for a week at our Texas motel until the doctor OK'd our new plans, a drive to Minnesota. We purchased a small car and began the trek, spending five weeks in the northland. Then we headed back to Texas to visit my eye surgeon, my dentist for the follow-up crown, and my urologist for an annual prostate exam.

Cyndi, not wanting to be excluded from such things, had her one-year colonoscopy after her cancer scare a year prior. This U.S. visit was productive, but not a lot of fun. The retina surgeon approved our drive over some small mountain passes to San Diego, even though the gas bubble hadn't entirely disappeared. We were scheduled to fly to St. Martin a few weeks later.

Two days before our return flight, the bubble, although increasingly smaller, remained. Not knowing if it would dissolve in days or weeks and needing to get back, I mapped a three-day trip to Miami via Greyhound bus, where I believed I could jump on a cruise ship. Cyndi, not wanting me on a bus despite her belief that it would make for a most interesting chapter in this book, convinced me to see a retina specialist in San Diego. The examining doctor predicted the bubble would disappear within a few days.

"If it doesn't, since it's so small, could I fly anyway?" I asked.

"I wouldn't if I were you."

"What happens if I do?"

"If the plane decompresses, you'll have tremendous pain in your eye as the gas expands, and it'll likely ruin the nerve, losing your sight for good."

"Does decompression happen often?"

"Only when someone with a gas bubble is on the plane. All of the doctors in our practice know of someone it's happened to. In one case, there was a doctor on the plane who put a needle into the eye to reduce the painful pressure."

Ouch. In the end, the doctor scared some sense into me, and I controlled my urgency. Cyndi boarded our scheduled flight to St. Martin, and I stayed back with high hopes of joining her a few days later. Sure enough, one day after she left, the bubble disappeared, and I jumped on another flight.

We've since had happier vacations to America. When we're back home and we tell people we're on vacation, they ask from where? They always laugh, wondering why someone from the Caribbean would vacation in the United States.

But now we no longer travel back to the States to see medical doctors. Our COBRA insurance, costing over $1,000 per month, ended June 2011, and in anticipation we tried in vain to get medical coverage. All but one turned us down, citing our pre-existing conditions, and the one that accepted us was prohibitively expensive, with a very high deductible.

Fortunately, by then we both had our hard-earned *Carte d'assurance maladie VITALE*, our French medical insurance that cost about two hundred euros annually. Not bad, although we were virgins to the French medical system. Neighboring restaurant owner Lara told us that it covered about 70 percent of our medical needs, and that a supplemental policy could be purchased to cover the balance, including dental and eye care. But Lara noted it was pretty expensive.

"How much? I inquired.

"About seven hundred euros per person."

"Per month or per year?"

"Per year, naturally."

"You've got to be kidding! That's nothing compared to what we pay in the States."

And unlike the States, it didn't abandon us because of pre-existing conditions. We opted to add the medical supplement, or *Complémentaire Santé,* which cost both of us combined €110 per month and covered 100 percent of medical, prescription drugs, dental, and eyeglasses, the latter up to €250 per year. *Vive la France.*

Cyndi first scheduled a physical and received a thorough checkup by a nice female French physician. I saw my buddy, Dr. Gibbs. So far so good, although we're unsure of specialists, knowing there aren't many on the island. If needed, we would fly to Guadeloupe or Paris, and some islanders claim the insurance not only pays for your flight, it pays for a companion. Hopefully, we'll never need to find out.

When we had medical insurance in the States, we had purchased medical-evacuation insurance as a couple for $360, which would fly us back to the States upon a doctor's order. Did we now need such air insurance to evacuate us back to St. Martin, or to France, where we had coverage? How ironic is that?

Here are the things we enjoy and appreciate most when we make our journeys back to America. They don't all seem significant, but they're most inviting when we go without them!

- Long, steamy showers. St. Martin is a typical Caribbean island, created by past volcanic activity. The only fresh water supplies are from rain or the desalination plants. This makes showers quick and economical, not relaxing and long.

- Browsing in a mega- bookstore

- Strolling inside the newest mega-mall or shopping at a sparkling new town center

- Endless selection possibilities at super grocery and hardware chains where convenience is expected and appreciated

- Not having to buy things in higher-priced euros

- People who understand our accents

- Roads without potholes

- Parking lots for cars

- The seasons. Depending on the time of year and what region we travel to, we enjoy the seasons, even winter, if it's for a brief period of time—very brief.

- Drive thru everything!

- Family members either a short drive or a quick flight away at a reasonable cost

- Phone calls that don't require Skype or a calling card with twenty-five numbers to punch in

- Customer service, expected rather than occasionally enjoyed

- Mail that arrives in a reasonable amount of time

- Electricity that stays on when the wind blows

Nevertheless, having dual residency has allowed us to enjoy the best of both worlds. We have a slower life with the luxury of nature's abundance in the Caribbean. We can go back for our fast-paced society's abundance in America. Traveling creates awareness and appreciation of both.

JOIE DE VIVRE

PERFUME FACT

More than any other of our senses, smell triggers the strongest memories.

Our dreams paralleled those of pioneers traveling similar paths, including the fascinating and famed French post-impressionist painter, Paul Gauguin. Gauguin was a financially successful stockbroker and self-taught amateur artist when he began collecting works by the impressionists in the 1870s. He took to the study of painting, comparable to my study of chemistry. In 1882, after a stock market crash and subsequent recession rendered him unemployed and broke, Gauguin abandoned the business world to pursue life as a full-time artist.

Gauguin made several attempts to locate a tropical paradise where he could "live on fish and fruit" while painting in his increasingly primitive style. One stop included a short stay on the nearby French-Caribbean island of Martinique.

In 1891, Gauguin, back in France, frustrated by lack of recognition and financially destitute, sailed to French Polynesia to escape "European civilization" and "everything that is artificial and conventional." He broke from a solid, middle-class world, abandoning family, children, and job. After stays on Tahiti, he settled on the Marquesas Islands where, but for one trip back to France, he lived until death.

Gauguin's art reflected his flight from civilization, searching for new ways of life, more primitive, more sincere, and real. The vogue for his work started shortly after his death.

I willingly left the corporate world in good financial stead, even though it was during the Great Recession of 2009. Naturally, we hoped that an appreciation for Tijon products would occur sooner. The likelihood of business success increases with passion, enthusiasm, and commitment. It's not about money; it's about *joie de vivre*, the joy of life. Establishing our dream and following our vision has allowed us to see that business success is possible. The worst-case scenario is still a life journey that will remain exciting and adventurous.

Dreaming was the easiest part of making Tijon and life in paradise a reality. It was the visualization and preparation that involved (past, present, and future) time and financial commitment with some well-laid plans. While failing *is* an option, we'll always believe that the biggest failure would be not to try. Our journey has incorporated many elements. We were strangers in a new land with a language we still don't grasp. The cultures and challenges of a life so different have overwhelmed us at times, but have never stopped us from moving onward. It's come with some laughter, tears, and memories.

We've learned to appreciate the luxury of being able to take a regular dip in the sea, hike up verdant hillsides, and stroll around our village, feeling a sense of belonging. Our neighbors, customers, and newfound friends are welcome additions to our memories in the making. They've made our experience truly special from day one. One of many defining moments of our arrival as members of the community came in an eloquent e-mail from our friend Dr. Victor Gibbs, who responded to Cyndi's e-mail after she thanked him for dinner while I was traveling off island:

Cyndi, your little note was full of warmth and friendliness. So nice of you. With Paul and Carol you are both now part of the Big Family. So, welcome home. . . . At this time we are going to wish you both a Happy and Healthy New Year 2011.

Vic and MClaude

Island living, as influenced by the French, is about enjoying life's simpler things. The coffee cups are tiny, as each sip is swirled and tasted in detail. Consuming a glass of chardonnay at lunch is civilized and common. Evening champagne is popular: we slowly sip a petite flute of the bubbly, savoring its effervescence.

We've found a way to make our own infusion: fast-paced America blends with laid-back island style. It's our perfect blend, and we enjoy letting people know that they do indeed have options when it comes to turning their dreams into a living, breathing choice.

One allurement of island life is the lack of enforcement of tedious laws and rules: no speed traps or code enforcement regarding the size of a light bulb. After all, the island has only one stoplight. It's all about less government making life more attractive. Sure, there are some things that would be nice, but force those on the island and they'll start eating away at the lifestyle.

When I make solo trips to the States, I bask in memories and the thought of my return to Cyndi and the island. She's always waiting outside baggage with a cold Heineken in hand. Once she even smuggled the full, cold green bottle in.

The memories all make it so special. There are many. I fondly recollect:

- The memory of an incredible buffet luncheon of conch, chicken, barbeque ribs, potatoes, and salad with our friends Jack and Jackie after the baptism of their son and our godson, Jaiyel

- Inviting Lara and Ciro, from Spiga restaurant next door, to a barbeque celebration the night after they closed their restaurant for a well-deserved six week holiday. Ciro brought over the steaks and lamb chops, and I happily let him do the grilling.

- Enjoying a delicious dinner of tomato gazpacho and lemon sole at L'Estaminet in Grand Case with our dear expat friends Paul and Carol. The French hosts/owners of the restaurant, Carole and Ina, sat down with us to open and share a complimentary bottle of Perrier Jouët Grand Brut champagne as they shared details about their recent trip to San Francisco.

- When our friends Steve and Marga sent us over a magnum bottle of champagne while we dined at their resort, celebrating our daughter's engagement with her fiancé and his parents

- Our first-ever Christmas without parents or children in 2010, when we received a dinner invitation from Jean Rich to dine with her and her friends at her fabulous restaurant, Bel Mar, in Simpson Bay. We returned home to find a painting placed on a chair by our artist friend Asif, with a handwritten note on the back: "Wishing you a happy holiday. Thank you for all your support over the short time you have known me and my family. May God bless you both and grant you many successes in all your endeavors."

- Spending a fabulous few days in St. Bart's with Mark and Robin in a beautiful open-air, two-bedroom villa, with pool, overlooking the ocean, given to us for the weekend by Jean Rich

- Getting a private tour and luncheon on the Azumura Journey cruise liner, docked in Marigot, by their guest-relations manager, who had taken our perfume class a few weeks prior

- Watching fireworks on *Le Jour de l'An* (New Year's) with our bare feet in the sand and our hands holding a tropical drink at midnight on Orient Beach

- Being invited into the closed restaurant of our neighbor Carl on New Year's Eve to enjoy a bottle of Pommery Brut Royal champagne with his family and our neighbors Vero and Jimmy

- Enjoying *galette des Rois* on January 6, 2011 at our regular Thursday Rotary meeting. This is a delectable puff pastry with almond cream, also known as *king cake*. Inside some of the pastries there's a trinket for which the finder becomes "king" for the day. January 6 in the Christian church is the Epiphany, or Twelfth Night, or as our Dutch friends call it, *Drie Koningen*.

- Simply waking in the morning to roosters crowing or goats crying, or driving along the main road and stopping to let cattle or goats pass

- And best of all, having customers at our parfumerie enjoy the boutique, products, and perfume classes. Some now return year after year.

A stunning luxury of life in a Third World paradise is seeing the setting sun as it paints the sky with a combination of fiery red and flaming orange, reflected by the warm, turquoise ocean. Grand Case Beach Club is a favorite spot; we sit above a small cliff with a tropical drink in hand, listening to the waves crashing against the rocks below as the sun melts into a sea of a million colors.

We try to make viewing the setting sun a regular excursion. We snap photos, naïvely hoping to best all our previous shots. We delete the photos with a "catch and release" mentality. There's no camera grand enough that can give us the same feeling that we get by viewing the sunset with our own eyes.

The exhilaration of an incredible sunset is followed by my favorite time of day, dusk, a middle degree between light and darkness. Technically, it's the time of evening when the sun achieves six degrees below the horizon, something we can't measure, only estimate and enjoy. Dusk brings an imperfect obscurity: objects are still distinguishable, but not detailed. Shadows take center stage, predicting the coming blackness of night. It's time ticking away.

Dusk is my tranquil, harmonious ending of another day on Mother Earth. Dusk peacefully reminds me of my mortality as I look forward to another island evening. It's another chapter in our life cycle.

By overcoming our own trepidations about living the life we wished, we have grown and enriched the days we have. As Sir Edmund Hillary once said, "It's not the mountain we conquer, but ourselves." Or as Odmanne Matheus, a corporate hospitality trainer originally from Haiti whom I met in St. Martin, proclaimed, "Dare to visualize the most magnificent and fulfilled life you can imagine. And dare to find a way to bestow that level of fulfillment on everyone you know."

What lies ahead on our broad horizon? We have a sense of conquest and contentment with the realization that our dreams have physically taken us thousands of miles, from chilly Minnesota to the cozy Caribbean. I sense a growing restlessness and the mystique of new dreams. I lovingly tease Cyndi that maybe it's the less-explored Nicaragua, or maybe it's the expansion of Tijon to the States. Or maybe . . . who knows? Until then, we enjoy the tranquility and beauty of St. Martin, its people, and its visitors. To stop dreaming is to die. Our dreams shall continue, as shall our enjoyment of our life.

OUR TOP-TEN LISTS

PERFUME FACT

Until the twentieth century,
all popular fragrances
were considered unisex.

Ten Tips for Living in a Third-World Paradise

1. Lose any real or perceived arrogance.
2. Become a local. When in Rome, do as the Romans.
3. Understand the land. While exotic in many ways, Third World standards are something most are unaccustomed to.
4. Learn the language, or at least make best efforts.
5. Follow the laws; pay the taxes.
6. Enjoy the land's beauty every day.
7. Enjoy the people of the land every day.
8. Take time to know your neighbors and visit others.
9. Stay healthy. Exercise and eat right.
10. Pray.

Ten Things We've Gotten Used to in Our Third-World Paradise

1. Red wine, chilled. Even at the better restaurants, our selection comes chilled, being the only way to ensure against spoilage in the tropical heat.
2. Outdoor urinals with three-sided walls at some French beach bars. The Europeans are less inhibited about these things. Local men are less inhibited yet, often simply finding a nearby bush.
3. Men walking along the road with a machete, used commonly as a cutting tool
4. Big potholes, better-labeled craters, intermixed with small potholes. Repairs are few and far between.
5. The island's narrow primary, two-lane circular road crowded with goats, houses, and stores. The road bumps are unmarked, and traffic can be slow (except for motorcycles). People also stop along the way to chat with friends as they drive down the road.
6. The color of the ocean, a beautiful, clear azure, and the beauty of the mountains hovering over the seashore

7.   Short showers to save on water costs, and using cistern water where possible

8.   Topless women at the beaches. At first I lost a contact, and later I stared. Now I hardly notice. This is likely due to assimilation or failing hormones—perhaps both.

9.   Giving a short car honk to let cars know they can cut in or to thank another car for letting us cut in

10.   Ti punches. We started drinking it because it's the local thing to do. We continued drinking it because it's the least expensive alcoholic drink. Now, we drink it because we actually like the taste.

ABOUT THE AUTHOR

John Berglund has had a varied and successful career, starting as a chief county prosecuting attorney at age twenty-four and transitioning into a lobbyist and trade-association executive. Immediately prior to his Caribbean relocation he was employed in the bowling industry, where one magazine survey voted him the most powerful person in the industry and another voted him the industry's most influential person for the entire decade. Throughout his career one relatively unknown interest remained consistent: Berglund's avocation for chemistry and the creation of chemical compounds.

Berglund, who studied chemistry in college and thereafter, initially focused his passion on fragrance and how nature interacts with the sense of smell. He visited parfumeries in Grasse, France, and elsewhere in addition to consulting numerous "noses," the industry word for perfumers. Berglund hired chemists and queried physicians to assist in the creation of revolutionary skin care and sun care products, all made at the Tijon laboratory in Grand Case, St. Martin, FWI.

Berglund's soul mate and business partner is his wife of over thirty years, Cyndi, who brings her popular personality and talents of jewelry design and customer service to Tijon. Cyndi has been John's primary assistant in his formulations and first responder to the many smell tests. Cyndi is a former physical-education teacher, award-winning bed-and-breakfast operator, retail manager, and corporate employee. In between, Cyndi, as the primary parent, proudly raised the couple's two children, Rachelle and T. J., both now living in San Diego, California.